THE ARCHAEOLOGY OF ENGLISH

THE ARCHAEOLOGY
OF ENGLISH

Martyn Wakelin

B.T. BATSFORD Ltd · London

For all my students, with affection and gratitude

© Martyn Wakelin 1988

All rights reserved. No part of this publication
may be reproduced, in any form or by any means,
without permission from the Publisher

Typeset by Lasertext, Stretford, Manchester M32 0JT
and printed in Great Britain by The Bath Press, Bath
Published by B.T. Batsford Ltd
4 Fitzhardinge Street, London W1H 0AH

British Library Cataloguing in Publication Data

Wakelin, Martyn F. (Martyn Francis), *1925*–
　The archaeology of English.
　1. English language to 1986
　I. Title
　420'.9

ISBN 0-7134-5556-X

Contents

List of Maps

Preface

Many books have been written on the history of the English language. This one is not intended to add to their number. Its true aim – to explore and expose the materials lying behind that history – is explained further in Chapter 1.

I have written the book with students in mind (they, I think, have not been offered this sort of approach before), but very much hope that it will appeal also to interested laymen. In places, it inevitably becomes rather technical (though I have tried to keep this to a minimum), and I have therefore supplied lists of symbols (p. 10), abbreviations (p. 9), and a brief glossary of the linguistic terms used (pp. 11–12). It may be helpful to glance at these before reading the book, as well as when necessity demands. The bibliographies will perhaps suggest further reading about some of the topics only touched on here.

Books have a tendency to write themselves in a way not quite envisaged by their authors. So it has been to some extent with this one, which has turned out to rely rather more heavily on illustrative texts, pictures and maps than I thought it might at the beginning. But these are quite clearly needed to display the essential 'physical' ingredients which lie behind the bare bones of the abstract history of English.

I have dedicated this book to my students, since they have been a constant source of solace and encouragement to me for more than twenty-five years of teaching. But I also want to thank Fran, Katie, and David, for their advice.

M.F.W.
Candlemas, 1988

Acknowledgements

The following are reproduced with grateful acknowledgement for permission. Maps: 1, from John Morris, *The Age of Arthur* (Weidenfeld and Nicholson, 1973), map 15; 2 and 4, from G.L. Brook, *English Dialects* (2nd edn., Basil Blackwell, 1965), maps 2 and 3; 3 and 10, from M.F. Wakelin, *English Dialects* (2nd, rev. edn., the Athlone Press, 1977), maps 2 and 8; 5, from Paul Thième, 'The Indo-European Language', *Scientific American*, 199, 1958, p. 70; 6, from R.I. Page, *An Introduction to English Runes* (Methuen and Co. Ltd, 1973), fig. 7 (adapted); 7, from M. Kirkby, *The Vikings* (Phaidon Press Ltd, 1970), p. 63; 8, from M.F. Wakelin, *Patterns in the Folk Speech of the British Isles* (the Athlone Press, 1972), p. 75 (adapted); 9, 11 and 12, from the Survey of English Dialects (base map); 13, from K. Sisam, *Fourteenth-Century Verse and Prose* (Clarendon Press, 1921), p. viii; 14, from M. Gilbert, *American History Atlas* (Weidenfeld and Nicholson, rev. edn., 1985), map 9; 15, from M.F. Wakelin, *Language and History in Cornwall* (Leicester University Press, 1975), map 23; 16, from W. Viereck, 'On the Interrelationship of British and American English', in W. Viereck (ed.), *Focus on: England and Wales* (John Benjamins, 1985), p. 279; 17, 18 and 20, from L.H. Burghardt (ed.), *Dialectology: Problems and Perspectives* (University of Tennessee, 1971), figs. 21, 10 and 17 (adapted); 19, H. Orton and N. Wright, *A Word Geography of England* (Seminar Press, 1974), map 10A (adapted).

The material from R.W.V. Elliott, *Runes* (pp. 18, 34, 38, 91–2), is reproduced by permission of the author and Manchester University Press (1959); the pages of Cawdrey's *Table Alphabeticall* from *Facsimile Reproductions* (with an Introduction by R.A. Peters); *OED* 'Kirk' is reproduced by permission of Oxford University Press, and the page of the Yorkshire *Olmenac* by permission of the Yorkshire Dialect Society.

The photograph of the Bridekirk Font inscription is by Dr. R.I. Page, and is featured here by his permission; the *Beowulf* and *Festial* reproductions are by courtesy of the British Library.

List of Abbreviations

General

acc.	accusative		O.H.G.	Old High German
adj.	adjective		O.N.	Old Norse
adv.	adverb		O.S.	Old Saxon
A.Fr.	Anglo-French		P.G.	Primitive Germanic
A.N.	Anglo-Norman		pl.	plural
A.S.	Anglo-Saxon		p.p.	past participle
dat.	dative		Pr.E.	present-day English
Du.	Dutch		pr.p.	present participle
Fr.	French		pr.sg.	present tense singular
I.E.	Indo-European		pr.t.	present tense
inf.	infinitive		p.t.	past tense
Kt	Kentish (O.E.)		sg.	singular
Lat.	Latin		St.E.	Standard English
L.G.	Low German		Sw.	Swedish
Mcn	Mercian		v.	verb
M.E.	Middle English		W.G.	West Germanic
Mod.E.	Modern English		W.S.	West Saxon
n.	noun			
Nb	Northumbria(n)			

Counties

Cambs	Cambridgeshire
Lancs	Lancashire
Lincs	Lincolnshire
Nb	Northumberland
Notts	Nottinghamshire
Yks	Yorkshire

nom.	nominative
Norw.	Norwegian
n.r.	not recorded
O.E.	Old English

Books, journals, etc.

ASC	The *Anglo-Saxon Chronicle*
DB	Domesday Book
EDD	WRIGHT, J., ed., *The English Dialect Dictionary*, OUP, 1898–1905
EDG	WRIGHT, J., *The English Dialect Grammar*, OUP, 1905
EEP	ELLIS, A.J., *On Early English Pronunciation, Part V*, EETS, 1889
EETS	Early English Text Society (O.S. = 'Old Series')
OED	*Oxford English Dictionary*
SED	ORTON, H., et al., *Survey of English Dialects*, E.J. Arnold, 1962–71
TYDS	*Transactions of the Yorkshire Dialect Society*

Key to Phonetic and Other Symbols

The letters b, d, f, g, h, k, l, m, n, p, s, t, v, w, z have approximately the values represented by English spelling. The values of the remainder are approximately as follows:

Vowels

a	cat		ɔi	coy
a:	same but lengthened		əu	road
æ	midway between ɛ and a			
æ:	same but lengthened		au	house
ɑ:	last		iə	hear
e	Fr. thé		ɛə	hair
e:	same but lengthened		ɔə	more
ɛ	pet		uə	gourd
ɛ:	air			
i	bit			
i:	beat			

Consonants

tʃ	church
dʒ	judge
ʃ	sheep
ʒ	leisure
ç	German nicht
x	German ach, Scots loch
ɣ	German sagen
θ	thin
ð	then
j	yes
β	Spanish Bilbao

o	Fr. eau
o:	same but lengthened
ɔ	bottom
ɔ:	bought
u	put
u:	rude
ə	china
ə:	bird
ø	Fr. peu
ø:	same but lengthened
œ	Fr. feuille
œ:	same but lengthened
y	Fr. tu
y:	same but lengthened

Diphthongs

ei	play
ai	kind

Others

/ /	enclose phonemic symbols (see p. 12, below)
[ ]	enclose phonetic symbols
~	'alternative with'
<	'descends from'
>	'becomes'
★	indicates a hypothetical form

Brief Glossary

[Note: the words listed below are defined only as used in this book.]

accidence: part of grammar which deals with endings of nouns, verbs, adjectives, etc.

Anglo-French (A.Fr.), **Anglo-Norman** (A.N.): Dialect of Fr. which developed in England after the Norman Conquest.

article, definite: in Pr.E. = *the*; **indefinite**: *a, an*.

assimilated: neighbouring sounds having become closer to each other, e.g. /n/ > /m/ in *comfort* < O.Fr. *confort*.

back vowel: vowel pronounced with the back of the tongue raised towards the soft palate near the back of the mouth, e.g. /aː/, /uː/. Cf. FRONT VOWEL.

back (or **velar**) **consonant**: the same, but for a consonant, e.g. /k/, /x/, /ŋ/.

bilabial consonant: consonant produced with both lips coming together, e.g. /p/, /b/, /m/.

centralization: movement of vowels towards the centre of the mouth.

cognate: derived from the same ancestor or root, and therefore related or allied.

'contain': a word at some stage of the language may be said to 'contain' a sound inherited from some earlier stage; thus, Pr.E. *make, grade* 'contain' M.E. *ā*.

diphthong: combination of vowel and glide (a sound made as the speech organs move from one position to another), e.g. /ei/ in *gate*, /au/ in *house* (to be distinguished from a **digraph**, which is a combination of two *letters*, e.g. æ, œ).

double plural: noun in which a new pl. ending is added to a pl. already existing, e.g. M.E. *childre* pl. + pl. ending *-en*.

final(ly): sound occurring at the end of a word, e.g. /t/ in *rat*. Cf. INITIAL(LY) and MEDIAL(LY).

front consonant/vowel: consonant or vowel pronounced with the front of the tongue raised towards the hard palate at the front of the mouth, e.g. /ç/, /j/, /iː/, /ɛ/.

fronting: movement of a sound to the front of the mouth.

glosses: in early works, explanatory translations of words in a text, usually given between the lines or in the margin; a **glossary** was originally a collection of these, and thus later became a kind of dictionary.

hypercorrect pronunciation: a pronunciation which, in aiming at correctness, adapts a feature which does not really belong to it, e.g. hypercorrect /h/ in *awful* or *onward*.

inflexion: variation in the ending of a word (e.g. noun, verb) to express grammatical relationship, e.g. plurality, tense, etc.

initial(ly): sound occurring at the beginning of a word, e.g. initial /t/ in *tractor*, initial /a/ in *action*.

intervocalic: a consonant occurring between two vowels, e.g. intervocalic /m/ in *coming*.

lexical: relating to the vocabulary or word-stock of a language or dialect.

loan-word: word adopted from another language or dialect, e.g. *window* < O.N. *vindauga, mushroom* < Fr. *mousseron*.

long vowel: vowel produced with approximately twice the length of a short vowel, e.g. /a:/ in *cart*. /u:/ in *fool* (cf. *cat, full*).

lowering: pronouncing a vowel in a lower or more open position in the mouth. A vowel may be **lowered** from, say, /ε/ to /a/. Cf. RAISING.

medial(ly): sound occurring in the middle of a word, e.g. /t/ in *bottle*.

Old Norse: name given to the older stages of the Scandinavian languages as a group.

palatal: referring to a vowel or consonant in which the front of the tongue touches, or almost touches, the hard palate near the front of the mouth, e.g. /y/, /ç/. A back vowel or consonant may be palatalized, e.g. /u:/ may > /y:/, /x/ may > /ç/.

phoneme: a minimal unit of contrastive sound within the system of a language or dialect, e.g. /a/ in *bad* as distinct from /ε/ in *bed*, /i/ in *bid*.

raising: pronouncing a vowel in a higher or closer position in the mouth. A vowel may be 'raised', e.g., from /a/ to /ε/.

retraction: the drawing of a vowel towards a back position in the mouth.

reverted /r/: type of /r/ pronounced, as in SW English, Ireland, and parts of America, with tongue turned towards the back of the mouth.

rounding: a 'rounded' vowel is one made by rounding the lips, e.g. /ε/ may be rounded to /œ/, /i/ to /y/. **unrounding** is the opposite process.

stressed vowel: a vowel used in the most prominent syllable of a word, e.g. *cábbage, achiéve*.

syntax: branch of grammar which deals with the way words are arranged in sentences.

voicing: phonetic term meaning the effect of vibration produced by air from the lungs passing through the vocal cords when brought close together in the windpipe; by causing them to vibrate, this gives rise to 'voiced' sounds, e.g. /v, z, b, g/, as distinct from voiceless sounds, e.g. /f, s, p, k/, which are made with the vocal cords in wide-open position. The process of 'voicing' means, thus, giving voice to voiceless consonants, e.g. /f/ > /v/, /p/ > /b/.

1 Archaeology

1.1 Introductory

'Archaeology', says Chambers' *Twentieth-Century Dictionary*, is 'the scientific study of human antiquities'. Of course the English language – like any other – is not a mere antiquity but an ever-living mode of communication and expression; nevertheless, precisely because it has a past it can be studied as 'archaeology', if we allow ourselves slightly to extend the meaning of the word.

In practical terms, archaeology means 'digging up the past', and this book aims to 'dig up' the English language of the past – both spoken and written – and to reconstruct it in archaeological fashion where necessary (especially for the earlier periods) in order to present the evidence for what English and its ancestors have looked like down the centuries. It is emphatically not a history of the English language, although that history – in abstract terms – is bound to emerge, if only for the purposes of summary and clarification, at certain points. It aims rather to present the 'physical' evidence which lies behind that history, in the form of inscriptions, manuscripts, place-names, writings of all kinds, descriptions of the state of the language at various times. But for readers who are coming to the subject afresh there is a brief outline of the history of English in the second part of this first chapter.

'History' implies change, and this is no less true of linguistic history than of any other sort. It has been aptly said that we are looking not at a lantern slide but at a moving picture (Foster, 1970). We are unsure of the precise reasons for language change, but they are many, and include social, political, economic, religious and technological factors, influence from other languages and dialects, fashion in language use, as well as those gradual – and therefore almost unnoticeable – changes in the movement of the human vocal organs which take place from one generation to another and ultimately produce sometimes quite radical changes in pronunciation. This is an immense subject, which can be safely left to the language historians, but the results of language change mean that, for convenience, we can divide languages up into historical periods: 'Old English', 'Old French', 'Middle High German', 'Modern Swedish', and so on. As far as English is concerned, we conventionally divide it into 'Old English' or 'Anglo-Saxon' (from the beginning to around

1150), 'Middle English' (up to about 1475–1500), 'early Modern' (up to about 1700) and 'Modern' English, bringing us up to the present day, The dates *are*, of course, conventional ones, since language changes continually, not at set times; nevertheless, major changes can be seen occurring round about the dates mentioned, and we shall be surveying these in due course.

As is well known, English also varies over space as well as in time: that is, at any particular period, the English of, say, Yorkshire, will be different from that of Cornwall, the English of Newcastle from that of Plymouth, the English of Great Britain from that of America. The evidence underlying these different varieties we shall also have to consider.

Language may exist in both spoken and written forms, and these are emphatically different, though, of course, related. The relationship between spellings and the sounds they represent is often commented on. The -*ough* spellings in, e.g., *bough, bought, rough* are notorious cases: the spellings (*ough*) are the same, but the pronunciations, because of the way the sounds of our language have developed, are different. So the histories of spelling and the histories of pronunciation are different, and we do not necessarily pronounce as we spell (though some people mistakenly think we should), otherwise we should find ourselves in appalling difficulties over works like, e.g., *knight* and *science*. In the first, the *kn* and *gh*, which were once actually sounded in the spoken language, have now disappeared but remain in the spelling. In the second, the same sound /s/ is represented first by *sc* and second by *c* alone.

Up to the Pr.E. period we have, of course, only written evidence, but we are able to reconstruct the sounds of the spoken language lying behind the written or printed page to a surprising extent, as I hope will become clear in the following pages. We also study language on three main levels: that of its sounds or *phonology* (including stress, rhythm and intonation), that of its *grammar* (word-endings, nouns, verbs, the way words are arranged in sentences and so on), and vocabulary or *lexis*. We also have to take into account, when dealing with the written language, the spelling and punctuation which represent the language on the manuscript or printed page.

To illustrate what I have written in the last few paragraphs, I give below four passages from the first five verses of St Matthew's Gospel, chapter 17, translated from the original Latin (the first two) or Greek (the other two) at various periods from the earliest times to the present day.

[Note: In the first passage, the 'macron' or length-mark is used to distinguish vowels pronounced 'long' from those pronounced 'short'. This is purely an editorial device, and does not appear in the original manuscript. It is important for the modern reader to understand the difference between, e.g., long *o* and short *o* (O.E. *ō* and *o*), even though this distinction is not made explicit by the original writers. The O.E. word spelled in the manuscript *god* (e.g. as in the first text, line 6) can mean two things, depending on the 'length' of the vowel. If it is long *ō* (= /o:/), the word means, and actually ends up as, Pr.E. 'good'; if it is short *o* (/o/), the word means, and actually ends up as, Pr.E. 'God'. The same applies to, e.g., O.E. *rīdan* (with long *ī*) 'to ride' and *ridon* (with short *i*) 'rode' (pl.).]

Text 1

And æfter six dagum nam[1] se Hælend[2] Petrum, and Iacobum, and Iohannem, hys brōðor, and lædde hig on-sundron[3] on ænne heahne munt,[4] and he wæs gehīwod[5] beforan him. And his ansȳn[6] sceān swā swā[7] sunne; and hys reaf[8] wæron swā hwīte swā snāw. And efne[9]! ðā[10] ætȳwde[11] Moyses and Helias, mid[12] him sprecende. Ðā cwæþ[13] Petrus to him, Drihten,[14] gōd ys ūs hēr tō bēonne. Gyf ðū wylt, uton[15] wyrcean[16] hēr þrēo eardung-stōwa,[17] ðē āne, Moyse āne, and Helie āne. Him ðā gyt sprecendum, and sōþlīce[18]! ðā beorht wolcn[19] ofersceān,[20] and ðā efne ! cōm stefn[21] of ðām wolcne, and cwæþ, Hēr ys mīn leofa[22] sunu, on ðām me welgelīcaþ,[23] gehȳraþ hyne.

[1]took [2]the Lord [3]together [4]mountain [5]transfigured [6]countenance [7]as [8]garments [9]lo, behold [10]then [11]appeared [12]with [13]said [14]Lord [15]let us [16]make [17]'dwelling-places' [18]truly [19]cloud [20]shone over [21] voice [22]dear, beloved [23]pleases well

(West Saxon Gospels, MS Corpus Christi College, Cambridge CXL, dated *c.* 1,000)

Text 2

And after sexe dayes Jhesus toke Petre, and Jamys, and Joon, his brother, and ledde hem asydis in to an hiȝ hill, and was transfigured bifore hem. And his face schoon as the sunne; forsothe his clothis were maad white as snow. And lo ! Moyses and Helye apperiden to hem, spekynge with hym. Sothely Petre answerynge seid to Jhesu, Lord, it is good vs to be here. ȝif thou wolt, make we here three tabernaclis; to thee oon, to Moyses oon, and oon to Helie. ȝit hym spekynge, loo ! a liȝty cloude shadewid hem; and loo ! a vois of the cloude, seyinge, This is my derworth sone, in whom I haue wel pleside to me; heere ȝe hym.

(Wycliffite version, *c.* 1382)

Text 3

And after six days Jesus taketh Peter, James, and John his brother, and bringeth them up into an high mountain apart, and was transfigured before them: and his face did shine as the sun, and his raiment was white as the light. And, behold, there appeared unto them Moses and Elias talking with him. Then answered Peter, and said unto Jesus, Lord, it is good for us to be here: if thou wilt, let us make here three tabernacles; one for thee, and one for Moses, and one for Elias. While he yet spake, behold, a bright cloud overshadowed them: and behold a voice out of the cloud, which said, This is my beloved Son, in whom I am well pleased; hear ye him.

(Authorized Version, 1611)

Text 4

Six days later, Jesus took with him Peter and James and his brother John and led them up a high mountain where they could be alone. There in their presence he was transfigured: his face shone like the sun and his clothes became as white as the light. Suddenly Moses and Elijah appeared to them; they were talking with him. Then Peter spoke to Jesus. 'Lord,' he said, 'it is wonderful for us to be here; if you wish, I will make three tents here, one for you, one for Moses and one for Elijah.' He was still speaking when suddenly a bright cloud covered them with shadow, and from the cloud there came a voice which said, 'This is my Son, the Beloved; he enjoys my favour. Listen to him.'

(The Jerusalem Bible, 1966)

The briefest of glances will discover the very obvious differences between the passages on all the 'levels' we have mentioned, the most obvious, apart from spelling, being that of vocabulary: to put it bluntly, the words are different, since there were considerable changes in the English vocabulary between the Old and Middle English periods. Quite apart from so-called grammatical words such as *hig* 'them', *þam* 'that' and 'whom', *hyne* 'him', there are some 23 different words which will be unrecognizable to the modern reader, and which I have therefore glossed. This does not include words such as *beforn* 'before' and *gehȳ-raþ* 'hear', since these are clearly the ancestors of our present words and not therefore 'different' from them.

Almost 400 years later, an astonishing change has taken place: there are very few words in the Wycliffite version which are not immediately recognizable to a modern reader, though some have a slightly unfamiliar look: *asydis, forsothe, ʒif, oon, liʒty,* etc. And from the early seventeenth century on, it is clear that the vocabulary, despite the archaic feel of the prose – *taketh, did shine, if thou wilt, spake,* etc. – is very much what it is today.

After vocabulary, it is probably the grammar which makes earlier English look so 'foreign' to a modern reader. Old English was a language with a grammatical form resembling that of Latin, Russian and German. That is, it used the various endings of words – what are called 'cases' – to express relationships between them: *æfter six dagum* 'after six days', for example, is a grammatical phrase with a pl. noun *dagum* in what is called the 'dative' case; on the other hand, *eardung-stōwa*, being the simple object of the verb *wyrcean*, is in the 'accusative' or objective case. It is clear that by the Wycliffite period the elaborate system of case endings with which English had begun had largely broken down.

The elaborateness of noun endings in Old English is matched by a similar complexity in the way the verbs work. The endings in particular look strange to the modern reader: p.p. *gehīwod* 'transfigured' (though here the *-od* ending is the ancestor of our Pr.E. *-ed* and therefore not so unfamiliar); pr.p. *sprecende* 'speaking': in the Wycliffite version the *-ende* has now become the familiar *-ing* form, though in older spelling; imperative *gehȳraþ* 'hear' has lost its *-aþ* ending in the Wycliffite version. One or two of the older forms remain in the fourteenth century, however: p.t.pl. *apperiden,* for example, which is an O.Fr. word accommodated into English, where it is found as early as 1250.

The O.E. and M.E. versions of the Bible are based on the 'Vulgate' translation rendered out of the original Greek into Latin by St Jerome in the fourth century, but the Authorized Version was translated from what original Greek manuscripts were known in the seventeenth century, and the verb forms follow the Greek original closely, changing from pr.t. to p.t. when the Greek does, whereas the earlier versions are rendered simply into the p.t. throughout. This gives us one or two examples of another old feature which originated in Old English, namely the 3 pr.sg. of the verb ending in *-eth: taketh, bringeth.* This was ultimately replaced by an *-es* or *-s* ending: *takes, brings.* Some of the old p.t. forms remain in the Authorized Version: *did shine, spake.*

In the O.E. passage the pronouns are sometimes different from those in Pr.E.: *hig* 'them' (accusative), *him* 'them' (dative); which remains as *hem* in the Wycliffite version); *hyne* 'him'; the definite article 'the' is *se,* which does not occur in the later versions – if it had, it would have appeared as *the.* In all the first three passages *thou, thee* (O.E. *ðū, ðē*) are retained, but *ʒe/ye* have appeared as the 'polite' form of the pl. in its subject form in the Wycliffite and Authorized versions. Finally under 'grammar' we might note that the syntax (the way the words are arranged) is sometimes different in earlier times: *nam se Hǣlend* 'the Lord took', with verb before its subject; *make we here three tabernaclis*; *then answered Peter*; *hear ye him*.

Three unfamiliar letters in Old English occur here, *æ*, *ð* and *þ*, with the values of, respectively, /æ/ and /θ/ ~ /ð/. In the ensuing passages *æ* appears as *a*, and *þ* as *ð* as *th*. The slightly modernized version of the first passage hides A.S. *ȝ*, but it is revealed in Wycliffe's passage, e.g. in *ȝif* 'if' and *liȝty* 'bright': in Middle English it is known as 'yogh', and has the value of *y* (in *ȝif*) or *ch* (in *liȝty*) as in German *nicht*; the latter value could also be expressed by *gh*, as it is in the Authorized Version passage (but the sound had disappeared altogether from English by this time).

Finally, one of the most obvious differences between the O.E. and the other passages is that words which were spelled with an *ā* (/a:/) in O.E. later have *o* or *oo* (= /ɔ:/): *āne* 'one' becomes *oon*. That is, the long /a:/ sound of O.E. (as in Pr.E. *hard*) had now become /ɔ:/ (as in Pr.E. *hoard*).

I hope the foregoing will have given some idea of how greatly English has changed over the centuries. As background to these changes, the brief historical survey below outlines the origins and development of the language.

1.2 The Anglo–Saxon invasion and settlement

The English language made its first appearance on these shores when the Angles, Saxons and Jutes, plus some Frisians, arrived here from the plains and forests of the Low Countries. They disturbed an indigenous Celtic-speaking civilization which, within perhaps a couple of centuries, was ousted from all of the Lowland Zone (except for a few scattered enclaves) and was henceforth confined to the Highland Zone, eventually splitting – on account of continued Anglo-Saxon penetration – into three geographically separate areas: roughly, present-day Devon and Cornwall; Wales; and 'Cumbria' (an area of SW Scotland and NW England). Another branch of Celtic was being spoken in northern Scotland and throughout Ireland.

The main thrust of the Anglo-Saxon invasion was in the middle of the fifth century, according to both the Venerable Bede and the *Anglo-Saxon Chronicle* (*ASC*), but, in fact, members of Germanic tribes had probably been here since the second century. The arrival of what we may now call the Anglo-Saxons was apparently in response to an invitation by a Celtic leader called Vortigern, who, after the departure of the Romans, called upon the Germanic tribes to assist him in repelling from Britain hostile invaders. The Anglo-Saxons responded – but, having arrived, decided to stay, with the result that the Celts, or Britons, were pushed further and further westwards as the English made their way up the great rivers flowing from the heart of the country into the North

1. The homeland of the English

Sea. Nevertheless, many Celtic enclaves remained in all parts of England, and place-names with an element *wal* (from O.E. *walh* or *wealh* 'foreigner', then 'Briton') in e.g., *Walcott, Walton*, often testify to this. Celtic dialects continued to be spoken in what is known as the Highland Zone, and survived in parts of this area up to modern times in relic form.

1.3 Primitive Germanic and Indo-European

The language spoken by the Germanic tribes was a West Germanic dialect related to others like Old Saxon and Old High German. In turn, the West Germanic dialects were all part of the larger Germanic family, which included the Scandinavian dialects (Swedish, Norwegian, Danish and Icelandic) and Gothic. And the Germanic family itself is part of one of the great families of languages, known as Indo-European, which includes other well-known branches such as Celtic (Welsh, Breton, Gaelic, etc.) and Italic (e.g. Latin and its descendants – Italian, Spanish, French, etc.) which probably originated in central Europe.

1.4 Written Old English

The earliest Anglo-Saxons were not literate, apart from their use of a very ancient form of angular script common to the Germanic peoples and known as runes, which, carved mainly on wood, stone or iron, were perhaps also intended to have a magical purpose; they continued in use well into Christian times, as, for example, on the famous Ruthwell Cross, where a fragment of *The Dream of the Rood* is found carved in this form.

The first Anglo-Saxon writing to be found in Roman script was introduced by Irish missionaries, who supplemented their Irish Latin form of alphabet in various ways: they used two of the old runes which had the names *thorn* (þ) and *wynn* (Ƿ), pronounced respectively /θ/ ~ /ð/ and /w/, and put a stroke through their Irish Latin *ð* to express the first of these as well. The Latin letters *æ*, *ae*, and *œ*, *oe*, variants of *e*, were used to express the O.E. sounds in, e.g., *æfter*, *wæs*, and (Nb) *groene* respectively.

1.5 The O.E. dialects

Anglo-Saxon occurs from the eighth century onwards in the form of several different dialects known as Northumbrian (Nb; written north of the Humber), Mercian (Mcn; roughly between the Thames and the Humber), Kentish (Kt; mainly in SE England) and West Saxon (W.S.; roughly south of the Thames). This last in the later Anglo-Saxon period, with the rise to prominence of King Alfred's Wessex, became a literary standard into which writings in other dialects tended to get translated. Behind this dialectal *written* diversity it is natural and sensible to presuppose a *spoken* diversity, even though this cannot, in the nature of things, be proven.

1.6 O.E. grammar

As I have already said, Old English was an 'inflected' language: it had four 'cases' of nouns in both singular and plural to express the ways in which they are related to each other; similarly for adjectives in masculine, feminine and neuter genders; several very full systems for pronouns and

2. Old English dialects

the definite article; and numerous different classes of verbs. This system – which may perhaps most nearly be compared with that of modern German – was greatly simplified in ensuing periods.

To give brief examples, the O.E. word for 'stone' looks like this:

Sg.   Nominative: *stān* – subject, 'this stone is heavy'.

Accusative: *stān* – object, 'I picked up a stone'.

Genitive: *stānes* – possessive, 'the stone's colour was beautiful'.

Dative: *stāne* – with, by, to, from, for (etc.) a stone.

Pl.   Nominative: *stānas* – subject, 'these stones are heavy'.

Accusative: *stānas* – object, 'I picked up some stones'.

Genitive: *stāna* – possessive, 'the stones' colours were beautiful'.

Dative: *stānum* – with, by, to, from, for (etc.) stones.

On the other hand, the O.E. word for 'door' declined as follows:

Sg. Nom. and Acc. *duru*; Gen. and Dat. *dura*.

Pl. Nom., Acc. and Gen. *dura*; Dat. *durum*.

While O.E. 'eye' is thus:

Sg. Nom. and Acc. *ēage*; Gen. and Dat. *ēagan*.

Pl. Nom. and Acc. *ēagan*; Gen. *ēagena*; Dat. *ēagum*.

I emphasize again that these are only three of the many classes of O.E. nouns. Others form their cases in different ways. I cannot give examples of the case systems of the adjectives, the personal pronouns (which include a 'dual' case for referring to just two persons rather than to many), the possessive pronouns, the demonstrative pronouns 'this', etc., and the definite article 'the', but I give below the most important forms of representative examples of the two great classes of verbs labelled 'strong' (those which make their p.t. by means of a change in the main vowel) and 'weak' (those which make their p.t. by adding a *-d*):

Helpan 'to help' (strong):

Pr.t.sg.: 1. *helpe*; 2. *hilpst*; 3. *hilpþ*; pl. *helpaþ*.

P.t.sg.: *healp* (but 2sg. *hulpe*); pl. *hulpon*; p.p. *(ge)holpen*; pr.p. *helpende*.

Lufian 'to love' (weak):

Pr.t.sg.: 1. *lufie*; 2. *lufast*; 3. *lufaþ*; pl. lufiaþ.

P.t.sg.: *lufode* (but 2sg. *lufodest*); pl. *lufodon*; p.p. *gelufod*; pr.p. *lufiende*.

1.7 Borrowings from other languages

From the earliest periods English 'borrowed' words from other languages: these are known as 'loan-words'. Indeed, even when the Germanic tribes arrived here, they brought with them some Latin words taken from their Roman overlords at the continental stage of their existence (e.g. *strǣt* < Lat. *strāta via* 'street'; *pytt* < Lat. *puteus* 'pit'); others came in later from Celtic speakers of Latin in Britain itself (e.g. *ceaster* (in place-names, e.g., *Chester, Irchester*) < Lat. *castra* 'camp', *Lǣden* < Lat. *Latīna* 'Latin'), and yet more through the influence of the Roman Church after the conversion to Christianity (e.g. *abbod* 'abbot' < Lat. *abbātem*; *nōn* 'noon' < Lat. *nōna (hōra)* 'ninth hour'; *munuc* 'monk' < Lat. *monachus*). Latin influence continued strong throughout the Middle Ages and beyond, but meanwhile another source of borrowings must be mentioned: at the end of the eighth century the first incursions from Scandinavian invaders made themselves felt on the English NE coast, and from the middle of the ninth century onwards there were Scandinavian settlements in England. Initial invasions and settlements in the east were followed by others to the west, until extensive areas of England were heavily

Scandinavianized. With settlement came intermarriage and complete fusion of the two peoples – a fusion which resulted, linguistically speaking, in a massive influx of loan-words into English (e.g. *window*, *keel*, the pronouns *they*, *them* and *their*), especially in northern dialect, but also in others, and of new place-names on the map (especially as represented by the ending *-by*: *Grimsby*, *Forby*, etc.). Scandinavian personal names are also well attested, and there are a number of inscriptions, including a few in the Scandinavian version of the runic alphabet.

1.8 The Norman Conquest

By the end of the Anglo-Saxon period, the Anglo-Saxons and their Norse guests were united in a common endeavour to combat another visitor, namely the Normans, themselves descended from Scandinavians who had earlier settled in northern France and adopted the form of French current there. But the O.E. period is generally felt to have gone on for another hundred years after this, since writings which are still demonstrably 'Anglo-Saxon' in language continued to be written until around 1150. Thus we come to the Middle English period.

1.9 Who spoke and wrote what?

Literature never ceased to be written in English all through the post-Conquest, French-dominated period, but the Norman Conquest, with its wholesale substitution of a French aristocracy and governing body for the superseded Anglo-Saxon one, led to Anglo-Norman (or Anglo-French), the dialect of French spoken in England, becoming *the* literary language. It also enjoyed a position of prestige in correspondence and legal transactions well into the fourteenth century, until English re-emerged as the sole 'official' language.

All through this period the lower classes probably continued to speak English, since there was no reason for them to do otherwise, even though it was Norman – and no longer Saxon – landholders who ruled the estates. Between these farmers and their labourers, and the French-speaking upper class, was an emergent middle class of different types: English 'squires', modest landowners who acted as linguistic intermediaries, often aspiring to marry into the middle and lower strata of Norman society; and the less-privileged Norman element itself – priests and servants, for example – who were glad to marry English women.

Although the Norman aristocracy had started off by being exclusively French speaking, it is likely that, by the twelfth to thirteenth centuries, many or most nobles were bilingual. Once this had happened, the way was open for the ultimate loss of this less useful 'upper' language and a come-back of the 'lower' one, i.e. English.

Latin, of course, continued to be the official language of the Church's liturgy and formal communication and of many legal documents, while

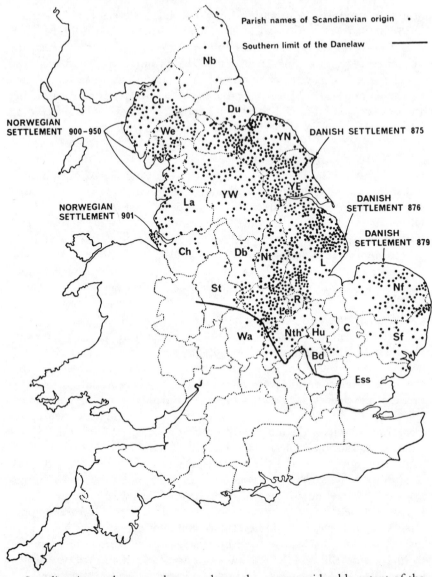

Parish names of Scandinavian origin •

Southern limit of the Danelaw ——

NORWEGIAN SETTLEMENT 900–950

NORWEGIAN SETTLEMENT 901

DANISH SETTLEMENT 875

DANISH SETTLEMENT 876

DANISH SETTLEMENT 879

3. Scandinavian settlements: the map shows the very considerable extent of the Scandinavian settlements in England – over 700 place-names in -by (<Old Danish bý 'village, town') are still known, over 200 in Yks, over 200 in Lincs, while there are also enormous numbers of names containing the elements -thorp (<O.N. þorp 'village'), -toft (<O.N. topt 'knoll', etc.) and -thwaite (<O.N. þveit 'clearing')

in the western half of Cornwall, in Wales, the Isle of Man, and much of Scotland and Northern Ireland, Celtic dialects persevered in speech and writing, though English had already penetrated all these areas.

1.10 Changes in spelling and sounds

The earliest Middle English was written by French scribes, who had the unenviable task of writing in a foreign tongue whose sound-system had – by the end of the O.E. period – undergone changes of such magnitude that the late O.E. spelling system was outmoded and needed drastic revision. This was attempted by such means as the use of the letter *k* for the sound in, say, *king, Kent* (i.e. to represent /k/ in the neighbourhood of front vowels), and reserving *c* for words like *cow, colour* (i.e. for /k/ in the vicinity of back vowels), *ch* being used for the sound in *inch, chair*. In the late O.E. period, *c* had, by and large, expressed all three. Older letters like *æ, þ, ð*, and *ƿ* gradually disappeared, being replaced by, respectively, *a, th* and *w*. These are but two examples, and vastly over-simplified ones at that; but the confusion which reigned over spelling in the early M.E. period will become abundantly clear in Chapter 4.

1.11 M.E. grammar

On this front by far the most important modification was in the drastic reduction of inflectional endings, so that, e.g., instead of the fully-inflected *stān* (1.6, above), we end up with simply *stoon* sg. (the vowel has also changed) and *stoones* pl. (and also gen. sg. and pl.); because most of the O.E. declensions eventually fell in with the *stān* class, the same applied to O.E. *duru*, which was now simply *door*, pl. *doors* or *doores*, and to O.E. *ēage*, which ended up as *eye*, pl. *eyes* – though some dialects preserved the old pl. form *een*. Verb endings, adjectives and pronouns were all similarly modified. In all this, of course, there is no intention of *deliberate* modification: no 'academy' existed to regulate the use of language. The cause was simple: English is a language whose words are usually strongly stressed on the first syllable – *cábbage, méeting, hárbour* – and even foreign words, e.g. *perfume, garage, envelope*, tend ultimately to adapt to this pattern. This means that the endings of words tend to become comparatively unimportant, so that, by the end of the O.E. period, the unstressed vowels in, e.g., O.E. *stānas, ēagan, helpan, lufian* had been reduced to an indeterminate vowel (most often expressed by the letter *e* in Middle English) like the first vowel in Pr.E. *afraid* or the last in *dearer*, and what phoneticians usually express by the symbol [ə]. From this root cause, the grammatical system, by the end of the M.E. period, had become a shadow of its former self, and very much as we see it today.

1.12 Vocabulary

The most distinctive aspect of the vocabulary of Middle English is its invasion in the wake of the Norman Conquest – with the consequent Frenchifying of the Court, the Church, and the legal system – by literally thousands of words from French. This happened to such an extent that it has been suggested (though infrequently, and nonsensically) that English lost its Englishness and become simply an amalgam of different tongues. The unfortunate Chaucer has been accused of introducing 'cart-loads' of French words into the language, but this – in spite of there being, e.g., 18 French words in the first 18 lines of the *Canterbury Tales* – is probably rubbish: the poet was far more likely to have been drawing on the rich stock of words which had already appeared in the language, either written or spoken, from an earlier period. Some of the earliest were connected with the law and its enforcement: *castle*, *prison* and *chancellor*, for example, all occur in the *Peterborough Chronicle* (1154; see 3.10); while other, later, words like *dance*, *carol*, *mansion*, *beef*, *mutton*, *riches*, and *prince*, trickled downwards into middle-class and lower-class society from the realms of upper-class high life and polite entertainment. Yet others were connected with the Church, the higher echelons of which were overwhelmingly French: *chapel*, *rosary*, *chasuble*, *vestments*, *sacrament*. A host of other subject areas were also well represented, and it now also became possible to combine native English elements with French and produce new compounds such as *unreasonable* (< O.E. *un-* + O.Fr. *raisonable*). Suffice it to say that the French language left a mark on the vocabulary of English such as to render it more radically and completely different than anything achieved by the Roman clerics of the late O.E. period, with their Latin, or the Scandinavian ruffians of the eighth century and beyond – whose vocabulary was, in any case, very similar to that of Old English both in social status and in sound-pattern and grammar.

Latin words also continued to come direct (i.e. not via French) into the language – examples being *pater* 'paternoster', *methacarpus* 'metacarpuls', *orphan* – and we also see an increase in contacts with the Low Countries. These had been taking place since Anglo-Saxon times, resulting in a not insubstantial element of Low Dutch (i.e. Flemish, Dutch, Frisian and Low German) origin entering the language, examples being *orte* 'leavings from food', *hobble*, *splint*, *firkin*, and dialectal *rean* 'furrow', *stull* 'large piece of food', *pad* 'path'.

1.13 The dialects and the rise of written Standard English

In the last few paragraphs I have been writing as if at this stage English was a unified language, but this was emphatically not so. After the dethronement of West Saxon as a written standard at the close of the O.E. period (1.5, above), literary English with this kind of status disappeared from the scene, submerged as it was by French literature.

When it fully re-emerged, in the fourteenth century, it did so as a collection of dialects – recognizably dependent on the territorial pattern of the four main Anglo-Saxon dialects, but with more subdivisions, as map 4 shows. Out of this melée, it was ultimately the prestigious official writing of the Chancery at Westminster which was to predominate from the early fourteenth century onwards, and it is this that becomes the basis of our present-day written Standard English, its historical evolution being completed in all essentials by about 1700. From the medieval period onwards, dialectal features began to disappear from written and printed English, except in so far as they were deliberately kept alive for literary or antiquarian purposes.

But what of the *spoken* standard which is used in England today?

4. Traditional classification of M.E. dialects

There is little evidence for the existence of this in the Middle Ages, though it may well have been that, with the growing mobility of the population which took place in the thirteenth and fourteenth centuries, some form of standard was already crystallizing. But no firm evidence is to be found before the early sixteenth century. As is clear from the continued existence of spoken dialect everywhere in Britain up to the present day, the drive towards a spoken standard has had only partial success: written standards are more easily achieved than spoken ones.

1.14 Early Modern English *c.* 1500–*c.* 1700

At the beginning of this period, there is still considerable diversity in the spellings found in manuscripts – and even, after the advent of printing, in printed works. Indeed, the invention of the printing press did not have such a swift and lasting influence for unification upon English as is often supposed. As the period wears on, however, we find more and more evidence that the written language was settling down, and by the beginning of the eighteenth century it had more or less crystallized once and for all, apart from minor differences, in the form we know it today.

While spellings gradually assumed a fossilized form, the spoken language obstinately refused to follow this example (though with the reservation that the passing of time saw an ever-increasing desire to conform in speech to what the written word suggested). As always, it continued to change – not so much in inflectional endings, which had virtually settled down, but in its sounds. The most far-reaching of the sound-changes (though there were others) is that known as the Great Vowel Shift. Briefly, and roughly, what happened was this: late Middle English had seven long vowels, expressed in spelling in different ways depending on date and dialect, but *conventionally* expressed editorially nowadays as: $\bar{\imath}$ pronounced /iː/; $\bar{u}$ /uː/; $\bar{e}$ /ɛː/; $\bar{e}$ /eː/; $\bar{\varrho}$ /ɔː/; $\bar{\varrho}$ /oː/, and $\bar{a}$ /aː/. From late medieval times onwards, all of them underwent a change, $\bar{\imath}$ eventually becoming the vowel in, e.g., Pr.E. *sky*, *tie*; $\bar{u}$ that in *brown*, *cow*; $\bar{e}$ and $\bar{e}$ (both) that in *bean*, *greet*; $\bar{\varrho}$ that in *nose*, *road*; $\bar{\varrho}$ that in *moon*, *boot*; *good*, *cook*; or *gloves*, *mother* (a triple development which went on sorting itself out through the early Modern period); and $\bar{a}$ that in *maze*, *sake*.

To name just one or two other important sound-changes, during this period the Pr.E. St.E. vowel sound in *some*, *butter*, etc. (/ ʌ /) developed from M.E. /u/ and spread from the east Midlands throughout the south (but not to the north and Midlands); M.E. short *a* /a/ in words like *grass*, *chaff* and *path* was lengthened to /aː/ in Standard English (with variants in the dialects); /r/ began to fade out before consonants and at the ends of words (e.g. in *cart*, *pear*); M.E. ʒ/*gh* also ceased to be pronounced (as in *bough*, *daughter*, *light*, *weight*) or became /f/ (*laugh*, *cough*); after /w/, /a/ became /ɔ/ (*what*, *was*, *wash*, etc.).

Spelling never caught up with these changes in pronunciation, so that, e.g., the 'new' sound in *brown* still has a medieval spelling, and so do *what, was* and *wash*; and – more noticeably – the *bough, laugh* group still have the medieval spelling indicative of earlier /x/.

1.15 The orthoepists and grammarians

One reason why we can be fairly definite about the sounds of English in this period is that we have a substantial body of writing *about* the language, which we do not possess for other periods. In the wake of the Renaissance, with its new-found enthusiasm for the Classics and the development of nation states, there also arose a new interest in national languages. This took several forms: one was the debate on the use or non-use of the many new words – some of them fantastic and absurd and now mercifully dead – which had flooded the language, either from foreign sources (this was the great era of discovery, and thus words came in from more exotic sources than simply French and Latin) or by composition from Latin elements. Another was antiquarian in orientation, rediscovering and studying Anglo-Saxon, and making an attempt to preserve dialects as forms of language of special historical interest. A third was descriptive/prescriptive: that is, its many writers – called 'orthoepists' from Greek *orthoépia* (< *orthós* 'upright, straight' + *épos* 'word') – attempted descriptions of English (as well as of other languages) as it was spoken, and, as often as not, also stated what they thought were right or wrong ways of speech. Such descriptions, collectively, provide reasonably sufficient information for us to be able to draw a convincing profile of the English of the sixteenth and subsequent centuries.

1.16 Dictionaries

All of these writers testify to the new interest in language and languages at the Renaissance period, and their work is an invaluable source for our knowledge of English at that time. A further consequence of such interest was the production of word-books and dictionaries. This had in fact been going on since medieval times, but at that period the works in question were simply glossaries of Latin words. From the sixteenth century onwards, compilations of 'hard words' appeared, i.e. of words which it was thought might be difficult to understand: these were, in many ways, an offshoot of the 'inkhorn' controversy, since they aimed to explain the many new terms which had been adopted or coined. They also aimed to put on record the 'best' words and were thus in essence a prescriptive movement. But as time went on, dictionaries began to become very much more all-embracing, their intention being to include the whole of the English lexicon, often its dialect element as well. This movement culminated in the great dictionary of Samuel Johnson (1755), but even after that there seems to have been an insatiable thirst for dictionaries, the compilation of which continued unabated throughout the next hundred years until the inception of the great *Oxford English Dictionary* in 1833.

1.17 The expansion of the vocabulary

Adventure, discovery and colonization led to the appearance of many new words in English. Contacts with France continued in many and different ways, though the influx of words from that source had reached its climax in the Middle Ages and was now diminishing. Contacts with the Low Countries continued fruitfully, and so did those with Germany, Germans playing a particularly prominent role in English mining. Words made their way into English from all these sources, as well as from Italian, Spanish and many other languages. Greek had been virtually unknown in the English medieval period, and during that time words from Greek usually got into English in Latin form, but with the renewal of interest in the Classics words passed directly into English from both languages independently of each other.

This was also a period of new invention and discovery, as well as of the rise of science and medicine in their modern forms, and it was thus necessary to accommodate new concepts in new words. These were mainly coined by a process of synthesis – i.e. by putting new words together from Latin and Greek elements.

1.18 Early Modern English grammar

In spite of some older forms remaining, early Modern English grammar was reaching an increasingly stable situation. During the period, the plural forms of most nouns settled into the familiar pattern of the *stone, stones* type, though some adopted different patterns which they retain today: *oxen, children, brethren* (plus many more such in dialect), *geese, mice, swine*, and so on. Adjectives had become completely uninflected, and pronouns had assumed more or less their present forms, except that *thou* and *thee* (as distinct from the 'polite' forms *you, ye*) were still in existence in conservative types of English (e.g. in the Authorized Version of the Bible, 1611) and for use by a superior to an inferior – but these died out during the period; conversely, the sixteenth century saw the rise of a new possessive pronoun *its*, at first colloquially, and then gradually in literary English around 1600. In the verb, -(e)st and -(e)th endings accompany *thou* and *he/she/it* respectively: *thou comest, he goeth, it seemeth*, etc., but these die out during the period. The -(e)th form had seen a continuous replacement by an -(e)s ending from the M.E. period onwards, and -(e)st disappeared as a natural consequence of the demise of *thou* and *thee*. In the past tenses, there was a continued shift from one class of verb to another: *chode* 'chided', e.g., still existed, as did *bote* 'bit', and older forms like *spake, stale* 'stole' and *brake* 'broke' were still common. These were gradually replaced in the course of the period by the forms we know today.

In general, speaking of grammar, we can view the period *c.* 1500 to *c.* 1700 as one of transition from the medieval period, when changes were beginning to take place, to the eighteenth century, by which time the grammatical level had stabilized.

1.19 Standard English and the spoken dialects in the early Modern English period

In 1589 George Puttenham, the reputed author of *The Art of English Poesy*, made his historic pronouncement that the best English was that spoken in the Court and within the sixty miles around London – i.e. educated Home Counties English. And he was not the first. The statement only confirms what had probably been taking place for some time – the rise of educated SE English as a prestigious type at the expense of others. From the sixteenth century onwards, northern, Midland and SW dialects continued only in a state of decline. They had, indeed, virtually ceased to exist in official *written* form from about 1500.

Our knowledge of the spoken dialects of the period depends on what stray regional spellings continue into sixteenth- and seventeenth-century documents; on various statements (in the main derogatory) by the orthoepists, grammarians and lexicographers; and on dialect as written for use on the stage and in other forms – monologues, dialogues, glossaries, etc. – which came to be composed from the sixteenth century onwards. The latter arose either from an antiquarian/philological motive or from the desire to preserve marginal forms of English for posterity, and reached a flood in the eighteenth and nineteenth centuries, especially from areas where dialect was especially strong – the north, the south-east, and, to a certain extent, East Anglia.

1.20 English abroad

Following the discovery and exploration of the New World in the previous century, in 1620 a band of travellers from various parts of England set sail – mainly in search of religious freedom – for the east coast of America. The mixture of dialects they were currently speaking was the basis of American English, and from this period onwards English was, for various motives, exported, so to speak, all over the known world – but in particular to North America, and later Australia and New Zealand.

We have now come virtually to the end of our summary of the history of English, leaving only the most recent period to be dealt with. There have naturally been changes in the language since 1700, and although written English has been virtually static since then, spoken English has changed a great deal. We shall need in due course to consider changes both in the dialects and in Standard English.

2 The pre-English period

2.1 Introductory: the reconstruction of languages

Linguistic reconstruction is a fascinating business and, of course, of the essence of linguistic 'archaeology'. I shall first try briefly to outline what can be reconstructed of an unrecorded period, namely Indo–European, and then deal at greater length with the Germanic period. First, though, we need to consider the notion of etymological relatedness, and an example will show what I mean by this. The English word *pilgrim* is taken – or 'borrowed' (1.7) – from Old French, but ultimately is of Latin origin – *peregrīnus* 'foreign', which gives us Provençal *pelegrin*, Catalan *pelegri/peregri*, Spanish *peregrino*, Italian *pellegrino*, Old French *pèlerin* (earlier *★pelegrin*). The words are clearly related to each other, though in the course of their evolution one family has changed the first original /r/ into /l/.

Putting the matter briefly and crudely, some words in certain languages appear so similar to each other that they are self-evidently related, and descend from a common parent. We need only take a word like Pr.E. *tooth*, written in Old English *tōþ*, and compare this older version with comparable ones such as O.Fris. *toth, tand*; O.S. *tand*; O.H.G. *zand, zan* to make this a demonstrable fact: all the forms can be clearly seen to go back to a common Germanic original. But since similar forms occur in the O.N. (*tǭnn*) and Gothic (*tunþus*) records, it is clear that *tooth* goes back not merely to West Germanic (perhaps in some such form as *★tanþ-*), but that it was part of the common stock of P.G. words, since otherwise these so-called 'cognate' forms could not occur in both east and west Germanic groups, which split from each other, and from West Germanic, centuries before the oldest records.

The story, however, does not stop here. It is obvious from a very cursory glance that other forms of this word, quite outside the Germanic family, are related to it: Sanscrit *danta*, Greek *odont-*, Lat. *dent-*, Lithuanian *dantis*, Welsh *dant*. True, the English forms have no *n*, but it appears in Gothic, the most primitive type of Germanic known to us, and Old High German, a W.G. tongue like English, had *zand, zan*.

Now, in the case of the Latin-derived words above, we were able simply to cite the Latin parent. But the W.G. and P.G. parent forms are unrecorded, so we have to rely on theoretical reconstruction, although from what we know of the sound-changes peculiar to Old English and Old High German, we can say for certain that both these old forms derive from a W.G. *tanþ- which had a different development in Old English and Old High German respectively. Using the same principles of etymological reconstruction, we can suppose that probably two base forms appeared in the parent P.G. language, namely *tanþ- and *tunþ-, and that going even further back the great I.E. family had a number of forms of the word *dent, *dont, *dnt, which gave rise to the Sanscrit, Greek, Latin, Lithuanian and Welsh forms cited above, as well as to the Germanic forms. It is this sort of reconstruction which allows us, in the first place, to recognize, accept, and talk about 'families' of languages.

The rule soon becomes obvious, in comparative philological study, that a given sound is always changed, in one and the same dialect, in the same way under the same conditions. Thus, for example, in Greek, I.E. initial s > h, and between vowels is lost altogether; in Celtic, initial p is lost; in Sanscrit, Persian and the Balto-Slavonic family a sound which appears as k in Greek and Latin and as h in Germanic develops into the sound of sh or s; Germanic has changed older p, t, k into f, þ, h respectively, and so we could go on.

I take a final illuminating example from the preface to H.C. Wyld's great etymological dictionary, to which I am indebted for this summary. It is the word stream, O.E. strēam, a word cognate with Greek hréein 'to flow', which in Indo-European would have been *srew-ein. We know that sr- > hr- in Greek and also that in Germanic it > str-. We know further that between vowels w disappears altogether in Greek, but > u, a vowel, when followed by another consonant. Hence we can say that Greek hreuma (with an -m- suffix) 'a flow, flux' is cognate with hréein, and that its earlier form must have been *srew-ma. This would > *streum in Germanic. It is very much like the P.G. form which gave O.E. strēam, but not quite the same, for the Germanic ancestor was *straum, and is preserved unaltered in O.H.G. straum (O.N. straumr). Now, this would be *sroum- in Indo-European, and we therefore have to assume two original I.E. types: this, and *sreum-, the ancestor of Greek hreuma. But it is known that in Indo-European the diphthongs eu and ou interchanged in the same 'base' or 'root' of a word by a principle known to philologists as 'gradation' (an interchange of vowels in words of the same original base, caused by differences in the position of accent, or in the tone, in primitive Indo-European). Further, a third possible form was u with loss of the first part of the diphthong, so that we have a postulated *sru- (or, with the -m- suffix, *sru-m-), actually found in Sanscrit sru 'to flow', and cognate with Sanscrit srávati 'flows', srótas 'stream' (= Greek rhóos), where the base had affixes different from the m (seen in Germanic) added to it.

Now, most of the languages clearly related together by a common

I.E. ancestor exist in very early forms; for example, Sanscrit – the earliest recorded language in the family, with texts from *c.* 2000 BC; Hellenic in its various dialects, recorded from *c.* 850 BC; the more recently discovered Hittite – the language of a people who flourished in Asia Minor and Syria in the second millenium BC, and whose language and culture were destroyed in the 12th century BC; and Tocharian, rediscovered in documents brought back this century from Chinese Turkistan, where it was apparently in use *c.* AD 700 in two dialects. It is from the ancient forms of words found in these and the other I.E. languages – the Italic, Germanic, Celtic and other groups – that it is possible, by the process of 'comparative philological method', to reconstruct with a fair degree of certainty the forms of Indo-European no longer recorded.

2.2 Who were the Indo-Europeans (1.3)?

We have to approach the Indo-Europeans themselves through their language or, rather, through the languages descended from the I.E. parent family. Linguists conjecture that, right from the beginning, Indo-European was not uniform, but a 'continuum' of closely related dialects, which nevertheless existed as some sort of recognizably single entity until the third millenium BC. It was apparently because of the widespread migratory habits of the speakers of Indo-European that ultimately the dialects became differentiated into quite separate languages, the relationship between them not being discovered until the end of the eighteenth century AD and then decisively reinforced in the nineteenth century with the rise of the study of comparative philology. The concept of 'Indo-European' then emerged to refer to the geographical location of the languages in question, i.e. a territory stretching from India to Europe.

There have been many conjectures as to the original homeland of Indo-European, but it now appears that it reached India from the west, so we have to locate it somewhere in Europe – perhaps for preference central and eastern Europe. Earlier opinion placed it in India or Asia, based on the idea of speech emerging first in the Garden of Eden, which was supposed to be in the neighbourhood of Mesopotamia. This seemed to be confirmed by the discovery of Sanscrit – situated in Asia and established as an I.E. language by the beginning of the nineteenth century. Sanscrit preserved features of the common language much older than most of those in any of the other I.E. tongues, but the supposition that early tribes, for various historical reasons, after emerging in the east, moved in a concerted direction westwards, was ultimately disproved: most of the languages of the I.E. group have been in Europe from the earliest times of which we know. It is surely therefore more likely that the fewer representatives of the family in Asia should have moved eastward than that nearly all the languages of Europe should have been brought to it from Asia.

It is natural that an original home for the Indo-Europeans should have been sought via an examination of their common vocabulary. Words which occur in a substantial number of the languages were presumably a part of the primitive I.E. vocabulary, and if the word existed so must the thing that the word denoted. This is a method which needs great

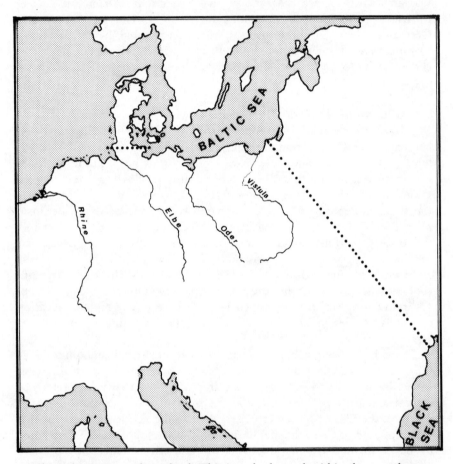

5. The Indo-European homeland. This is to be located within the area shown on the map. Since the Indo-Europeans had a word for 'beech', they must have lived within the beech-bearing area of Europe: the eastern boundary of this area is shown by the line on the right-hand side. There was also apparently an I.E. word for 'turtle': in ancient times turtles did not live north of the line at upper left. We can thus roughly define the original I.E. area by these two words. The location is substantiated by the I.E. word for 'salmon' (perhaps originally 'the leaping fish'): salmon are found in rivers flowing into the Baltic and North Seas, but not those into the Black Sea or the Mediterranean.

care, but, handled cautiously, can probably tell us something about the original home and culture of our I.E. forbears. The fact that there are common words for winter, snow and rain, for example, suggests a climate which could sometimes be cold. There is apparently no common word for 'sea' (though there is for 'ship', and rivers and streams seem to have been common), which suggests that the Indo-Europeans were an inland-dwelling community. There are common words for both cattle and sheep, which figure prominently in the early writings of the various I.E. languages. Other domestic animals included the horse, the dog, and perhaps the pig, goat and goose. On the other hand, there is no complete agricultural vocabulary, though there are common words for grain, and Greek and Sanscrit have common words for the plough and furrow, so they have had some acquaintance with agriculture. There are a number of common words for tools and weapons, including arrows.

This is only a very small selection of the evidence available, but the cumulative affect of the whole corpus suggests to most modern scholars that we are dealing with a nomadic or semi-nomadic people living somewhere on the plains of central or eastern Europe – a loosely-linked group of communities with common gods and similar social organization – until, about 2500 BC, they began to expand in all directions.

I close this section with the final, illuminating, example from Paul Thième's article on the I.E. languages: it is an old Lithuanian proverb which a Protestant minister translated into Latin in 1625 to show the similarity of the two languages. The proverb means, 'God gave the teeth: God will also give bread.' In Lithuanian this reads: *Dievas dawe dantis: Dievas duos ir duonos*; in Latin: *Deus dedit dentes: Deus dabit et panem*. Translated into an old form of Sanscrit, it would be: *Devas adadāt datas: Devas dāt* (or *dadāt*) *apidhānas*. A possible reconstructed I.E. version might be *Deivos ededōt dntns: Deivos dedōt* (or *dōt*) *dhōnās*.

2.3 The Germanic languages (1.3)

The Germanic languages represent, generally speaking, that branch of the I.E. group which remained longest in, or near, the original home of the Indo-Europeans where, apart from their gradual expansion, they remained during the pre-Christian era. According to Prokosch (pp. 25ff.; presumably on archaeological evidence), it was in territory between the Elbe and the Oder, north of the Hercynian Mountains and extending into southern Scandinavia, that these peoples developed the linguistic, cultural and physical characteristics that made them a separate branch of the I.E. family. However, he admits that this view is not in accord with that of early historians (e.g. Jordanes, historian of the Goths, writing in AD 550, or the Frank, Frechulf, *c.* 830), according to whom – in agreement with long tradition – the Goths, or even all Germanic tribes, came from 'Scandinavia'. But the fact that the name *Scandinavia* is apparently a compound probably meaning something like 'perilous shores' (perhaps referring to navigational dangers from sudden squalls and rocky cliffs) suggests that the name originally referred not to the present-day territory of Scandinavia, but to the lands around the southern Baltic – at least southern Sweden, the Danish Isles, and Jutland, and probably also northern Germany around the Elbe.

Shortly before the first century AD the Germanic group of languages, though with divisions, appears to have been a relatively homogeneous linguistic and cultural unit. Subsequent overpopulation, leading to frequent emigration and expansion, led to an ultimate grouping – approximately at the beginning of the Christian era – into what linguists now term North, East, and West Germanic.

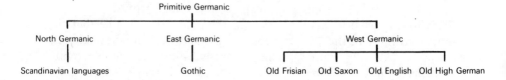

2.3.1 North Germanic (1.3)

This is the language of the Scandinavian north, Jutland becoming North Germanic (Danish) after a large part of its Anglian (part of the W.G.-speaking group) population had emigrated to England during the A.S. invasions of the fifth and sixth centuries. Later, Norse settlements (from about the ninth century onwards) were founded in Iceland, Greenland, the Faroes, Orkneys and Shetlands, and, of course, in Great Britain.

Over one hundred early runic inscriptions, showing little dialect variation, are our evidence for 'Primitive Norse' (from the end of the third century AD to c. 800); after this period, the division first into Norwegian, Swedish and Danish, and then their later offspring, becomes increasingly more evident. We are concerned with this branch of Germanic only in so far as it had a decisive influence on English in the O.E. and M.E. periods.

2.3.2 East Germanic (1.3)

This is the language of the tribes, most importantly the Goths, that settled on the SE shores of the Baltic, east of the Oder, during the last two to three centuries BC. The Goths appear to have taken their name from their original homeland (Gotland) in south Sweden. About AD 200, forced by overpopulation, they migrated south-east and settled in the plains north of the Black Sea, where they separated into two groups, the Ostrogoths east of the Dnieper, and the Visigoths west of it. The Gothic kingdoms were destroyed by the Huns, and later the Goths disappeared in the Roman Empire; but some Gothic settlements survived the Hunnish invasions and existed up to the sixteenth century. We look at Gothic in more detail below (2.5).

2.3.3 *West Germanic (1.3)*

This reflects the expansion of the continental stock between the Elbe and the Oder to the west and south-west, whose tongues are attested to by the Roman historian Tacitus in his *Germania* (AD 98). Their expansion was fan-like in pattern, and led to the formation of several dialect groups which we may divide into two main ones – the German and Dutch group, in its various sub-divisions; and, more important for our purposes, Anglo-Frisian. The tribal situation is very complicated (Prokosch, p. 31), but we end up with various groups known to history as Anglians, Saxons, Jutes and Frisians. I shall be content, with Prokosch (*ibid.*), to enter all these under the label of 'Anglo-Frisian'. These were the first Germanic peoples to occupy Britain and to bring about that dialect which is known as 'Anglo-Saxon' or 'Old English'.

2.4 *Primitive Germanic: inscriptions*

Together with the legitimate theoretical inferences about the descent of the P.G. vowels and consonants that we can make as they came down from Indo-European, our earliest *tangible* evidence for the Germanic period comes in the form of runic inscriptions in languages related to Old English: Gothic, Norse and Frisian. I am indebted for much of the following summary to R.W.V. Elliott's *Runes: an Introduction.*

Runes were an ancient form of writing, now often incomprehensible, consisting of angular characters scratched on wood, stone or metal and, later, incorporated into manuscripts. It is possible – probable even – that they were believed to have magical significance. Their origin has been much disputed, but present theory believes that they came from scripts used in the Alps, descendents of the old Etruscan alphabet – which is itself of obscure origin. At some early stage, a Germanic tribe (we do not know which) was in touch with this North Italic writing, since a runic alphabet, or 'fuþark' – as it is known, from its first six letters – had been carried north to reach Scandinavia by the third century AD.

A valuable archaeological piece in this ancient jigsaw puzzle is an inscription on one of 26 bronze helmets found in 1812 at Negau near the Austro-Yugoslav frontier. It bears in third-century BC *North Italic* letters the *Germanic* words *Hariχasti teiva*, generally interpreted as a votive inscription 'to the god Herigast' (*teiva* being related to O.N. *Týr* 'Tiw'). This suggests that at some time some speaker, or speakers, of Germanic, most probably in the third to second century BC, knew North Italic writing well enough to use it for the words of their own language, and we may probably date the evolution of the fuþark somewhere between this date and the first century BC, say between *c.* 250 and *c.* 150 BC. For from the second century onwards Latin influence grew, causing a steadily increasing mingling of North Italic and Latin letters until, during the first century BC, the alpine alphabets ceased to be used. Latin influence can, indeed, be seen in the creation of the fuþark, especially in the runes *f* and *b*.

From north Italy, the fuþark spread to the Goths (who, originating in south Sweden – 'Gotland' – had migrated south to Poland and the Black Sea area by the third century AD), to the North Sea Germanic tribes, and to Scandinavia. Our knowledge of its traditional sequence and the shapes of the individual letters of the common Germanic fuþark, which consists of 24 runes, is based on five runic inscriptions in which it is wholly or partially represented. The earliest of these, and the only one to show the entire sequence of 24 runes, is the stone from Kylver (Gotland) of *c.* 400, followed by two sixth-century Swedish medallions, and a silver brooch from Charnay (Burgundy) of the same period; and then part of a stone pillar from Breza (near Sarajevo), with only 19 runes but probably from earlier in the sixth century.

It is from these early fuþarks that we can partially construct the first forms of Primitive Germanic (although they by no means present the whole picture), and I give them opposite in summary form from Elliott (p. 18), with his suggested sound value for each rune, and some additional explanation based on the three pages leading up to his summary.

2.5 Gothic
We are not totally dependent on inscriptions for the 'pre-English' or Germanic period, since Germanic exists in various manuscript forms as well. Scandinavian does not concern us at this point, since manuscripts in those dialects relevant to English are available only from the late, 'Viking', period; Frisian, the closest relative to English, also exists in records only from the fourteenth century onwards. Gothic is the oldest extant Germanic language in manuscript, the text comprising fragments of a biblical translation from the Greek, originally made in the fourth century by Ulfilas (or Wulfila), Bishop of the West Goths. The chief value of Gothic, linguistically speaking, is in reconstructing the earliest form of Primitive Germanic, since Gothic is closest to that parent language.

The most well-known manuscript of the translation is in the sixth-century Codex Argenteus (in the University Library, Uppsala). Elaborate in appearance, it is written in silver letters on purple vellum, decorated in gold and silver, using a unique mixture of Greek uncials (large manuscript letters, used from the fourth to the ninth centuries AD), runes and Roman letters. Here is a specimen passage (Mark ix.2–7), recounting part of the story of the Transfiguration, as in the passages in Chapter 1. The accents are included to show vowel length, or to show the sounds

	Kylver		Vadstena		Grumpan		Charnay		Breza	
1	ᚠ	f	ᚠ		ᛈ		ᚠ		ᚠ	
2	ᚺ	*u*	ᚢ		ᚢ		ᚢ		ᛁᚢ	
3	ᚦ	*þ*	ᚦ		ᚦ		ᚦ		ᚦ	
4	ᚨ	*a*	ᚨ		ᚨ		ᚨ		ᚨ	
5	ᚱ	*r*	ᚱ		ᚱ		ᚱ		ᚱ	
6	ᚲ	*k*	ᚲ		ᚲ		ᚲ		ᚲ	
7	ᚷ	*g*	ᚷ		ᚷ		ᚷ		ᚷ	
8	ᚹ	*w*	ᚹ		ᚹ		ᚹ		ᚹ	
9	ᚺ	*h*	ᚾ		ᚺ		ᚺ		ᚺ	
10	ᛏ	*n*	ᛏ		ᛏ		ᛏ		ᛏ	
11	ᛁ	*i*	ᛁ		ᛁ		ᛁ		ᛁ	
12	ᛃ	*j*	ᛃ		ᛑ		ᛃ		ᛉ	
13	ᛈ	*p*	ᛚ	*ė*	ᛌ	*ė*	ᛌ	*ė*	ᛌ	*ė*
14	ᛌ	*ė*	ᛒ	*b/p*	ᛈ	*p*	ᚹ	*p*	ᛥ	*p*
15	ᛉ	*z*	ᛊ				ᛉ		ᛦ	
16	ᛞ	*s*	ᛊ				ᛦ		ᛊ	
17	ᛏ	*t*	ᛏ		ᛣ		ᛏ		ᛏ	
18	ᛒ	*b*	ᛒ		ᛒ		ᛒ			
19	ᛖ	*e*	ᛖ		ᛖ		ᛖ		ᛖ	
20	ᛗ	*m*	ᛗ		ᛗ		ᛗ		ᛗ	
21	ᛚ	*l*	ᛚ		ᛚ					
22	ᛜ	*ŋ*	◇		ᛦ					
23	ᛞ	*đ*	ᛟ	*o*	ᛟ	*ṣ*				
24	ᛟ	*o*			ᛞ	*đ*				

2. *u* is /u/; 3. *þ* is /θ/; 7. *g* is /ɣ/, also (rarely) /g/; 9. *h* is either the 'spirant' which later appears as O.E. /x/ or /ç/; or else 'aspirate' /h/ as in Pr.E. *hat*; 12. *j* is /j/; 13. *ė* (= *p* at Kylver) is probably somewhere between /e/ and /i/, and is here distinguished from /e/ by placing a point above it; 15. *z* is a sound probably half-way between modern English /r/ and /z/ – it is often transliterated *R*; 18. *b* is /β/, also (rarely) /b/; 23. *đ* is /ð/, also (rarely) /d/.

·Mд· ПNTЄGдБдIдꜰдЄTIψMдNNдM
MD. UNTE YABAI AFLETIþ MANNAM
xliv. Enim si remittitis hominibus

MISSдdЄдINSïZЄ·дꜰдЄTIψGдh
MISSADEDINS ÏZE, AFLETIþ YAH
transgressiones eorum, remittit et

ïZYISдTTдïZYдꝶSдNꝼдꝶhIMINд·
ÏZWIS ATTA ÏZWAR SA UFAR HIMINAM.
vobis pater vester ó super coelis.

ïψGдБдINIдꝼдЄTIψMдNNдMMIS
Ïþ YABAI NI AFLETIþ MANNAM MIS-
Autem si non remittitis hominibus trans-

SдdЄдINSïZЄ·NIψдNдTTдïZ
SADEDINS ÏZE, NI þAU ATTA ÏZ-
gressiones eorum, neque pater ves-

YдꝶдꝼдЄTIψMISSдdЄдINSïZYд
WAR AFLETIþ MISSADEDINS ÏZWA-
ter remittit transgressiones vest-

·MЄ· ꝶƧS:дψψдNБIψЄꝼдSTдIψNIYдIꝶ
ME. ROS. AþþAN BIþE FASTAIþ, NI WAIR-
xlv. tras. Autem quum jejunatis, non fia-

Facsimile of a portion (Matthew vi.14–16) of the Gothic Codex Argenteus, with transcription, and the Vulgate Latin text. (Reproduced from *The Gothic and Anglo-Saxon Gospels* (ed. J. Bosworth), 2nd edn., London, 1874)

of different diphthongs: as with Old English, they are not present in the manuscript itself.

Jah afar dagans saíhs ganam Iēsus Paítru jah
Iakōbu jah Iōhannēn, jah ustáuh ins ana faírguni háuh sundrō áinans:
jah inmáidida sik in andwaírþja izē,
Jah wastjōs is waúrþun glitmunjandeins, hweitōs swē snáiws,
swaleikōs swē wullareis ana aírþái ni mag gafíeitjan.
Jah atáugiþs warþ im Hēlias miþ Mōsē; jah wēsun rōd-
jandans miþ Iēsua.
Jah andhafjands Paítrus qaþ du Iēsua: rabbei, gōþ ist unsis
hēr wisan, jah gawaúrkjam hlijans þrins, þus áinana jah
Mōsē áinana jah áinana Hēlijin.
Ni áuk wissa hwa rōdidēdi; wēsun áuk usagidái.
Jah warþ milhma ufarskadwjands im, jah qam stibna us

þamma milhmin : sa ist sunus meins sa liuba, þamma
háusjáiþ.

2.6 Summary

Finally, using the same comparative method outlined at the beginning
of this chapter (2.1), we may offer the following examples of one or two
words which exist in several Germanic languages, and trace them back
to their common, postulated source. We shall then be on the brink of
primitive Old English. (Note: the other Germanic forms are included as
showing the closest recorded evidence to Old English; they are not, of
course the *progenitors* of the O.E. forms, as Indo-European and Primitive
Germanic are, but are cognate, or parallel, forms.)

(i) Gothic *taíhun*, O.N. *tíu*, O.S. *tehan*, O.H.G. *zehan*, O.E. *tīen*,
P.G. **teχan, -un* (= Lat. *decem*, Greek *déka*); Pr.E. *ten*.

(ii) Gothic *hunds*, O.N. *hundr*, O.S. and O.E. *hund*, O.H.G. *hunt*,
P.G. **hundo-z* (= Lat. *canis*, Greek *kúon*); Pr.E. *hound*.

(iii) *Gothic fisks*, O.N. *fiskr*, O.S. and O.H.G. *fisk*, O.E. *fisċ*, P.G.
*fisko-z (= Lat. *piscis*, Greek *ichthús*); Pr.E. *fish*.

(iv) Gothic *dags*, O.N. *dagr*, O.S. *dag*, O.H.G. *tag*, O.E. *dæg*, P.G.
*daʒ-az; Pr.E. *day*.

(v) Gothic *baíran*, O.N. *bera*, O.S. and O.H.G., O.E. *beran*, P.G.
stem **ber-* (= Lat. *feran*, Greek *férein*); Pr.E. *bear*.

(vi) Gothic *ga-dēþs*, O.N. *dáð*, O.S. *dād*, O.H.G. *tāt*, O.E. *dǣd*, P.G.
*dǣdi-z, Pr.E. *deed*.

(vii) Gothic, O.S., and O.H.G. *fāhan*, O.N. *fā*, O.E. *fōn*, P.G.
*faŋχanan 'to seize'; no Pr.E. equivalent.

3 Old English

(to c. 1150)

3.1 Introductory (1.4)

Our earliest evidence for Old English as a distinct W.G. dialect comes from the form of the O.E. runic alphabet, together with eighth- and ninth-century manuscripts from various areas of England, especially, at this early period, from Northumbria and Mercia; rather less so, until later, from Wessex.

We shall, however, start centrally with the W.S. manuscript tradition of the tenth and eleventh centuries, and work out from there, earlier and later, in both time and space. This West Saxon is what students of Old English are customarily reared on in the beginning – and very sensibly, too, since there are more works in this later form of 'standard' Old English than in all the other dialects put together.

3.2 The formative influences behind late West Saxon (1.5)

The initial clue to the rise of late West Saxon is to be found in King Alfred's famous, but gloomy, words on his accession to the throne (871), found in the Preface he wrote to his translation of St Gregory the Great's *Cura Pastoralis* ('Pastoral Care'):

> So entirely had it [sc. learning] declined in England that there were
> very few this side of the Humber who could understand their
> missals in English, or even translate one letter from Latin into
> English, and I think that there were not many beyond the Humber.
> There were so few of them that I cannot think of a single one south
> of the Thames, when I succeeded to the kingdom.

To stem this decline, which was due, no doubt, mainly to the impact of a long period of Scandinavian invasion and settlement, Alfred initiated a programme of educational reform – writing a number of works himself – which resulted in the largest stretches of W.S. prose which we possess (including the *Anglo-Saxon Chronicle*, probably initiated by Alfred in about 890). That programme gave the main impetus to the post-Alfredian monastic revival, whose most prominent literary figures were abbot Ælfric of Eynsham (c. 955–c. 1020) and archbishop Wulfstan of Worcestor and York (d. 1023).

The importance of Alfred's scheme lay in the circulation of documents from Wessex to the rest of England, his intention being to have a copy of each new work, as it became available, sent to every diocese. The names of the scribes who produced this vast body of material are, of course, unknown, but, even if they were Wessex men, they must have been trained by non-Wessex scholars, since there were apparently no literate W.S. writers to speak of! They were probably trained as a group, which is why the documents they produced share a common character – a character indeed not *purely* West Saxon, and containing elements of inconsistency suggesting that the writers were using conventions not consonant with their own speech habits. Nevertheless, the standard written language with which they familiarized the whole country – 'early', or 'Alfredian' West Saxon – is the source of the standard written form used by the writers of the tenth-century renaissance.

With this briefest of background summaries in mind, we may take a look at a page from the only surviving manuscript of the most monumental of all O.E. poems, *Beowulf* (MS Cotton Vitellius A XV). The poem was copied into West Saxon in about the year 1000 from an eighth-century version in a Mcn or Nb dialect. In 1731, the manuscript was damaged in the famous Cottonian fire, which accounts for the frayed edges. These were, however, not as badly frayed in 1787, when a Danish scholar, G.J. Thorkelin, copied the text for the first time ever, and the lacunae can therefore often be restored by modern editors.

A literal transcription of the first half-dozen or so lines of the facsimile, preserving the lines as they are here in the manuscript, runs as follows (modern editors would, of course, set the text out as in the version of Cædmon's *Hymn*, 3.3.1, below).

> Hƿæt ƿe garde
> na ingear dagum þeod cyninga
> þrym ge frunon huða æþelingas ellen
> fremedon oft scyld scefing sceaþen
> þreatum monegum mægþum meodo setla
> ofteah egsode eorl syððan ærest ƿearð
> feasceaft funden

Note especially the forms of the 'special' letters þ, ð, æ, ƿ; and of *g* ('insular' *g*), *r*, *s* and *d*. These are discussed more fully in 3.3, below.

Having seen what a representative specimen of classical West Saxon looks like, we may now consider this important dialect a little further.

Early West Saxon occurs only in the names and boundaries of two Latin charters, some genealogies, and two fragments of a martyrology, all of the ninth century. Indeed, we know virtually nothing of West

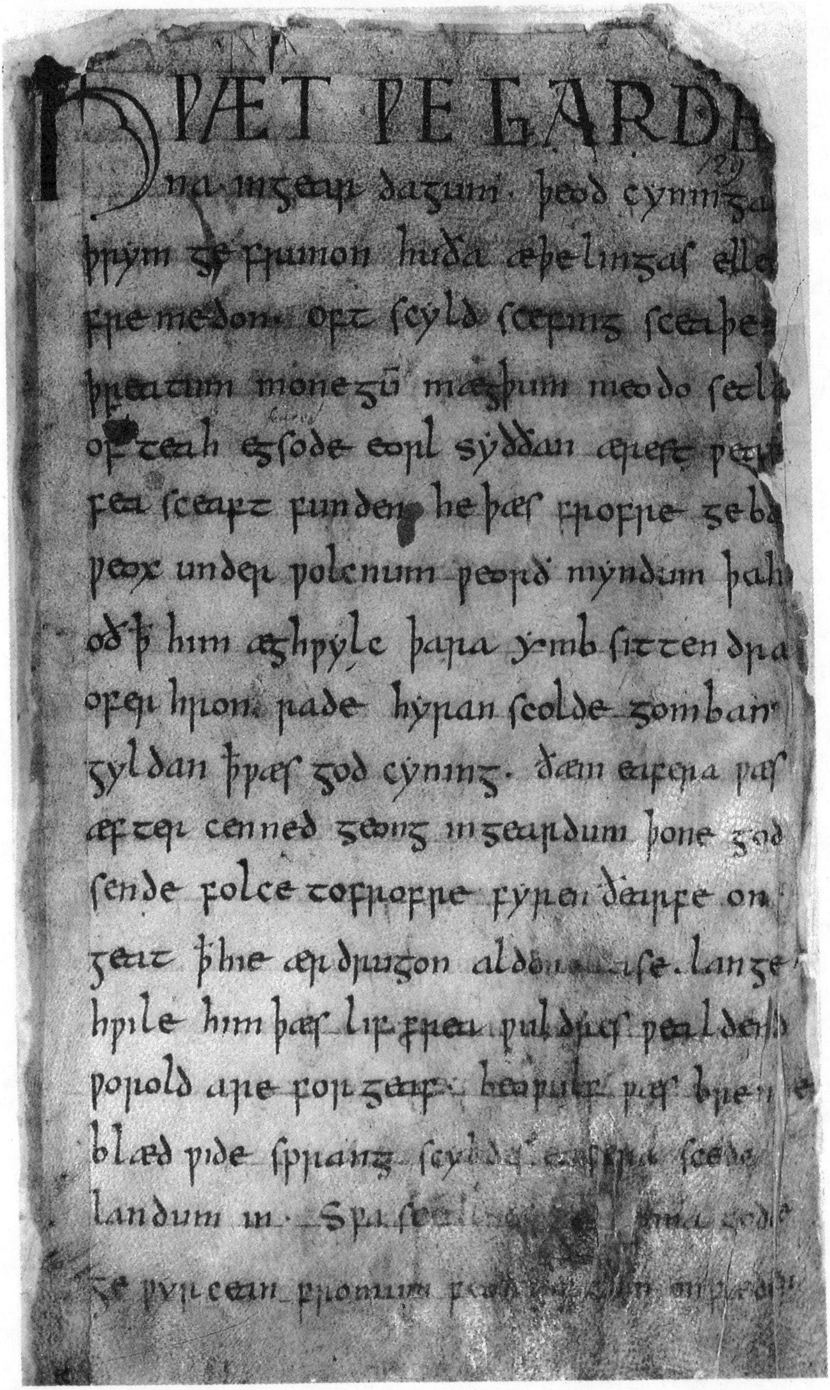

The opening of *Beowulf*

Saxon until the time of Alfred. Later, however, the material becomes much more abundant. From the end of the ninth or the early tenth century we have the Parker manuscript of *ASC*, the two oldest manuscripts of Alfred's translation of the *Cura Pastoralis* (above), and the Lauderdale manuscript of the O.E. translation of his 'Orosius'. The Works of Ælfric (*c.* 1000) constitute the bulk of later W.S. writing, and to these must be especially added the gloss on the *Junius Psalter* and the *Leech Book* (both early tenth-century manuscripts); the Abingdon manuscripts of *ASC* (late tenth and eleventh centuries); the W.S. Gospels (the early manuscripts are dated *c.* 1000); the Abingdon copy of the O.E. 'Orosius' (eleventh century); MS 'A' of the Benedictine Rule (*c.* 1000); the boundaries in the charters of W.S. kings, and the numerous royal writs.

We should emphasize again that, even in its later stages, when West Saxon became well established as a literary standard, it nevertheless shows forms of words characteristic of provincial dialects. This lack of dialectal uniformity is perhaps best seen in most of the extant O.E. verse, which is mainly preserved in the four great codices written *c.* 1000. These, while mostly late West Saxon in language, are very rich in dialectal forms.

The contrast between West Saxon and the other dialects will emerge clearly enough from the examples that follow, and W.S. specimens will also appear in the versions of *Cædmon's Hymn* and the *Dream of the Rood*, which occur in W.S. form as well as Northumbrian.

3.3 The rest of the O.E. manuscript tradition (1.5)

We are naturally reliant upon the traditional division of Old English into about four main dialects, as they appear in their written forms. There is not enough evidence to allow us to draw firm boundary lines between the dialects, but sufficient is available to allow us to distinguish their individual features (with due attention to the question of 'borrowing' from one dialect into another): these are usefully outlined by G.L. Brook (pp. 44–50), and the dialects, as far as we can assign them to different areas, appear on map 1. There may have been more varieties of Old English than the surviving evidence is able to tell us, and we may assume that the regional differences in writing reflect underlying differences in speech but, by the nature of the evidence, that is as far as we can go. They are better regarded as evidence for local scribal practice at a number of monastic centres. We find, e.g., that the tenth-century *Durham Ritual* comes from the Durham area, so we can say something about the way in which scribes wrote there; similarly, the *Vespasian Psalter* (see 3.3.2) – which can be defined as a Mcn work by comparison with independent sources – affords us a knowledge of one specific centre in the Mcn area, even though where it is is still unknown. I should repeat that, since Old English extended over several centuries, dialectal differences may be due to date as well as to region. Indeed, it is hard, if not impossible, to separate dialectal characteristics from archaic ones. Before looking at dialect samples, however, we should return a little more fully to the A.S. alphabet.

As we have said (1.4), the Irish Latin form of the alphabet used by the first missionaries needed certain additions and modifications. The most important arose in the following ways.

(i) 'Roman' had no symbol for the sounds of O.E. /θ/ and /ð/. Early non-runic inscriptions and manuscripts used *d* or *th* for them, but later the runic letter þ, together with a crossed Irish ð were adopted and used indiscriminately – i.e. without distinguishing the sounds /θ/ and /ð/. Both of these appear first in the eighth century: /ð/ lasted until the thirteenth, but þ lasted until the sixteenth.
(ii) At first, for /w/ *u* or *uu* were used, but in the eighth century the runic symbol ƿ 'wynn' began to appear – according to Denholm-Young (p. 19) in a charter of 692, and lasted until the thirteenth century.
(iii) Other now unfamiliar letters and clusters of letters were adopted from 'Roman', notably *oe* (for Nb /œ/ ~ /œ:/) and *ae* or *æ* (for /æ/ ~ /æ:/), which in Latin had been variants for the expression of the sound /ɛ/.
(iv) For *f* (which was pronounced /f/ initially, but /v/ medially), the earliest spelling was *b*: this was because /f/ had evolved from a sound half-way between /b/ and /v/, and at first *b* was thought to express the sound better (it may have been that in the earliest Old English /f/ still had something of this quality). But in the eighth and ninth centuries *b* and *f* alternate.

3.3.1 *Northumbrian*

In addition to runic inscriptions (3.4.2), the dialect of this area is represented by: the glosses on the *Lindisfarne Gospels*, on the *Rushworth Gospels* (except for the part which is apparently in north Mcn) and the *Durham Ritual* – all quite long texts of the tenth century; in earlier (eighth to ninth-century) works by the two earliest manuscripts of Cædmon's famous *Hymn*, and the earliest manuscripts of Bede's *Death-Song* – a fragment of five lines of verse – and of the *Leiden Riddle* (so called because it is found in a manuscript now at Leiden, in the Netherlands), a poem of 14 lines.

We will illustrate this dialect by following G.L. Brook's example (p. 51), and citing Cædmon's *Hymn* in its Nb version, and to make the contrast between dialects sharper, will also give the W.S. version (which is more than two centuries later). This is quoted by the Venerable Bede (672–735), the famous monk of Jarrow, in his *History of the English Church,* as the earliest work of one Cædmon, a lay brother of Whitby abbey in the seventh century who was apparently miraculously endowed with the gift of composing religious verse.

> Nu scylun hergan   hefaenricaes uard,
> Metudæs maecti   end his modgidanc,
> uerc uuldurfadur;   sue he uundra gihuaes,
> eci Dryctin,   or astelidæ.
> He aerist scop   aelda barnum,
> heben til hrofe,   haleg Scepen;
> tha middungeard,   monncynnæs uard,
> eci Dryctin,   æfter tiadæ
> firum foldu,   Frea allmectig.

West Saxon version:

> Nu we sculan herian   heofonrices weard,
> Metodes mihte   and his modeþonc,
> weorc wuldorfæder;   swa he wundra gehwæs,
> ece Dryhten,   ord onstealde.
> He ærest gesceop   eorðan bearnum
> heofon to hrofe,   halig Scyppend;
> ða middangeard,   moncynnes weard,
> ece Dryhten,   æfter teode
> firum foldan,   Frea ælmihtig.

> [Now we must praise   the Guardian of the heavenly kingdom,
> the Lord's might   and his thought,
> the work of the Father of Glory;   as he, of wonderful things,
> the eternal Lord,   made a beginning.
> He first created   for the children of men [W.S. 'of earth']
> heaven as a roof,   the holy Creator;
> then 'middle-earth'   mankind's protector,
> the eternal Lord,   afterwards created
> the earth for men,   God almighty.]

The following are the most important differences between the two versions: æ and i appear in unstressed position (*hefaenricaes, maecti, tiadæ, dryctin*); ia (in *tiadæ*) is the Nb version of W.S. *eo* in this text; in the spellings of the consonants, u or uu are used for W.S. þ /w/, th for W.S. þ or ð /θ/ (*tha*), c for W.S. h before t (*maecti, Dryctin*), and d (the second one in *modgidanc*) and b (*heben*) as the equivalents of, respectively, W.S. þ or ð /ð/ and intervocalic f (pronounced /v/ in these positions). All of these are well-known early Nb features. We may also add *uard, barnum*, and *uerc*, whose W.S. equivalents are *weard, bearnum*, and *weorc*, showing diphthongal forms. In vocabulary, the preposition *til* is a rare O.E. northern word, but was later 'reinforced' by O.N. *til* and > Pr.E. *till*.

3.3.2 *Mercian*

Here the earliest texts are several glossaries of the eighth to ninth centuries: the *Corpus, Épinal* and *Erfurt Glossaries*, and other eighth-century glosses (there are also some later ones – the *Royal Glosses* of *c.* 1000); later, there is a part of the gloss on the *Rushworth Gospels* (tenth century), but by far the largest single source for our knowledge of Mercian is the extensive series of glosses on the psalms and hymns of the mid-ninth-century 'Vespasian Psalter' (MS Cotton Vespasian A.I in the British Library). Again, I illustrate by using the same part of the text as Brook (p. 53), the gloss on the psalms in Isaiah, chap. 12, but with the Latin text as well (following Sweet, rev. Hoad, p. 117). Note that '7' is a manuscript symbol for 'and'.

ic ondettu ðe dryhten fordon eorre ðu earð me ge-
Confitebor tibi Domine, quoniam iratus es mihi. con-

cerred is hatheortnis ðin 7 frofrende earð mec sehðe god
versus est furor tuus, et consolatus es me . ecce Deus

hęlend min getreowlice ic dom 7 ne ondredu forðon
salvator meus; fiducialiter agam , et non timebo . quia

strengu min 7 herensis min dryhten, 7 geworden is me
fortitudo mea et laudatio mea Dominus, et factus est mihi

in haelu gehlaedað weter in gefian of *wellu haelendes
in salutem. aurietis aquas in gaudio de fontibus salvatoris,

7 cweoðað in ðæm dege ondettað dryhtne 7 gecegað
et dicitis in illa die : confitemini Domino ; et invocate

noman his cyðe duð in folcum gemoetinge his ge-
nomen ejus. notas facite in populis adinventiones ejus ; me-

munað forðon heh is noma his singad dryhtne
mentote quoniam excelsum est nomen ejus. cantate Domino

forðon micellice dyde seggað ðis in alre corðan
quoniam magnifice fecit ; adnuntiate hoc in universa terra .

gefeh 7 here eardung Sione forðon micel in midum
exulta et lauda habitatio Sion, quia magnus in medio

ðin halig Israel
tui sanctus Israhel .

[The following translates only the Old English, which occasionally deviates from the Latin.

I will praise thee, Lord, because (*sic*) thou art angry with me. Thy fury is turned back, and thou art comforting me. Behold, God is my Saviour; I act faithfully, and do not fear, because God is my strength and (object of) praise, and has become my salvation. You shall draw waters in joy frm the wells of the Saviour, and shall say in that day, 'Praise the Lord, and call upon his name. Make known his deeds among the peoples in his assembly; declare that his name is exalted. Sing to the Lord because he has worked magnificently; say this in all the earth. Rejoice and give praise, oh dwelling of Sion, for great among you is the Holy One of Israel.']

A summary of the most important distinctive Mcn features would include: long *e* in *heland* (W.S. long *æ*); short *e* in *weter* and *dege* (W.S. short *æ*); the archaic symbol *oe* (= /œ:/) in *gemoetinge* (which also occurs in early Nb, e.g. as represented by runes on the Ruthwell Cross (below)) would be *e* (/e:/) in West Saxon; archaic *u* in final unstressed syllables = W.S. *e*, and occurs in, e.g., the 1sg. of the vowel in *ondettu*, *ondredu*, and n. *haelu*; archaic *d* is used for *ð* or *þ* once only in this passage: *singad*. Perhaps the most curious of all the dialectal characteristics, however, is *dom*, literally 'do' – with the Anglian addition of -*m* on the analogy of *eam* 'am'.

These are not by any means all the specifically Mcn features present in the passage; for a fuller summary, see Brook (p. 53).

3.3.3 *Kentish*

This dialect occurs in the eighth century only in names in Latin charters, but in the ninth it is used for the language of a series of charters themselves. The glosses on one of the manuscripts of Bede's *History* (3.3.1) may contain Kt elements (*c.* 900), and four Latin charters again have Kt names. After 900, Kt Old English is represented only by the *Kentish Psalm*, the *Kentish Hymn*, and the glosses to *Proverbs* (all preserved in MS Cotton Vespasian D VI, late tenth century), but we shall meet the dialect again in M.E. times.

Part of a charter of Ealhburg
(MS Cotton Augustine II. 52) *c.* 850

Ðis sindan geðinga Ealhburge 7 Eadwealdes et ðem lande et Burnan hwet man elce gere ob ðem lande to Cristes cirican ðem hiwum agiaban scel for Ealhburge 7 for Ealdred 7 fore Eadweald 7 Ealawynne: XL ambra mealtes, 7 XL 7 CC hlaba, I wege cesa, I wege speces, I eald hriðer, IIII weðras, X goes, XX henfugla, IIII foðra weada. 7 ic Ealhburg bebiade Eadwealde minem mege an Godes naman 7 an ealra his haligra, ðet he ðis wel healde his dei, 7 siððan forð bebeode his erbum to healdenne, ða hwile ðe hit

cristen se. 7 suelc mon se ðet lond hebbe eghwylce sunnandege XX
gesuflra hlafa to ðare cirican or Ealdredes saule 7 for Ealhburge.

[These are the agreements of Ealhburg and Eadwald with regard to
the land at *Burna*—what every year is to be donated from that land
to Christ's Church to the monks for Ealhburg and for Ealdred and
for Eadwald and Ealawynn: 40 measures of malt and 240 loaves, one
'weigh' of cheese, one 'weigh' of spice, one mature ox, four
wethers, ten geese, 20 hen-fowls, four fothers of wood, And I
Ealhburg bid Eadwald, my son, in the name of God and all his
saints, that he keep this well during his own day, and thereafter
entrust it to his heirs to hold, as long as it be Christian. And
whoever owns that land [is to give] each Sunday 20 loaves (?) of
fine flower to the church, for Ealdred's and Ealhburg's souls.]

Here the most obvious differences from West Saxon are short *e* instead
of short *æ* (a peculiarity it shares with Mcn), in e.g. *et, scel, mege, hebbe*;
likewise long *e* for long *æ* (*ðem* = W.S. *ðæm*); and the archaic *b* that we
have already met, instead of *f*, in *ob* 'of', *agiaban* (= W.S. *agiefan*), *hlaba*
(cf. *hlafa*, almost at the end of the passage). See further, Brook, p. 54.

3.4 Runes

The word *rune* means 'mystery', 'secret' in Old and Middle English, and
is used in various ways, e.g. of the deliberations in secret conclave of
A.S. chieftains, and later in *derne runes* 'secret love-songs'. The sense was
kept alive until the seventeenth century in the word *roun* or *round* 'to
whisper in the ear', and even later by antiquarian writers like Scott,
Carlyle and Kingsley. One of the earliest references to their use in A.S.
times is in *Beowulf* (referring to a sword);

Swā wæs on ðǣm scennum scīran goldes
þurh rūnstafas rihte gemearcod.
[Also the hilt-plates of glittering gold
were carefully inscribed with runic letters.]

By the time of the main A.S. invasions of the mid-fifth century, the
runes we discussed in the last chapter were quite widespread in Norway,
and occurred elsewhere in Scandinavia, with further examples from
eastern Europe, the USSR, Poland and Hungary. Most important for
O.E. runology is a group from Frisia, since the early Frisian dialects are
the closest linguistic neighbours to Old English.

The whole corpus can be divided into two groups, North Germanic
and West Germanic, the two groups having similar fuþarks apart from
a few letters. The earliest inscriptions in England suggest that two strains
arrived here, one from the northern Germanic territories and the other
a West Germanic one probably direct from Frisia. Unfortunately, the

early Frisian runes are mainly incomprehensible, and therefore of little use in reconstructing the W.G. dialect nearest to Old English.

3.4.1 *A.S. runic inscriptions*

The main body of these is naturally a prime source for early Old English. There are about 65, but ignoring those which are either so damaged or so fragmentary that they tell us little, or are known only through early (possibly inaccurate) drawings, or are of doubtful authenticity, or are in magical gibberish, or are of doubtful interpretation, we are left with under thirty significant texts, several of which consist only of personal names. Runes also occur in some O.E. manuscripts, being indeed the basis of the famous 'Runic Poem'. They occur also individually or in small groups, sometimes being used in the manuscripts when scribes wanted for some reason to make individual letters stand out. They are used in the A.S. *Riddles* to give clues to their meanings and, most famous of all, there are the runic signatures embedded in the end of the writer Cynewulf's poems.

The longest runic inscriptions in Britain are those on the Ruthwell Cross in Dumfriesshire (320 characters), the carved whalebone box known as the 'Franks Casket' (over 260), a memorial stone at Thornhill, Yorks (54), the reliquary or casket now at Mortain in Normandy (38), and a bone plate traditionally ascribed to Derby (24). This body is diverse in both time and space (stretching from Edinburgh to Kent), and there are many uncertainties, e.g. with regard to the sounds which are being represented. But for the moment we will return to the beginning.

The A.S. settlers presumably brought with them from the Continent a modified version of the older Germanic fuþark, which shows an increase in the number of runes (reaching in Northumbria a maximum of 33), a process which probably began on Frisian soil prior to the A.S. settlement of Britain. Nevertheless, the oldest inscriptions are extremely short: on an *astragalus* (the ball of an ankle-joint) from Caistor-by-Norwich of the fourth or early fifth century, which obscurely reads *raihan*; on a sixth-century brooch from Wakerley (Northants); and on the famous sixth-century coin found in George III's cabinet bearing the (perhaps) personal name *skanomodu*—however, this may not be Anglo-Saxon at all, but possibly Frisian. Runology is a subject fraught with uncertainties.

3.4.2 *Fuþork alphabets*

Our longest early stretches of A.S. runic inscriptions come only in the eighth and ninth centuries, with the fuþork (now so called because of the change of Germanic *a* to O.E. *o*) of 28 runes on the short sword—or *scramasax*—from the river Thames, and those recorded, together with the names and phonetic values of each rune, in the 'Salzburg Codex' (now Codex 795 of the Österreichische Nationalbibliothek in Vienna). Both preserve substantially the same order, which clearly derives from

Two of the panels on the Franks Casket

The Caistor-by-Norwich runes

the older Germanic fuþark (but with four additions – ƿo, ƿa, ƿy, and ƿea).
I reprint those from the Thames sword here, together with Elliott's (p.
34) transliteration into A.S. letters.

ᚠ ᚢ ᚦ ᚩ ᚱ ᚳ ᚷ ᚹ ᚻ ᚾ ᛁ ᛄ ᛖ ᛈ ᛉ ᛋ ᛒ
f u þ o r c g w h n i j ė p x s t b
            5   10   15

ᛗ   ᛝ   ᛞ ᛚ ᛗ ᛟ ᚪ ᚫ ᚣ ᛠ
e ŋ (=ng) d l m œ a æ y êa
        20   25

The fuþork on the Thames scramasax

Later a further five runes were gradually added to this system, but perhaps only in the Nb dialect: the early eighth-century Ruthwell Cross uses 31, but the final 33-letter version appears only in George Hickes's *Linguarum Veterum Septentrionalium Thesaurus* (1705), fortunately copied from the runes of MS Cotton Otho B X, which perished in the British Museum fire of 1731. The five further runes are: *þia* or *io*, *þk*, *þg* /ɤ/, *þq*, and *þst*. We thus obtain the following 33-letter fuþorc in use in Northumbria around A.D. 800:

ᚠ ᚢ ᚦ ᚩ ᚱ ᚳ ᚷ ᚹ ᚻ ᚾ ᛁ ᛄ   ᛋ   ᛤ ᛣ ᛉ ᛏ
f u þ o r c g! w h n i j ė/[ç] p x s t

ᛒ ᛗ ᛗ ᛚ ᚸ ᚫ ᚸ ᛗ ᚱ ᚠ ᚩ ᚣ ᚷ ᚻ ᚳ ᛋ ᛥ
b e m l ŋ œ d a æ y êa îo k gⁿ q ŝt

3.4.3 *Dates and places*

The dating and localization of runic inscriptions is a hazardous task, but R.I. Page has two excellent distribution maps of inscriptions located in England before and after 650, the weight of distribution in the first being the south-east and the east Midlands, in the second north Mercia and Northumbria. But Page is careful to point out that portable objects in particular (coins, swords, rings, boxes, brooches and the like) could easily have originated elsewhere, and are therefore not totally reliable evidence for O.E. dialects. I take it, however, that the inscriptions on the northern rune-stones (especially the huge stones at Ruthwell and Bewcastle), give us every indication as to what later Nb Old English looked like, especially when taken in conjunction with the language of O.E. manuscripts of known Nb provenance. Most of these stones are clearly of Christian origin, Christianity in this area having accepted the old pagan method of writing.

3.4.4 Runic evidence for O.E. language

The longer runic texts are basic data for our knowledge of early Old English, while even the shorter ones tell us something about primitive sound-change, about the pronunciation and grammar of the very earliest Old English of which we know, and supply some additions to its vocabulary. The following examples of what is offered by the runes are indebted to Page's analysis.

One example of an ingenious interpretation which Page (p. 183) thinks may illustrate extremely primitive O.E. forms is the aforementioned *raihan* of the Caistor-by-Norwich *astragalus*, which he links to P.G. **raiho*, which gives O.E. *raha* and *rā*, Pr.E. *roe* (the *astragalus* does, indeed, come from a roe). If this interpretation is correct, then the inscription shows two very early characteristics: namely primitive O.E. *h* preserved between vowels where it was later to be lost, and P.G. *ai* retained, whereas later it > O.E. *ā*.

Again, the runic inscriptions draw attention to 'the vast mass of the [O.E.] language that once existed but is not recorded because it stands outside the main manuscript traditions of Anglo-Saxon England' (p. 219). Sometimes, for example, the inscriptions, as with the early manuscripts, show the language as it was before the unstressed vowels -*æ* and -*i* fell together in late O.E. -*e*: a memorial stone from Great Urswick (Lancs north of the sands) retains such spellings as *setæ* (W.S. *sette*) 'set up' (p.t.) and *saulæ* (W.S. *saule/sawle*) 'soul' (dat.), and these endings contrast with that of *Tūnnini* (= W.S. *Tūnwine*), a personal name on the same stone.

The specific local features that can be distinguished on the runic monuments are virtually all Northumbrian and Mercian, since these are the main geographical areas where the non-portable objects are, and their language is clearly similar to that of early manuscripts known to come from those regions. One simple example of this is the impressive number of words recorded in runic letters which show what linguists call 'glides' – that is, a vowel which develops between two consonants: the Mortain Casket's *gewarahtæ*, the Kirkheaton (Yks) stone's *worohtæ* (both of which = W.S. *(ge)worhte* 'became') are examples, and these may be evidence that the spoken version of Old English (as distinct from the written) had more glides of this sort than the manuscripts record.

Finally, the inscriptions supply some additions to A.S. vocabulary, though the words in question are often difficult to interpret, as three

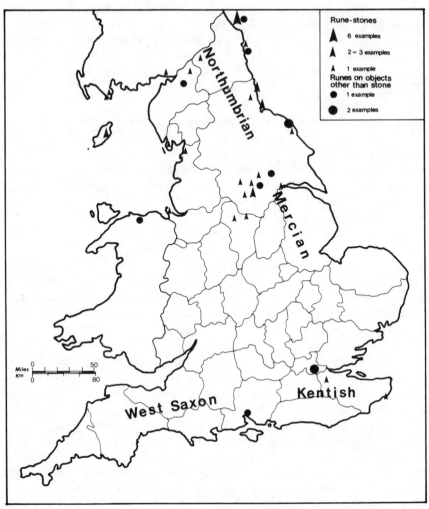

6. Post-650 runic monuments

examples from the Franks Casket easily demonstrate: *fergenberig* (apparently 'cliff-bank'); *gasric* (? 'ocean', 'rager', 'impetuous creature', 'spear-wounded', or 'whale': the word has been variously interpreted); *grorn* (either 'turbid', if referring to the sea, or 'sad', if referring to the whale out of whose bone the box was made). We are on somewhat easier ground when we consider the contribution the runes have made to otherwise unrecorded personal names, or to recording variants upon known names – *Pada*, *Epa/Æpa*, *Æþiliræd* (= W.S. *Æþelræd*), *Wigræd*, and so on – since these are clearly recognizable as such, and need no further interpretation.

3.4.5 *The Ruthwell Cross*

Finally, we may briefly consider the extensive series of runes on the Ruthwell Cross, as a simple but comprehensive illustration of how much such inscriptions contribute to our knowledge of Primitive Old English – and in a dialect far removed from the more familiar late West Saxon. They are thus both archaic and dialectal. The following is based on R.W.V. Elliott's description and transliteration of the runes (pp. 90–96), though the translation of the Vercelli version into modern English is my own. (Note that in Elliott's system of transliteration (following that of Bruce Dickins) $\bar{g}$ is intended to mean /g/ or /ɤ/ as distinct from /j/ (a value the letter had before front vowels), and k transliterates a special Ruthwell rune denoting front or palatalized /k/, i.e. /k/ in the context of a front vowel such as *e* /e/.

In addition to lavish sculptural ornamentation, this 18-foot tall stone cross, a splendid specimen of early eighth-century Nb art, and certainly the best-known and most imposing of all the English runic stone monuments, bears inscriptions in both Roman and runic characters. The former refer to the ten main sculptured panels which show Christian figures and biblical scenes.

The main runic inscription is carved on the two narrower sides of the cross and is devoted entirely to certain passages, in early eighth-century Nb Old English, from *The Dream of the Rood.* In these the Cross itself speaks of the agony and glory of the Crucifixion. For convenience, Elliott (pp. 91–2, reproduced in the box below) gives the runes in separate words and in lines corresponding to those of the full text of the poem, which is found, mainly in W.S. dialect, in the Vercelli Codex (*c.* AD 1000). No marks of division are, however, used on the cross. Some likely readings are added in brackets, and points are used to indicate the probable number of missing runes.

The equivalent lines in the fuller Vercelli text run as follows:

Ongyrede hine þa geong hæleð (þæt wæs god ælmihtig)
strang ond stiðmod. Gestah he on gealgan heanne,
modig on manigra gesyhðe, þa he wolde mancyn lysan.
Bifode ic þa me se beorn ymbclypte. Ne dorste ic hwæðre bugan to
     eorðan,
Rod wæs ic aræred. Ahof ic ricne cyning,
heofona hlaford, hyldan me ne dorste.
Bysmeredon hie unc butu ætgædere. Eall ic wæs mid blode bestemed,
begoten of þæs guman sidan, siððan he hæfde his gast onsended.
cwiðdon cyninges fyll. Crist wæs on rode.
     Hwæðere þær fuse feorran cwoman
to þam æðelinge. Ic þæt eall beheold.
Sare ic wæs mid sorgum gedrefed, hnag ic hwæðre þam secgum to
     handa,

The Ruthwell Cross, south side

standan steame bedrifenne; eall ic wæs mid strælum forwundod.
Aledon hie ðær limwerigne, gestodon him æt his lices heafdum,
beheoldon hie ðær heofenes dryhten, ond he hine ðær hwile reste.

[Then the young Warrior (who was almighty God) stripped himself

The Ruthwell Cross, east side

Strong and courageous of heart. He ascended onto the high gallows,
Brave in the sight of many, when he intended to redeem mankind.
I trembled when the Hero embraced me. But I dared not bow to
   the earth,
I was raised up as a cross. I bore the noble King,

Line 39 ..ᚷᛖᚱᛖᛞᚨᛖ ᚻᛁᚾᚨ ᚷᛟᛞ ᚨᛚᛗᛖᛉᛏᛏᛁᚷ

        geredæ hinæ g̅od almeᵹttig

East
side
(north-
east)

40 ᚦᚨ ᚻᛗ ᛈᚨᛏᚻᛗ ᛗᚻ ᚷᚨᛚᚷᚢ ᚷᛁᛋᛏᛁᚷᚨ

    þa he walde on g̅algu gistig̅a

41 .ᛗᚻᛁᚷ ᚠ... .....ᛗᚻᛗᛁ

    (m)odig f[   ] men

42 .ᚢᚷ. [about thirty characters lost]

    (b)ug̅(a)

Line 44 ....ᛁᚻ ᚱᛁᛁᚻᚨᚠ ᚲᚢᚾᛁᚲᚻ

    ic riicnæ k̅yniŋc

45 ᚻᛏᚠᚢᚾᚨᛋ ᚻᛚᚨᚠᚨᚱᛈᚻ ᚻᚨᛚᚦᚨᚱ ᛁᚻ ᚻᛁ ᚻᚨᚠᚱᚢᛏᚨ

East
side
(south
east)

    hêafunæs hlafard   hælda ic ni dorstæ

48 ᛒᛁᚢᛗᚨᚱᚨᛞᚢᚾ ᚢᚲᚲᛖᛏ ᛗᛖᛗᛁ ᛒᚨ ᚠᛏᚷᚨᛞᛗᚻ.. ᛁᚻ ...

    bismærædu uŋk̅et   men ba ætg̅ad(ræ) ic (wæs)

        ᛗᛁᚦ ᛒᛚᛗᚻᚨᚠ .ᛁᚢᛏᛗᛈᛁ.

        miþ blodæ (b)istemi(d)

49 ᛒᛁ [about forty characters lost]

    bi

Line 56 ᚨᚱᛁᚢᛏ ᛈᚠᚢ ᛗᚻ ᚱᛖᚻᛁ

    krist wæs on rodi

57 ᚻᛈᛖᛗᚦᚱᚨ ᚦᛗᚱ ᚠᚾᚢᚠ ᚠᚢᚱᚱᚨᛁ ᚨᛈᛖᛈᚢ

West
side
(south-
west)

    hweþræ þer fusæ fêarran kwomu

58 ᚠᚦᚦᛁᛚᚨ ᛏᛁᛚ ᛗᚨᚾᛈᛗ ᛁᚻ ᚦᚨᛏ ᚨᛏ ᛒᛁᚻ...

    æþþilæ til anum ic þæt al bih(êald)

59 ᚢ... ᛁᚻ ᚦᚠᚢ ᛗᛁ. ᚢᚠᚱᚷᚢᛈᛗ ᚷᛁᚻᚨᚱᚲ..ᚻ

    s(aræ) ic wæs mi(þ) sorg̅um gidrœ(fi)d

        ᚻ.ᚠᚷ [about eighteen characters lost]

        h(n)ag̅

Line 62 ᛗᛁᚦ ᚢᛏᚱᛗᛚᚢᛈᛗ ᚷᛁᚦᛁᛈᚻᛗᚠᚻ

    miþ strelum   giwundad

West
side
(north-
west)

63 ᚠᛏᛗᚷᚦᚨᚾᛁ ᚻᛁᚠ ᚻᛁᚻᚠ ᛚᛁᛗᚠᚷᚱᛁᚷᚾᚨ ᚷᛁᚢᛏᛈᚻᛈᚢᚾᛁ

    alegdun hiæ hinæ limwœrignæ   gistoddun

        ᚻᛁᛗ.....ᛚᛁᚻᚠᚢ ..ᚠ..ᛈᛗ

        him.....licæs (hêa)f(du)m

64 ..ᚻᛏ.ᚻᚢ. ᚻᛁ.ᚦᛗ [about twenty characters lost]

    (bi)hêa(l)du(n) hi(æ) þe(r)

The Lord of the heavens, I dared not bend.
They mocked us both together. I was all soaked in blood,
Streaming from the man's side, when he had sent forth his spirit.
They★ bewailed the King's death. Christ was on the cross.
But eager ones came there from afar
To that Prince. I beheld all that.
I was bitterly grieved with sorrows, but I bowed to the hands of
    men,
Standing bespattered with blood; I was utterly wounded with spears.
Then they laid down the limb-weary one, stood at the head of his
    body,
Then they looked at heaven's Lord, and he rested himself there a
    while.]

★i.e. all Creation

Some contrasts between the two O.E. versions will be evident straight away, the most obvious perhaps being that the Nb text sometimes has archaic *æ* and *i* when unstressed, whereas the W.S. text has *e* for both: *riicnæ* as cf. *ricne*, *bismærædu* as cf. *bysmeredon*, etc., *rodi* as cf. *rode*. Nb *œ* for W.S. long *e* is typical: *gidrœ(fi)d* as cf. *gedrefed*, *limwœrignæ* as cf. *limwerigne*. In inflexions, the most obvious feature is the loss of final *-n* in infinitives and p.t.pls.; this disappeared early in Nb Old English: *hælda* as cf. W.S. *hyldan*, *bismærædu* as cf. *bysmeredon*, *kwomu* as cf. *cwomon* (the p.t.pls. also show archaic *u* for W.S. *o*, and in this respect are closer to the O.N. forms: cf., e.g., O.N. *kwomu*).

3.5 Non-runic inscriptions

These inscriptions are found on a variety of materials: frequently on stone, but also on many objects made of metal, ivory, whalebone and wood, the vast majority dating from *c.* AD 700 to *c.* AD 1100. Their geographical provenance is of some interest to us, especially those on stones which, like the runic stones, we can assume to have probably remained *in situ* since they were raised. Elizabeth Okasha, who produced a complete hand-list of all the inscriptions, points out (p. 4) however that, as evidence for O.E. dialect, they are not necessarily reliable: although some carvers may have been local men, perhaps employed on a full-time basis by a local monastery, many were probably itinerant. But when their language corresponds to the language of manuscripts of known provenance, we may surely accept it as reliable.

About 80 per cent of the inscribed stones are found roughly north of a line from the Wash to the Wirral (their distribution pattern follows closely that of the runic inscriptions on stone and of A.S. carved stones). This is possibly due to the cultural sophistication of the 'golden age of Northumbria' (seventh and eighth centuries) but more likely, according to Okasha, to the large quantities of suitable stone available in that region as compared with the south.

The non-runic inscriptions are useful for various reasons, in the same way that, as we have already seen, the runic inscriptions help to extend our knowledge of O.E. vocabulary. This is less so in the case of those in Roman letters, but like the runes they 'give a contextual meaning' (Page, p. 219) for a word like *becun* [Pr.E. *beacon*] which occurs so often that it must have been a current one. The word occurs only in inscriptions and not in the manuscripts. A cross of the eighth to ninth centuries, for example, found in about 1830 at Dewsbury (Okasha, no. 30), reads:

 −RHTAE BECUN A[E]FTER BEORNAE GEBIDDAD
    D[A]ER SAULE

(the square brackets, here and elsewhere, enclose a damaged letter where restoration of it is fairly certain.)

> '−a monument in memory of his child (*or* lord); pray for the (i.e. his) soul.'

The incomplete first word is probably part of an O.E. name in the dat. sg. and BEORNAE may be the dat. of O.E. *bearn* 'child' (Pr.E. *bairn*) or *beorn* 'lord'.

Becun apparently has three implications in the runic monumental verse inscriptions (Page, pp. 159–60), and these probably apply to the non-runic ones also: 'token' or 'symbol' (of the deceased); 'something impressive and conspicuous'; and 'brilliance' − literally a shining beacon (like some Scandinavian stones, the English ones may have been brightly painted originally). Here we have, then, a word unique to inscriptional practice, thus extending our knowledge of Old English in the same way that the glossaries and certain elements in place-names do. A second example, allied to this one, is the use of the unique Latin word *signum* 'token, symbol' in the Yarm (north Yks) inscription of the eighth to ninth centuries (Okasha, no. 145), a borrowing into Old English which occurs nowhere else.

Many of the personal names in the inscriptions are known to us also from the manuscripts, e.g. *Æðelmǣr*, *Ceolfrið*, *Ēadburg*, *Godwine*, *Wǣrmund* and many more in Old English, and *Brandr*, *Grímr*, *Iarl*, *Ormr*, *Ulfr*, etc., in Old Norse, but there are several unrecorded ones, e.g. O.E. *Costaun* at York (Okasha, no. 152), *Torhtswīð* at Hartlepool (Okasha, no. 46), and about half-a-dozen more uncertain ones. Others are only rarely found, e.g. *Ēawynn* on the 'Eawen ring', probably of the ninth to tenth centuries (Okasha, no. 155), otherwise recorded only once. All are included in Okasha's comprehensive lists (pp. 152–4), which also include Old Irish *Muiredach* from Alnmouth (Nb; Okasha, no. 2) and possibly

Old Welsh *Oue(i)n* (unless this is O.E. *Ōwine*) from Haddenham (Cambs; Okasha, no. 43).

Some of the earlier inscriptions show forms comparable to those on the runic stones, e.g. *beornæ* (above), with -*æ* instead of -*e*; likewise such forms as Nb *æftær* (later *æfter*), *eomæ* (later *eome* 'uncle'; Okasha, no. 39). This (as other stones) also uses *D* in its inscription, the archaic spelling for *Ð*/ð/.

There are one or two items of more random interest. The Lanteglos cross shaft (Okasha, no. 69) is of some significance in that its eleventh-century or post-Conquest inscription contains the only extant Old English from Cornwall, though its now fragmentary form tells us virtually nothing about late Old English in that county.

One or two of the inscriptions show O.N. influence. That on the late tenth-to-eleventh-century sun-dial from Aldbrough, Humberside (Okasha, no. 1) probably contains the O.N. dat. pronoun *hanum* 'him' used as a reflexive 'himself'; while the much longer three inscriptions dated 1055–65 on the Kirkdale (north Yks) sundial (Okasha, no. 64) has names of Scandinavian origin – *Orm*, *Gamal*, *Tosti*, *Brand*. This is a very important monument in that it gives a fairly exact dating by reference to both Tosti, earl of Northumbria (1055–65) and King Edward the Confessor (1042–66). The three texts show the lack and confusion of late O.E. inflections which is reflected in the manuscript evidence.

Finally, here is the inscription (late tenth to eleventh centuries) on a circular silver disc brooch (Okasha, no. 114) found at Sutton (Cambs.):

+ ÆDVÞEN ME AG   AGE HYO DRIHTEN
DRIHTEN HINE AÞERIE   ÐE ME HIRE ÆTFERIE
BUTON HYO ME SELLE   HIRE AGENES ÞILLES

Probable translation:

+ Ædvwen owns me   may the Lord own her.
May the Lord curse him   who takes me from her,
unless she gives me   of her own will.

This is an 'owner formula', followed by a Christian curse, as occurs in wills and charters. The first line is in traditional O.E. alliterative verse, the second in rhyme, perhaps reflecting the typical mixing of these two types which was taking place at the time.

In the text the letter þ is still being used for later *w*: and the interesting form *hyo* 'she' occurs, which students of classical Old English are more used to seeing as *heo* or *hio*: presumably the *y* is simply an interchange for the letter *i*, as occurs frequently at this period and in Middle English. On the whole, the text is in the 'normal' West Saxon that we should expect from its period.

3.6 Inscriptions on coins

This concludes our consideration of inscriptions, runic and non-runic, except for one other type, namely those found on coins. These consist solely of the personal names of the moneyers, but some mention must be made of them, since this corpus of well over 5,000 late A.S. coins bears impressive testimony to sound-change at a crucial time – the transition between Old and Middle English. In a long paper on this subject, Fran Colman examined the linguistic evidence to be gleaned from the personal names found on the coins minted in the reign of Edward the Confessor (1042–66), and although coin inscriptions, runic and non-runic, are to be found from an earlier period, I confine myself for purposes of example to this well-documented one. The following remarks and examples are based on Colman's summary of the late O.E. evidence found on coins.

First of all, however, one or two preliminaries. Coin-spellings have a special value for our purpose because they can be dated within far more precise limits than can manuscripts (those under consideration here, within three years), and are thus records of O.E. spellings at the time of minting. There is also a substantial body of such evidence: about 350 different moneyers' names in various spellings, for example, are recorded for the reign of Edward the Confessor alone. These are mainly of O.E., but also of Scandinavian and Continental Germanic, origin – there are also some with possibly Celtic, and other, etymologies. They may consist of two elements (O.E. *Ladmær*, O.N. *Spraceling*) or of only one, e.g. O.E. *Manna*. The heaviest distribution of the Scandinavian names is predictably in the Danelaw, especially in its northern half, although, due to the mobility of the population, Scandinavian names have been found at places as far south as London and Winchester: *Spraceling*, above, is a case in point, perhaps in origin a type of nickname – the first element may be connected either with O.N. *spraka* 'to creak, rattle', or with *sprakki* 'a dandy or a woman'. Although common in early Old English, they were extremely common in Scandinavian, as witness the most famous of all, king *Haraldr Fagrhár* 'Harold of the beautiful hair'.

More specifically, then, how do coin-names add to our knowledge of late Old English and the sound-changes which took place in it? Here are one or two examples.

1. During the transition from Old to Middle English, the sound expressed by the O.E. letter *æ* (1.4, 3.3) and that expressed by *a* became one, without any distinction between them; both ended up symbolized by the latter, which also had the sound associated with it in modern English. The coin-spellings give impressive pre-Conquest evidence of this change, and Colman is able to cite *Alfsie* beside *Ælfsige* from Chester, *Alfnað* beside *Ælfnoð* from Lincoln, *Alfwald* and *Alfwold* from Salisbury, and *Alfwold* beside *Ælfwold* from Wilton, all names with the first element O.E. *ælf* 'elf'.

2. During the late O.E. period, the consonant /ɣ/ (as in German *sagen*) changed to the semi-vowel /w/, so that, e.g., O.E. *fugol* > *fowl*, *sorg* > sorrow. The second element in some name-forms on coins from York shows this change actually taking place: *-fuhel*, *-fuhl*, and *-fuel* exist side by side with the older *-fugel*, suggesting the gradual 'weakening' of /ɣ/ to /w/.

3. Finally, the coins testify to one of the most important changes in late Old and early Middle English, namely the weakening of the vowel in final unstressed syllables, ending up as the 'neutral' sound [ə] (1.11): by late O.E. times, the sounds expressed by the letters *u, o* and *a* in, e.g., the inflectional endings of words, namely [u] [o] and [a], had all coalesced in [ə]. Coins from Lincoln show the name *Gife* (< O.E. *gifu* 'gift'); from London *Godesune* beside *Godsunu*; from Canterbury *Manne* beside *Manna*; from York the three parallel forms *Scule, Scula* and *Sculæ*. Alternations of *u* and *e*, of *a* and *e*, and of *a, æ* and *e* are well-known in early M.E. manuscripts, and show scribal confusion between the late O.E. unstressed vowels, since they were all tending in speech to coalesce in one sound [ə]; the pre-Conquest coins give additional and very dateable testimony to this movement.

3.7 Interim summary

The passages and inscriptions in the several O.E. dialects provide ample evidence for written Old English as outlined in Chapter 1. The material we have looked at so far gives us the possibility of also reconstructing spoken Old English, for, looking at the written form of a language, we can often get behind its surface to infer what its sound-*system* is, even if we cannot reconstruct the individual sounds in minute detail. In conclusion, therefore – rather than giving a synopsis of Old English sounds – I give as a specimen a phonemic transcription of the Lord's Prayer in the language as it is thought to have sounded in the classical W.S. period. Note that /r/ is trilled. Theoretically the letter *e* = /e/, but in unstressed position I have transcribed it /ə/, since it had almost certainly reached this more indeterminate sound by the late O.E. period.

Fæder	ūre	þū	þe	eart	on	heofonum,	sī	þīn	nama
fædər	*u:rə*	*θu:*	*θe*	*eart*	*ɔn*	*heovonum*	*si:*	*θiin*	*nama*

gehalgod.	Tō	becūme	þīn	rīce.	Gewurþe	ðīn	willa
jəhalɣod	*to:*	*bəku:mə*	*θi:n*	*ri:tʃə*	*jəwurðə*	*θi:n*	*willə*

on	eorðan	swā	swā	on	heofonum.	Ūrne	gedæghwāmlīcan
ɔn	*eorðan*	*swa:*	*swa:*	*ɔn*	*heovonum*	*u:rnə*	*jədæjhwa:mli:tʃan*

hlāf	syle	ūs	tōdæg.	And	forgyf	ūs	ūre	gyltas,
hlɑ:f	*sylə*	*u:s*	*to:dæj*	*and*	*fɔrjiv*	*u:s*	*u:rə*	*gyltas*

swā swā wē forgyfað ūrum gyltendum. And ne gelæd
swa: swa: we: forjivaθ u:rum gyltəndum and ne jəlæ:d

þū ūs on costnunge, ac alȳs ūs of yfele.
θu: u:s on kostnuŋgə ak aly:s u:s ov yvələ.

3.8 Place- and personal names in manuscripts

The presence of names in A.S. charters has already been mentioned, but they also occur in other documents. For the earlier A.S. period one of the most important sources for place- and personal-names is *ASC* (3.2) in its several versions; the first sections of it appear to have been compiled towards the end of the ninth century, though names are, of course, also found in the manuscripts of Latin works like Bede's *History* (3.3.1). Some of these latter are of an early (eighth-century) date and preserve archaic and dialectal (often Nb) spellings such as those we have already met. Undoubtedly, however, the most important source for our knowledge of such names is *Domesday Book* (*DB*), compiled by 1086, although this immensely valuable source has to be treated with caution since the scribes were Norman, trying to represent English sounds by the nearest equivalent in their own pronunciation.

DB, together with the invasion of England which produced it – the Norman Conquest of 1066 – falls well inside the O.E. period from the linguistic point of view; but the neatest method of dealing with it will, I believe, be to illustrate by giving a conspectus (4.6, below) – from A.S. times, through *DB*, up to late Middle English – of half-a-dozen names, to show how this sort of material may be used as an ancillary to the main sources for the history of English. First however I want to suggest, by looking at some place-names, how we can supplement our knowledge of Old English. The examples are taken from the Introduction to Ekwall's *Dictionary of Place-Names* (pp. xxx–xxxii). Ekwall notes four particular values of place-names for linguistic study:

1. They frequently contain personal names found nowhere else outside place-names, and are therefore of great importance for our knowledge of A.S. nomenclature, including the personal names of the early tribes. The name *Godhelm* (< O.E. *god* or *gōd* + *helm*, both of which are elements, though occurring separately, in personal names), e.g., has been found only with certainty in the Surrey name *Godalming*. Women's names are quite common: *Ēadburg* is especially common (in *Aberford*, e.g.), but there are many others, e.g. *Beaduburg* (in *Babraham*), *Ēadgifu* (in *Eddington*).

2. Place-names contain many old words unrecorded elsewhere, showing that Old English preserved some words found in other Germanic languages but not found in O.E. literature; e.g. *Beeston, Bessacar*, etc. contain an element O.E. *bēos* 'reed, rush' (= Du. *bies*, L.G. *bēse*). *Doiley*

shows that Old English had an adjective corresponding to O.N. *digr* 'thick', while *Sompting* testifies to an O.E. *sumpt* (= O.H.G. *sunft* 'marsh').

Again, other place-names prove the existence of O.E. words otherwise unrecorded in *any* Germanic language. Here, Ekwall's special example is the element O.E. *ēan* 'lamb', found in *Enham* and *Yen Hall*. This corresponds to Lat. *agnus*, but is otherwise found only in derivatives (O.E. *ēanian* 'to lamb', *geēan* 'with lamb').

Finally, under this second heading, some place-names testify to otherwise unknown side-forms of O.E. words, e.g. *hagga* beside *haga* 'haw', found in *Hagley* and in *Haglow* (interestingly, the O.E. form with *-gg-* is, in fact, a common element in some modern dialect forms of the word, e.g. *hag, hagag, haggle*).

3. Place-names often afford far earlier references for words than those found in literature, e.g. *Hunter* (first quotation in *OED*, c. 1250) occurs in a *DB* place-name (*Hunston*, Suffolk). *Potter* is found in a charter place-name of 951 (*Potteresleag*) otherwise not until 1284 (*OED*).

4. Place-names are valuable for the history of English sounds, often helping in the dating and localization of sound-changes, the fixing of dialect boundaries, and the like, e.g. the geographical distribution of place-name forms such as *Stratford, Stratton*, as cf. *Stretford, Stretton*, gives information on the O.E. dialects in which the word 'street' appears as O.E. *strǣt* or *strēt*, i.e. it helps in drawing the line between W.S. (*strǣt*) and Anglian (*strēt*) territory. Likewise, one of the chief tests for the distribution between Midland and northern English is the development of O.E. *ā*, which > M.E. *ǭ* in the Midlands and south, but remains as *ā* in the north. The *ā/ǭ* line can be drawn with some accuracy with the help of place-name material.

3.9 The Scandinavian impact

3.9.1 *Evidence for the Scandinavians in England: historical*
Our earliest, and prime, source for the Vikings in England is *ASC*, which reports Danish plundering in the north from the end of the eighth century, and thereafter chronicles the Viking presence – at first sporadic and occasional, but later (from the middle of the ninth century) more permanent. A further important point already noted is the establishment of the 'Danelaw' (cf. map 3, p. 24, a territorial division agreed between king Alfred and Guthrum, king of the East Anglian Danes, and embodied in a treaty known as the *Treaty of Alfred and Guthrum*. But Viking incursions continued, including, from about 900 onwards, a new penetration by Norwegians into the north-west. Warring between the Scandinavians and the English went on until almost the end of the tenth century, when there was a new, highly-organized, second wave of Viking attack.

In 1013 the Dane, Swein Forkbeard, became the first Scandinavian king of all England, but he died in the following year; there followed a series of campaigns, until in 1016 all England was under the rule of the famous Cnut, Swein's younger son. Danish rule continued until 1042, when the old line of Wessex was restored under Edward the Confessor. Thus much pure history is essential if we are to understand the vast *linguistic* impact which the Scandinavian dialects had on English, especially in the north of England.

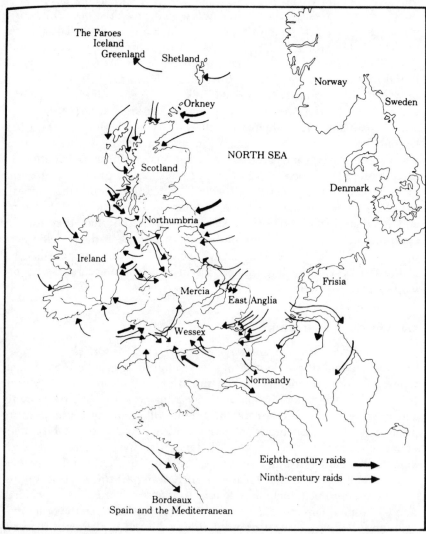

7. Viking raids on western Europe in the eighth and ninth centuries

ASC is not the only English chronicle to chart the 'progress' of the Viking invasion and settlement of England, especially in its later phases, and there are also relevant Scandinavian documents. These all appear in *English Historical Documents c. 500–1042*, the most important examples, after *ASC* (1), being: the *Historia Regum* of Simon of Durham (3); Roger of Wendover's *Flores Historiarum* (4); Florence of Worcestor on the reigns of the Danish kings of England (9); the A.S. poem *The Battle of Maldon* (10); various literary O.N. sources in prose (*Egil's Saga*) and poetry (11–19); other annals and chronicles in short extracts (20–28); Cnut's letter to the people of England (48) and his Laws (50); the Life of St Oswald (236; with an important section on 'the renewal of the Danish attacks', p. 843); and finally, Archbishop Wulfstan's A.S. homily known as *Sermo Lupi ad Anglos* 'the Sermon of the Wolf to the English' (240). Between them, these documents give us a vivid reconstruction of the history underlying the Scandinavian influence on the English language. We may add that there is also a large amount of archaeological evidence for the Vikings in England, seen nowhere better than in the important sites uncovered at York. Such evidence naturally supports and illuminates the direct linguistic evidence, to which we now turn.

3.9.2 *Evidence for the Scandinavians in England: linguistic*
Various types of linguistic evidence emphasize the profound and lasting Scandinavian influence on English, which survives to this day in the vocabulary both of the dialects and of Standard English. The northern dialects were also affected in their sound systems.

The problem here is frankly one of methodology: that the Scandinavian dialects were already having a decisive influence on spoken English even in A.S. times—at the very least from the later part of them—can scarcely be doubted, but that influence hardly appears at all in the O.E. writings, except in a small number of inscriptions, a few loan-words in the literature, and some names in *ASC*, the charters and *DB*. The main body of evidence does not emerge until the Middle English and later periods, and consists of a large number of loan-words in M.E. manuscripts, of numerous place-names, and of the Scandinavian words still in Standard English and the dialects. Apart from the place-names (4.7) I have, nevertheless, decided to deal with this later evidence here, even though some of it does not make a 'physical' appearance within the period, since the great bulk of Scandinavian influence, recorded or unrecorded, must have taken place during the O.E. period, and it seems sensible to tie the evidence firmly to it. Let us first, however, take a very brief look at the Scandinavian runic inscriptions.

3.9.3 *Scandinavian runes*
The northern Germanic peoples had altered the original fuþark in a way different from the A.S. peoples—by cutting it down to 16 characters,

instead of increasing it, and by simplifying some shapes. Thus, by the time the Viking hordes poured into England, their runes were markedly different from those of the Anglo-Saxons, and also emerged in various forms. This so-called younger fuþork is well dealt with by Page (chap. 12).

Many of the purely Norse runic inscriptions (i.e. in a Scandinavian dialect) in England are obscure or illegible. Some of them are, indeed, in the Norse tongue itself, and as such hardly concern us, but they are important evidence for the duration of time that the Scandinavian dialects were being spoken in England, since they date from the eleventh and twelfth centuries. One example is a sculptured burial stone from St Paul's churchyard. It reads:

(KI) [or (FI)] LET LEKIA STIN ÞENSI AUK TUKI
'Ginna (or Finna) and Toki had this stone placed'

There is one monument, however, where Scandinavian runes are used for an inscription which is definitely English. This is the font at Bridekirk (Cumbria). The elaborate carving on the font can be dated to the twelfth century, and the inscription, on the east face of the pedestal, is in the form of a rhyming couplet. We may regard it as a very early form of Middle English, and it is evidence that at least here, in NW England, Viking runes were so far naturalized as to be used by speakers and readers of English. The inscription (slightly simplified here from Page's detailed version, p. 196) reads:

+ RICARÞ HE ME IWROCTE 7 TO ÞIS MERÐ GER [..] ME BROCTE
'Richard he made me and Ger .. brought me to this splendour'

In the more familiar form of early Middle English known to students, this would look like:

+ Ricard he me iwrohte,
And to þis merðe Ger .. me brohte

Note that the archaic spelling c is retained for /x/ in iwrocte and brocte, but that the old Nb endings in -i have now become the later -e. Ger [..] is probably a second personal name, recording the man who commissioned the font or a second craftsman who embellished it further, perhaps with paint.

3.9.4 *Loans from Scandinavian into Standard English and the dialects (1.7)*
As already noted, a Scandinavian element appears in the manuscripts mainly from early M.E. times, though some words had doubtless been in use orally from at least the ninth and tenth centuries. They form an important body of evidence for influence on both the English vocabulary

The Bridekirk Font, east side

Close-up of the Norse runes on the Bridekirk Font

and its sounds. For example, *window* (O.N. *vind-auga*, literally 'wind-eye') is simply a word borrowed from Scandinavian into English, whereas Nb dialect *flick* (= St.E. *flitch*) is probably an example of Scandinavian influence on the northern English sound system, giving /k/ where Standard English has /tʃ/ (the Scandinavians had no /tʃ/, and substituted their nearest sound /k/ for it); likewise Norse /g/ in Pr.E. *give, get*, which has replaced O.E. *ġ* /j/. Grammatical influence is not lacking either, as we shall see later.

The standard histories list large numbers of Scandinavian words found in Middle English, but it is not my purpose to do that here: the question is – how do we *discover* the Scandinavian element in English? The answer is, of course, by looking at the manuscripts and writings. Let us therefore consider some examples. In the passages that follow, words of Scandinavian origin and those whose forms seem to have been influenced by cognate Scandinavian ones are italicized, and, where possible, in the case of the pure lexical items, the first occurrences of them in English, as recorded in *OED*, given below.

1. Richard Rolle, *Ego Dormio, c.* 1343
(ed. H.E. Allen, *English Writings of Richard Rolle*, Clarendon Press, 1931, p. 61)

This prose work of some 3,500 words, on the subject of complete devotion to heavenly love, is addressed by the Yorkshire writer Richard Rolle (*c.* 1300–49), to a nun (this particular manuscript dedicated it to a nun of Yedingham, a small nunnery a few miles south-east of Pickering, north Yks).

1   Ego dormio et cor meum vigilat. Þai þat lyste[1] lufe,

herken, and here of lufe. In þe sang of lufe it *es*
writen: 'I slepe, and my hert wakes[2].' *Mykel* lufe
he schewes, þat never *es* irk[3] to lufe, bot ay stand*and*,
5 sitt*and*, gang*and*[4], or wirk*and*, *es* ay his lufe thynk*and*
and oftsyth[5] þarof *es* drem*ande*. Forþi[6] þat I lufe, I
wow þe, þat I myght have þe als I walde[7], noght to me,
bot to my Lorde. I will become þat messanger to bryng
þe to hys bed þat hase made þe and boght þe, Criste,
10 þe keyng sonn of heven. For he wil with þe dwelle,
if þou will lufe hym: he askes þe na mare bot þi lufe.
And, my dere *syster* in Criste, my wil þou dose if þou
lufe him. Criste covaytes noght els bot *at* þou do his
wil, and enforce þe[8] day and nyght þat þou leve al
15 fleschly lufe,[9] and al lykyng þat lettes[10] þe *til* lofe
Jhesu Crist verraly[11].

[1]whom it pleases to [2]keeps watch [3]weary [4]going (= walking) [5]often
[6]Because [7]want [8]exert yourself [9]desire; [10]prevents [11]in truth

Lines:
1   *þai* < O.N. *þeir* (*c.* 1200).
2   *es* < O.N. *es*.
3   *mykel* < O.N. *mikill* (*-k-* forms from *c.* 1200; = O.E. *miċel*, Pr.
E. *much*).
4ff *-and(e)* (*standand*, *sittand*, etc.) < O.N. *-andi* pr.p. (= O.E.
-ende).
12   *syster* < O.N. *systir* (= O.E. *sweostor*). In view of the O.E.
cognate, impossible to date: see the entries in *OED*.
13   *at* < O.N. *at* (*c.* 1325; = O.E. *þat*).
15   *til* < O.N. *til* (in Old English, *c.* 800 (Ruthwell Cross)).

2. *Sir Gawain and the Green Knight*, *c.* 1350–75; *GGK*
(ed. J.R.R. Tolkien and E.V. Gordon, 2nd rev. ed. by N. Davis,
Clarendon Press, 1967; see further 4.3, Text 6)

The Scandinavian words in this text are numerous, possibly for
poetic purposes: the alliterative technique, in its search for synonyms,
constantly needed, and used many. In this passage, e.g., *carp* is added
to the traditional stock of words for the notion of declaring, speaking,
etc. See further Tolkien and Gordon (above), pp. 125–8; Davis (above),
pp. 138–41.

1   On þe morne, as vche mon *mynez*[1] þat ty.ne
Þat Dryȝtyn[2] for oure destyne to *deȝe* watz borne,
Wele waxez[3] in vche a *won*[4] in worlde for his sake;
So did hit þere on þat day þurȝ dayntes mony:

5   Boþe at mes and at mele, messes ful quaynt
     Derf men vpon dece drest of þe best.
     Þe olde auncian wyf[5] heȝest ho[6] syttez,
     Þe lorde lufly[7] her by lent, as I trowe[8];
     Gawan and þe gay burde[9] togeder þay seten[10],
10   Euen inmyddez, as þe messe metely come,
     And syþen þurȝ al þe sale, as hem best semed,
     Bi vche grome at his degre *grayþely* watz serued.
     Þer watz mete[11], þer watz myrþe, þer watz much ioye,
     Þat for to telle þerof hit me tene[12] were,
15   And to poynte hit ȝet I pyned me parauenture.
     Bot ȝet I wot þat Wawen and þe *wale burde*[13]
     Such comfort of her compaynye caȝten[14] togeder
     Þurȝ her dere dalyaunce of her derne wordez,
     Wyth clene cortays carp closed fro fylþe,
20   Þat hor play watz *passande* vche prynce gomen,
          in vayres.

[1]remembers [2]the Lord [3]Joy springs up [4]every dwelling [5]woman [6]she (ho)
[7]courteously [8]think [9]lady [10]sat [11]food [12]burden, trouble [13]fair lady [14]took

5–6 Both at dinner and less formal meals, very finely prepared dishes of
    food stalwart men on the dais served in the best manner
10 Right in the middle, as the food duly came
11–12 And then through all the hall, as seemed best to them, each man
    was promptly served according to his rank.
15 If to describe it in detail I perhaps made the effort
18–20 In the pleasant courtly conversation of their private words, with
    pure and gracious talk free from defilement, that their playful words
    surpassed every princely game, in truth

Lines:
1.   *mynez* < O.N. *minna* 'remind', *minnask* 'remember' (*c.* 1200,
    but in this sense only from the fourteenth century; see *OED*,
    Min, v.²).
2.   *deȝe* ? < O.N. *deyja* (unless < an O.E. form *$\star d\bar{e}g(i)an$, etc.;
    c. 1135).
3.   *won* < O.N. *ván* (this meaning from *c.* 1275: see *OED*, Wone,
    sb.²).
6.   *derf* < O.N. *djarfr* 'bold' (*c.* 1200).
12. *grayþely* < O.N. *greiðliga* (before 1300 as adv., *c.* 1205 as adj.;
    see *OED* Gradely).
16   *wale* adj. < O.N. *val* n. 'choice' (*c.* 1250).
19. *carp* < O.N. *karp* 'bragging' n., *karpa* 'to brag' (*c.* 1325 n., but
    carp v. from before 1240).
20. *passande*: -ande < O.N. -andi pr.p. (= O.E. -ende).

3. George Meriton, *A Yorkshire Dialogue*, 1683
(ed. A.C. Cawley, Yorkshire Dialect Society Reprint II, 1959)

For my final example, I have taken the somewhat unusual course of choosing a passage right outside the medieval period. The *Dialogue*–one in a tradition of humorous dialect dialogues intended to display, and perhaps preserve, north Yks dialect–nevertheless contains plenty of certain or probable Scandinavian words of a much earlier origin (see notes below).

In the passage, *M.* = 'Mother', and *F.* = 'Father'. The odd-looking spellings, e.g. *deau* 'do', *cawd* 'cold', represent local dialect sounds (see further 5.9.4).

1   *M.* Come tack up'th Beefe Tibb, ist Dubler ready,
Thy Father and Hobb *mun gang*[1] to'th Smiddy[2],
And fetch the Specks[3], *Sock*[4], and Coulter hither,
Seedtimes now come, they *mun* Sawe *Haver*[5];
5   Stride Tibb, and *clawt*[6] some Cassons[7] out 'oth Hurne[8],
Then geay[9] Thy wayes and fetch a *Skeel*[10] of Burne[11]
And *hing* the pan ore'th Fire, ith *Rekin-crewke*[12]
And Ise wesh'th *Sile*[13], and dishes up 'ith *Newke*[14]
And than wee'l all to Bed; here's a cawd Neet
10   But Husband Ise cling close, and weese *blend*[15] Feet,
   F. Pray thee deau[16] Pegg, than Ise git up 'ith Morne,
and *late*[17] some pokes[18], and put up our Seed Corne;
Than thou may sarra'th[19] Goats and Gilts[20] with *draffe*[21],
And Ise give *Yawds*[22] some Hinderends and *Caffe*[23],
15   Than for our Breakfasts, Thou may haet[24] some Cael[25],
Til I lye[26] by my Shackfork[27] and my Flail:
And Hobbs mack ready my Harrows and my Plewgh[28]
And he and I Pegg, sall deau weel aneugh;
Ive hard it tauk'd, and now the Trueth Ive fund,
20   *Amell*[29] tweay[30] Steauls[31], the Tail may fall to'th grund.
[1]must go [2]smithy [3]long, thin pieces of iron nailed to the plough to stop it wearing [4]ploughshare [5]oats [6]rake [7]dried cow-dung [8]fireplace corner [9]go [10]pail [11]water [12]pot-hook [13]strainer, sieve [14]corner [15]put together [16]do [17]look for [18]sacks [19]give food to the [20]young pigs [21]pig-swill [22]horses [23]chaff [24]heat [25]broth [26]lay [27]threshing-fork [28]plough [29]among [30]two [31]stools

Lines:

2.   *mun* < O.N. *munu* (*c.* 1200); *gang* < O.N. *ganga* (= O.E. *gangan*).

4.   *haver* ? < O.N. *hafre* (1362).

5.   *clawt* ? < O.N. (all northern quotations in *EDD*, s.v. Claut, sb.1 and v.).

6. *skeel* < O.N. *skjóla* (*c.* 1330).

7. *hing* < O.N. *hingja* (before 1300; see *OED* Hang, v., para. A2); *rekin* < O.N. *rekendr* pl. (sg. *★rekandi*, unrecorded: see *OED*, s.v. Rackan, 1400) + *crewke* (= 'crook') < O.N. *krókr* (*c.* 1290).

8. *sile* < O.N. *★síl*; cf. modern Norw. and Sw. *síl* (1459–60); *newke* (probably) < O.N., cf. Norw. dialectal *nōk* 'hook, bent figure', etc. (before 1300).

10. *blend* (probably) < O.N. *blanda* (before 1300).

12. *late* < O.N. *leita* (before 1300: see *OED*, Lait, v.²).

13. *draffe* (probably) < O.E. *★dræf*, but cf. Icelandic *draf* (*c.* 1205).

14. *yawd* < O.N. *jalda* 'mare' (only from early sixteenth century); *caffe* shows /k/, presumably by O.N. influence, as cf. St.E. *chaff.*

20. *amell* < O.N. *á milli*, etc. (before 1300).

From these examples, I hope it may be clear what a great influence Old Norse had on late Old English – on its vocabulary, and also on its sounds and grammar. An examination of more documents would give us hundreds of further examples, but we may supplement this material by looking at the Scandinavian words in Pr.E. dialects, which also, of course, go back to the medieval period. Again, first occurrences of words are shown recorded in *OED*. A small selection of the information available from dialect sources is presented over the following pages in a few maps based on the data collected by the Survey of English Dialects in the 1950s. See also the map of *I am* in Chapter 5 (map 15, p. 145).

3.10 The Norman Conquest

The purely historical side of the Conquest hardly concerns us further: the relevant sources are to be found in *English Historical Documents*, II (1042–1189), and see also the bibliography to Chapter 1.9. Suffice it to say here that the advent of the Conqueror produced a decline in English literary works and also the end of the W.S. dialect as a literary standard. When English literature fully emerged from its transitional period, it did so in a wide variety of different forms, no single dialect having predominance.

We may therefore end with an extract from the *Peterborough Chronicle*, which nicely marks in every way the untidy transitional period between Old and Middle English.

The *Anglo-Saxon Chronicle* was continued into late O.E. and early M.E. times at Canterbury, Worcester and Peterborough, but that of the last-named, continued up to 1154, is of the greatest interest historically and linguistically. I give here part of the annal for 1137 (the misery of

8. Occurrences of *kirk* (recorded from *c.* 1200; <O.N. *kirkja*) [N.B., in maps 8, 9, 11, 12, (and also 15, 17–20) the dots mark the localities investigated by *SED.*]

KIRK

0   50
Miles
Km
0   80

the country during the anarchy under king Stephen), which is included in most M.E. text-books (e.g. Dickins and Wilson, pp. 4ff.). Words and phrases derived from French, apart from proper names, are italicized. Others are commented on in the notes below.

1   Ðis gære for þe king Stephne ofer sæ to Normandi and
    ther wes underfangen, forþi ðat hi uuenden ðat he
    sculde ben alsuic alse the eom wes, and for he hadde
    get his *tresor*, ac he todeld it and scatered it *sotlice*.
5   Micel hadde Henri king gadered gold and syluer, and na
    god ne dide me for his saule tharof.
    Þa þe king Stephne to Englalande com, þa macod he
    his gadering æt Oxeneford, and þar he nam þe biscop
    Roger of Sereberi, and Alexander, biscop of Lincol, and
10 te *canceler* Roger, his neues, and dide ælle in *prisun*
    til hi iafen up here *castles*. Þa the suikes undergæton
    ðat he milde man was and softe and god, and na *iustise*
    ne dide, þa diden hi alle wundor. Hi hadden him manred
    maked and athes suoren, ac hi nan treuthe ne heolden.

9. Occurrences of *kirn* 'churn' (recorded from 1338–9; cf. O.N. *kirna*)

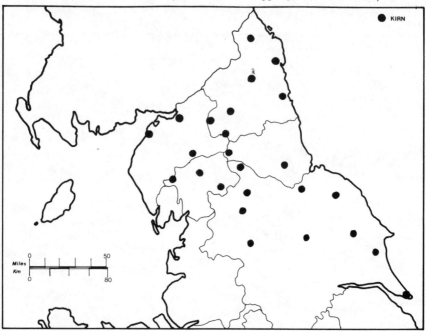

15 Alle he wæron forsworen and here treothes forloren, for
æuric riceman his *castles* makede and agænes him heolden,
and fylden þe land ful of *castles*. Hi suencten suyðe þe
uureccemen of þe land mid *castel*-weorces. Þa þe *castles*
uuaren maked, þa fylden hi mid deoules and yuele men.

20 Þa namen hi þa men þe hi wenden ðat ani god hefden, bathe
be nihtes and be dæies, carlmen and wimmen, and diden
heom in *prisun* efter gold and syluer, and pined heom
untellendlice pining, for ne uuæren næure nan *martyrs*
pined als hi wæron.

[This year, king Stephen went over sea to Normandy and was received
there, because they thought that he would be just like his uncle was,
and because he still had his treasure; but he divided it and scattered [it]
foolishly. King Henry had gathered much gold and silver, and no good
was done for his soul with it.

When king Stephen came to England, then he made his counsel at
Oxford, and there he seized bishop Roger of Salisbury, and bishop
Alexander of Lincoln, and the Chancellor Roger, his nephews, and put
[them] all in prison till they gave up their castles. When the traitors
realized that he was a mild man, and soft and good, and inflicted no
punishments, then they did all [sorts of] atrocities: they had given him
homage and sworn oaths, but they kept no faith. They were all

10. Four Scandinavian loan-words:

steg 'gander' (1483; <O.N. *steggi*, steggr)
lea 'scythe' (1483; <O.N. *lê*)
ket 'rubbish' (*c.* 1220; <O.N. *kjǫt*)
stee 'ladder' (before 1300; <O.N. *stige*, etc.)

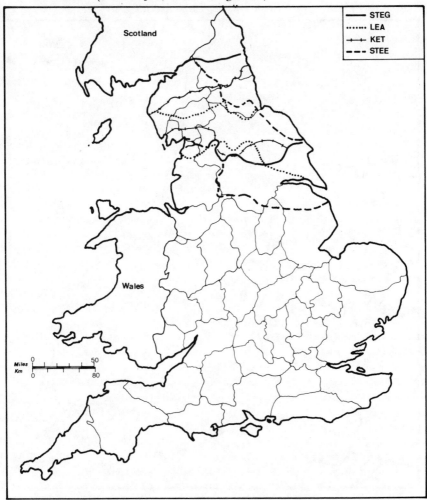

perjured, and their promises of loyalty worthless, for every powerful
man built his castles, and held them against him, and filled the land full
of castles. They greatly oppressed the wretched men of the land with
forced labour on castle-building. When the castles were built, then
they filled them with devils and evil men. Then they took those people
whom they thought had any wealth, both by night and by day –
ordinary men and women – and put them in prison for gold and silver,
and tormented them with unspeakable torture, for no martyrs were
ever so tortured as they were.]

11. Distributions of a different pattern: *lathe* and *lop*. Dots show occurrences of *lathe* 'barn' (*c.* 1250; <O.N. *hlaða*). Boundary line shows general limit of *lop* 'flea' (*c.* 1460; probably <O.N. **hloppa*). Whereas the most familiar pattern of Scandinavian words in twentieth-century dialect is in the form of a diagonal band across the country from north-east to north-west (as seen on other maps here), other types of pattern also occur. Two such are seen here.

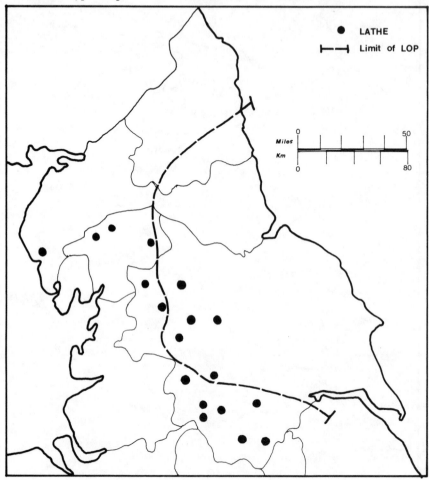

The text shows the written English language at this stage in a state of considerable flux, O.E. spelling conventions surviving side by side with new innovations. Here are some examples.

Sounds and spellings
The most interesting complex here is the use of the letters *a*, *æ* and *e* to represent a number of late O.E. sounds, e.g.: *gære* (1; = O.E. *gēar*); *sæ* (1; = O.E. *sǣ*); *ther* (2; = O.E. *þær*; cf. *þar* 8); *ðat* (2; = O.E. *ðæt*); *ac*

12. Distribution of *lait* 'look for' (before 1300; <O.N. *leita*) and *laik* 'play', etc. (*c.* 1300; the n. from *c.* 1200; <O.N. *leika*)

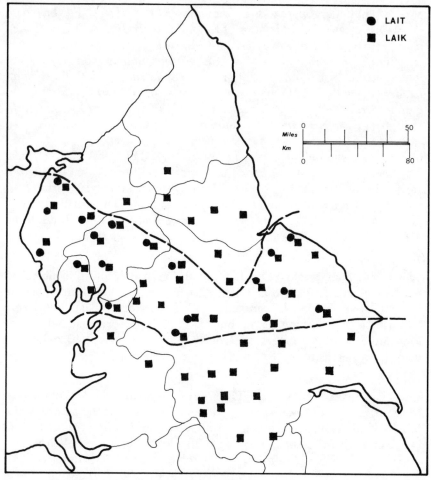

(4; = O.E. *ac*); *hadde* (5; = O.E. *hæfde*, cf. the pls. *hadden* 13 and *hefden* 20 < O.E. *hǣfdon*); *þa* (7; = O.E. *þā*); *ælle* (10; = O.E. (Anglian) *all*, cf. *alle* 13). This is only a very small selection, and the whole text shows the confusion of the situation in much greater detail.

In consonants, we may note the continued use of the letter *c* for /tʃ/ (*riceman* 16); of *sc* for /ʃ/ (*biscop* 9), though *k* is now in use in *king* (1; O.E. *cyning*); *ð* and *þ* also continue in use (*ðat* 2; *þar* 8) beside *th* (*ther* 2, *athes* 14); O.E. front *ġ* /j/ is now represented by either *i* or *g* (*gære* 1, *iafen* 11, *iustise*–a Fr. loan-word, 12); *uu* or *u* are used to represent /w/ (*uuenden* 2, *suencten*, *suyðe* 17, but cf. *forsworen* 15); *t* represents /θ/ at line 10 in the definite article, cf. *the* (3).

Inflections and syntax

Verbs: these are still recognizably Old English in form, though endings have often undergone modification: p.t.sgs. *for* (1; = O.E. *fōr*), *com* (7; = O.E. *c(w)ōm*), *hadde* (3; = O.E. *hæfde*), *macod* (7; = O.E. *macode*), *nam* (8; = O.E. *nam*), *was* (12; = O.E. *wæs*), etc.; p.t.pls.: *uuenden* (2; = O.E. *wēndon*), *iafen* (11; = O.E. *gēafon*), *undergæton* (11; = O.E. *undergēaton*, N.B. -*on* is still preserved), *diden* (13; = O.E. *dydon*), *hadden* (13; = O.E. *hæfdon*), *uuaren, uuæren* (19, 23; = O.E. *wæron*), etc.; p.ps. *underfangen* (2; = O.E. *underfangen*), *gadered* (5; = O.E. *gaderod*), *maked* (14; = O.E. *macod*), *suoren* (14; = O.E. *sworen*), *forloren* (15; = O.E. *forloren*), *pined* (22; = O.E. *pīned*), etc.

Pronouns: the old pl. forms *hi* (2), *he* (22) 'they' (< O.E. *hīe*), *here* (15) 'their' (< O.E. *hiera, heora*) and *heom* (11) 'them' (< O.E. *heom*) are still in use, not having been replaced by the Scandinavian forms *þeir*, *þeira* and *þeim*, which were ultimately to become standard by the end of the M.E. period, *ða* 'those' (20; < O.E. *þā*) also remains, though the definite article now appears as *þe* (1; Pr.E. *the*) rather than O.E. *sē*.

Word order

This is still recognizably Old English: the verb precedes the subject in *for þe king* (1), *þa macod he* (7), etc., cf. Pr.E. 'the king went', 'then he made' (but also cf. *þer he nam*, etc., with Pr.E. word order); *Henri king* (5), with title following name, but cf. Pr.E. word order already in *þe king Stephne* (1, 7), *þe biscop Roger* (8–9), etc.; *þa* … *þa* 'when … then' (11 … 13) is the O.E. 'correlative' construction.

Vocabulary

This is almost entirely still late Old English in nature; the few (italicized) Fr. words, as is common at this period, and because of the nature of the text itself, are mainly concerned with law and order. Note that O.E. *eom* (3) survives, A.Fr. *oncle* not having been adopted in this text; *bathe* (20), however, is < O.N. *báðir, efter* (22) probably owes something to O.N. *eptir* (= O.E. *æfter*), and *carlmen* (21) is < O.N. *karl* + O.E. *menn* (though O.E. also has *hūs-carl* 'house-carl'). One or two other notable items include: *sotlice* (4), which is a combination of Fr. *sot* and O.E. -*līce* (Pr.E. -*ly*), showing the early possibility of combining Fr. and English; *ne dide me* (6) – *me* is shortened *men* 'one', cf. Fr. *on*, used in the same way, i.e. 'was done'; *na iustise ne dide* (12–13) is apparently a partial translation (of which there seem to have been a number in Middle English) of Fr. *faire justise* 'to inflict punishment' (see Dickins and Wilson, p. 155); *wunder* (13) is an O.E. neuter pl. form – these had no endings to mark the pl., however, and this old form is retained here. The sense 'atrocity' is a development from an earlier sense 'omen, portent', a sense apparently not infrequent in Middle English.

4 Middle English
(to c. 1475–1500)

4.1 Introductory

It is natural that this chapter, like the previous one, should be concerned mainly with the language found in manuscripts, since these form the most important concrete evidence for the English of the period. The manuscripts range in date from c. 1150 to c. 1450–75, which is a long period of time, and we shall not therefore expect to find total uniformity over either time or space. The texts given here are only a small selection, intended to show the *sort* of information at our disposal, not by any means a full conspectus of medieval English.

All the M.E. texts here, four early and four later, are such as can be found in the most accessible text-books and selections or well-known editions, and for convenience I have appended the relevant references (number and page reference) to B. Dickins and R.M. Wilson, *Early Middle English Texts* (3rd rev. ed., Bowes and Bowes, 1956; abbreviated 'DW'), J.A.W. Bennett and G.V. Smithers, *Early Middle English Verse and Prose* (2nd ed., Clarendon Press, 1968; 'BS'), and K. Sisam, *Fourteenth-Century Verse and Prose* (Clarendon Press, 1921; 'Sis.'). This should facilitate reference to the further details about them which I do not have space to give here. Each text is followed by a translation or is glossed, and there is also a brief summary of its distinctive linguistic features.

4.2 The production and dissemination of M.E. manuscripts

When one first comes to look at, say, a M.E. lyric or one of Chaucer's *Canterbury Tales* in a text-book or collection of extracts, it is perhaps difficult to realise that what one sees on the printed page is physically only a shadow of the original that lies behind it. Before the days of printing arrived, in the fifteenth century, works were written out by hand on prepared and ruled parchment (the skin of sheep, goats, etc.), vellum (a fine calf-skin parchment) or, from the fourteenth century on, paper (but this was not in common use until the fifteenth century), and then further copies made, usually in monastic cloisters or scriptoria. The process of copying means that, unless we are fortunate enough to possess a 'holograph' (i.e. the manuscript actually written by the author himself), of which there are few – Text 5, below, is a very notable example – we are looking at a work which may be several times removed from the author's original. It may contain mistakes made in the copying process, or 'corrections' of what the scribe, rightly or wrongly, took to be mistakes in his exemplar. This results in what is called 'textual variation' between the manuscripts of a work.

Dialectal variation is, of course, also present. In the recent *Linguistic Atlas of Late Mediaeval English* (vol. I, p. 3), it is acutely pointed out that

> Middle English represents that stage in the history of the language most highly characterised by diversity of written forms; while dialects have been spoken at all periods, it is only during late mediaeval times that local usage is regularly reflecting in writing ... almost any Middle English written before *ca.* 1430 is 'dialectal' as a matter of definition.

Dialectal 'translation' also takes place, because a manuscript from, say, Canterbury may be copied out by a scribe from perhaps Beverley and thus 'translated' from a Kentish dialect, either fully or partially, into a northern one. This might be done quite consistently and thoroughly, with, for example, every occurrence of southern *siche* (etc.) 'such' turned into northern *sike, swilke*, etc., every example of *schulde* turned into *ssolde* or the like, *muche* becoming *mikil*, and so on, or it may be only partially 'converted', so that a mixed dialect results, and this makes it hard to disentangle word-forms belonging to the original dialect from those of the copyist. We also have to deal with variation caused by time. A work originally written in, say, 1325 may be copied out in 'updated' form in 1450, so that the language is of the latter date in general, although the scribe may have perpetuated some older forms of words.

Taking all these considerations into account, it will be obvious that we rarely meet what we might call a 'pure' M.E. dialect, i.e. one uncontaminated by copying or revision. It is thus not easy to state precisely where a manuscript is likely to have been produced, though careful textual study, combined with a scrutiny of any 'external' evidence relating, for example, to the manuscript's present-day location or its known history, and of the various items included in it (since many manuscripts are collections – of poems or sermons, religious pieces, romances and so on), can often achieve a surprising degree of success.

Neither is it always particularly easy to give a date to a manuscript (and such a date will not, of course, necessarily be the same as the date of composition of what the manuscript contains), unless we have a holograph or there is other external evidence. Usually we are dependent upon the palaeographical experts, and even these can date a hand only to within about a quarter of a century. We are thus left with datings like '1425–50' or, perhaps, more precisely, 'mid-fifteenth century, probably *c.* 1440–55 from the style of the illuminated border': the latter example incorporating 'external evidence', namely the style of the illumination (decoration in colour) with which some manuscripts are embellished.

It has become possible more recently, however, to determine the probable provenance of the written dialect of M.E. manuscripts with more precision than hitherto, thanks to over thirty years of research carried out by Professors Angus McIntosh and M.L. Samuels, which has now culminated in the publication of their magisterial *Atlas* (above). For this the characteristics of several thousand manuscripts of between roughly 1350 and 1450 were subjected to scrutiny. McIntosh and Samuels used a procedure which they call the 'fit' technique, which, by comparing the total dialectal characteristics of non-localized texts with those of texts of known provenance, enabled them to localize manuscripts, or portions of manuscripts, in appropriate positions on a map of England. Naturally, the more localizations that could be made, the greater would be the possibility of making even more, which would provide a series of maps 'with ever denser and denser coverage'. The aim of the investigation was primarily to locate and map a large number of *scribal* varieties: i.e. the language of a manuscript is seen first and foremost as a written variety of English, not primarily as one which, so to speak, encodes a form of speech. The editors are as interested in a scribe who wrote *itt* or *ytt* for 'it', which cannot conceivably represent a dialectal pronunciation different from that of *it* or *yt*, as they are in one who wrote *mon* for 'man', which probably does reflect a dialectal pronunciation. There are, in any case, numerous occasions on which it is not clear whether a written form represents a special pronunciation or not, northern *qui* 'why' being an interesting example: does the *qu* represent a very heavily aspirated form of /w/ in the word written in non-northern texts more usually as *hwi*, *hwy*, etc., or is it merely the result of a scribal tradition, handed down over the years, and not necessarily indicating any special spoken form? In the face of such uncertainties, McIntosh and Samuels sensibly decided that – in a period from which we have *only* written, and no spoken, evidence – the written word must have priority in any M.E. dialect survey. The dialectal nature of Middle English should emerge forcefully enough in the following selection of texts.

4.3 Texts

1. Twelfth-century SW Midland: *The Worcester Fragments*
   (DW, I, p. 2; DW's editorial emendations are ignored.)

The Worcester Fragments are the remains of a manuscript, some leaves of which had been cut up and pasted together to form a cover for another book in the Chapter Library at Worcester. These leaves have been collected and now form MS 174 in that collection. When complete, the manuscript apparently contained a copy of Ælfric's *Grammar* and *Glossary*, the short poem here, and a longer one on the *Debate of the Soul and the Body*. The surviving leaves are written in a single hand, dated *c.* 1180, though the language shows that the various pieces were composed at a much earlier date, probably in the late O.E. W.S. literary dialect – though after the Conquest – and then roughly modernized by a later scribe probably writing at Worcester. Nothing is known of the original author. The text printed below is about the disuse of English.

1   Sanctus Beda was iboren her on Breotene mid us,
     And he wisliche bec awende
     Þet þeo Englise leoden þurh weren ilerde.
     And he þeo cnotten unwreih, þe *questiuns* hoteþ,
5   Þa derne diʒelnesse þe deorwurþe is.
     Ælfric abbod, þe we Alquin hoteþ,
     He was bocare, and þe fif bec awende,
     Genesis, Exodus, Vtronomius, Numerus, Leuiticus,
     Þurh þeos weren ilærde ure leoden on Englisc.
10 Þet weren þeos biscopes þe bodeden Cristendom:
     Wilfrid of Ripum, Iohan of Beoferlai, Cuþbert of Dunholme,
     Oswald of Wireceastre, Egwin of Heoueshame, Ældelm of
     Malmesburi, Swiþþun, Æþelwold, Aidan, Biern of Wincæstre,
     Paulin of Rofecæstre, S. Dunston, and S. Ælfeih of Cantoreburi.
15 Þeos lærden ure leodan on Englisc,
     Næs deorc heore liht, ac hit fæire glod.
     Nu is þeo leore forleten, and þet folc is forloren.
     Nu beoþ oþre leoden þeo læreþ ure folc,
     And feole of þen lorþeines losiæþ and þet folc forþ mid.
20 Nu sæiþ ure Drihten þus, *Sicut aquila prouocat pullos suos ad*
       uolandum, et super eos uolitat.
     This beoþ Godes word to worlde asende,
     Þet we sceolen fæier feþ festen to Him.

[Holy Bede was born here in Britain with us,
And he wisely translated books
Which the English people were taught through.
And he revealed the 'knots' which are called questions,
The secret mystery which is precious.
Abbot Ælfric, whom we call Alhwine,
He was a writer, and translated the five books,
Genesis, Exodus, Deuteronomy, Numbers, Leviticus,
Through these our people were taught in English.
These were the bishops who preached Christianity:

Wilfrid of Ripon, John of Beverley, Cuthbert of Durham,
Oswald of Worcester, Egwin of Evesham, Ældhelm of
Malmesbury, Swithin, Æþelwold, Aidan, Birinus of Winchester,
Paulinus of Rochester, St Dunstan, and St Ælphege of Canterbury.
These taught our people in English,
Their light was not dark, but it glowed brightly.
Now the teaching is abandoned, and that people is damned.
Now there are other people who teach our folk,
And many of the teachers are damned and the people as well.
Now Our Lord says thus, 'Like an eagle stirs up its young for
Flying, and flits about over them',
These are God's words sent to the world,
That we should place our full trust in him.]

The language looks typically 'western' in its features, and, perhaps, because of the conservative area in which it was written, still bears a strong resemblance to Old English.

Sounds and spellings
O.E. æ usually remains, but e occurs in *þet* (3, 10, etc.), perhaps an unstressed form, and a in *was* (1, 7); typically, western u reflects a continued pronunciation of O.E. y /y/ in *Cantoreburi* (14; O.E. *-byrig*); O.E. eo (representing both the long and short sounds) is still in use in, e.g., *leoden* (3, 18), *deorwurþe* (5), *deorc* (16), *beoþ* (18), *feole* (19), *sceolen* (22); O.E. sc /ʃ/ continues to be represented by sc in *Englisc* (9, 15), *biscopes* (10), but cf. *Englise* (3); þ continues from O.E. times throughout the text, but cf. *this* with th (22). This early text therefore shows features which are still virtually either 'Old English' or 'western'.

Grammatical features
These are much as they were in Old English.
    Nouns: note the old pl. *bec* 'books' (2, 7); *-en* pls. in *cnotten* (4) and *leoden* (3, 9, 18), *leodan* (15; this word did not have the *-n* pl. ending in Old English (see 1.6, 1.11), but has adopted it here (which sometimes happened in the south)); no pl. ending in *word* (21).
    Pronouns: O.E. *heore* 'their' (16) continues, as does the relative pronoun *þe* 'which' (4, 5, etc.).
    Verbs: *-eþ* ending in 3pr.sg. *sæiþ* (20) and pl., e.g. *hoteþ* (4, 6), *losiæþ* (19), *beoþ* (21); *i-* (< O.E. *ge-*) occurs in p.p. *iboren* (1).

Vocabulary
This is nearly all of native O.E. stock, including one or two Latin loan-words already present in Old English: *abbod* (6), *biscopes* (10). But *sanctus* (1) is present in its pure Latin form (cf. *sannt* < Lat. *sanctus* in Text 3, line 5, below).

2. Early thirteenth-century SW Midland: *Ancrene Wisse*
(MS Corpus Christi College Cambridge 402; BS, XVIII, p. 241.)

Ancrene Riwle ('the Rule of Anchoresses', i.e. nuns) has been described
as 'the most influential and important of the prose works of the early
ME period'. Written originally at the request of three noble maidens
who had left the world to live as recluses, it was revised – as the
Ancrene Wisse ('the Guide of Anchoresses') – for the use of a larger
community. Its influence continued in devotional literature as late as
the sixteenth century. The M.E. manuscripts are certainly of SW
origin, probably from Herefordshire. The language is still (as in Text
1) conservative.

1 Fowr heaued luuen me ifind i þis world: bitweone gode iferen;
   bitweone mon and wummon; bi wif & hire child; bitweone
   licome & sawle. Þe luue þet Iesu Crist haueð to his deore
   leofmon ouergeað þeos fowre,
5 passeð ham alle. Ne teleð me him god fere þe leið his wed i
   Giwerie to acwitin ut his fere ? Godd almihti leide him seolf for
   us i Giwerie & dude his deorewurðe bodi to actwitin ut his
   leofmon of Giwene honden. Neauer fere ne dude swuch fordede
   for his fere.

[One finds four chief loves in this world: between good friends; between
man and woman; with a woman and her child; between body and soul.
The love that Jesus Christ has for his dear loved one surpasses these four,
exceeds them all. Does one not count him a good friend who lays his
pledge in Jewry to buy out his friend ? God almighty laid himself for us
in Jewry and gave his precious body to buy his lover out of Jews' hands.
Never did friend do such service for his friend.]

Sounds and spellings
There is no longer any trace of O.E. *æ*; again, western *u* represents O.E.
y /y/ in *dude* (< O.E. *dyde*; 7, 8), *swuch* (< O.E. *swylč*; 8); and again,
O.E. *eo* still appears in its old form: *bitweone* (1, 2, etc.), *deore* (*wurðe*)
(3, 7), *leofmon* (4, 8), *þeos* (4), *seolf* (6); western *o* is present in (-)*mon*
(2, 4, 8 (*o* in the *honde* (8), *lond*, etc. class is regular in the M.E. period
throughout the south)); these are all typically western M.E. features. In
this text, *ð* continues to represent /θ/ ~ /ð/.

Grammatical features
These are, again, precisely conservative and southern.
   Nouns: *-en* pls. in *luuen* (1), *iferen* (2), *honden* (8).
   Pronouns: *ham* 'them' (6; = O.E. *him*, *heom*).
   Verbs: 3pr.sg. in *haueð* (3), *ouergeað*, *passeð* (5), *teleð*, *leið* (5).

Vocabulary
The vocabulary is uniformly of native origin in this passage.

3. Early thirteenth-century eastern: the *Orrmulum*
[Bodleian MS Junius I; DW, XV, p. 83.]

Orrm, or Orrmin as he sometimes calls himself was, like his brother, apparently an Augustinian canon, who wrote his work at the request of his brother. The unique autograph of this remarkable work is dated *c.* 1210, and the dialect is that of Lincolnshire. It is an unfinished collection of homilies – a course of sermons intended to be read aloud in church, the (20,000) lines being modelled on the Latin 'septenarius', with exactly 15 syllables each.

The metre of the *Orrmulum* has been described, with some justification, as 'monotonously regular ... and soporific' but from the linguistic point of view it is one of the most important works in early Middle English. It has a very distinctive orthographical system, especially the frequent doubling of consonants and the use of various diacritics, which were probably devised to help preachers in reading aloud to the congregation.

1   Nu broþerr Wallterr, broþerr min, affterr þe flæshess kinde,
    Annd broþerr min i Crisstenndom þurrh fulluht annd þurrh trowwþe,
    Annd broþerr min i Ḡodess hus, ʒêt o þe þride wise,
    Þurrh þatt witt hafenn tăkenn ba an reʒhellboc to follʒhenn,
5   Unnderr kanunnkess had annd lif, swa summ Sannt Awwstin sette;
    Icc hafe don swa summ þu badd, annd forþedd te þin wil,
    Icc hafe wennd inntill Ennḡlissh Ḡoddspelles hallʒhe láre,
    Affterr þatt little witt þatt me min Drihhtin hafeþþ lenedd.
    Þu þohhtesst tatt itt mihhte wel till mikell frame turrnenn
10 ʒiff Ennḡlissh follc, forr lufe off Crist, itt wollde ʒerne lernenn,
    Annd follʒhenn itt, annd fillenn itt, wiþþ þohht, wiþþ word, wiþþ dede.

[Now, brother Walter, my brother, after the nature of the flesh,
And my brother in Christendom, through baptism and through faith,
And my brother in God's house, yet in the third way,
Because we two have both undertaken to follow the rule of an order,
Under the order and life of a canon, just as St Augustine established,
I have done just as you bade, and furthered your will for you,
I have translated into English the Gospel's holy teaching,
According to that little intelligence that God has granted me.
You thought that it might well turn to great benefit
If English people, for love of Christ, would learn it readily,
And follow it, and fulfil it, in thought, in word, in deed.]

Sounds and spellings

In this passage, Orrm uses these diacritics: $\bar{g}$ = /g/; $\hat{e}$ (in the manuscript this is actually a double or treble acute accent) = /e/; $\breve{a}$ = short /a/; $\acute{a}$ = long /a:/.

Orrm is especially ingenious in his use of the symbols ʒ and g to represent the different sounds /j/ (ʒet (3), ʒiff (10)); /g/ (Ḡodess (3), Englissh (7)); /gg/ (i.e. a 'double' /g/, as in Pr.E. dialectal fog-grass); /ɤ/ (reʒhellboc, follʒhenn (4)); /dʒ/, etc. (see DW, pp. 82–3).

Other items: the short O.E. æ has totally disappeared and is invariably a, but long ǣ is still represented by the symbol æ in this extract: flæshess (1; < O.E. flǣsc); O.E. a/o before a nasal is always a (cf. the western texts); O.E. y is invariably i (cf. u in the western texts), as in kinde (1; < O.E. (ġe-)cȳnd), fillenn (11; < O.E. fyllan); O.E. eo appears as e (cf., again, the earlier western texts, which have eo), as in ʒerne (10; < O.E. ġeorne). Orrm uses t to denote initial þ /θ/ after a word ending in t or d, as in te (6), tatt (9; cf. þatt 8); he uses the form mikill, with k, presumably by Scandinavian influence (O.N. mikill).

The language here is, therefore, in sharp contrast to that found in the earlier, and western, texts 1 and 2, and represents a slightly later eastern type of Middle English.

Grammatical features

There is very little of distinctive interest in this particular passage, but in pronouns, note the retention of the O.E. dual forms (1.6) in witt 'we two' (4); and in verbs the Midland pl. form hafenn (4), with an -en ending, as distinct from -eþ; -eþ (< O.E. -eþ) continues, however, for the 3pr.sg. hafeþþ (8).

Vocabulary

Note: kanunnkess (5; < O.E. canonic < Lat. canonicus), sannt (5; < O.E. sanct < Lat. sanctus), and inntill (7; < O.E. in + O.N. til); turrnenn (9) is < O.E. tȳrnan/tūrnian, supported by O.Fr. to(u)rner.

4. Late thirteenth-century northern: the Cursor Mundi
[DW, XXII, p. 115.]

This work, a poetic history of the Hebrew and Christian world in some 30,000 lines, surviving in at least ten manuscripts, is said by DW (p. 114) to be 'the most comprehensive versification of biblical material and early Christian legend during the ME period.' The anonymous author was certainly a cleric, who wrote somewhere in the north, perhaps in County Durham, during the last quarter of the thirteenth century.

The most complete version of the poem is that preserved in B.L. MS Cotton Vespasian A III (1300–50), which probably best represents the dialect of the original and is the source of the following text.

1   Man yhernes[1] rimes for to here,
And romans[2] red on maneres sere[3],
Of Alisaundur þe conquerour;
Of Iuly Cesar þe emparour;

5   O Grece and Troy the strang strijf,
     Þer[4] many thosand lesis þer lijf;
     O Brut þat bern[5] bald[6] of hand,
     Þe first *conquerour* of Ingland;
     O Kyng Arthour þat was so rike[7],
10   Quam[8] non in hys tim was like,
     O ferlys[9] þat hys knythes fel[10]
     Þat *aunters* sere[11] I here of tell[12],
     Als[13] Wawan, Cai and oþer stabell[14],
     For to were[15] þe *ronde tabell*;
15   How Charles kyng and Rauland faght,
     Wit Sarazins wald þai na saght[16];
     O Tristrem and hys leif[17] Ysote,
     How he for here be-com a sote[18],
     O Ioneck and of Ysambrase,
20   O Ydoine and of Amadase.
     Storis als o serekin[19] thinges
     O *princes, prelates* and o kynges;
     Sanges[20] sere of selcuth[21] *rime*,
     Inglis, Frankys, and Latine,
25   To rede and here ilkon[22] is *prest*[23],
     Þe thynges þat þam likes[24] best.

[1]longs [2]romances [3]many [4]where [5]warrior [6]bold [7]powerful [8]whom [9]marvels
[10]fell to his knights [11]various adventures [12](i.e. tell of) [13]such as [14]steadfast
(warriors) [15]guard [16]reconciliation [17]dear [18]madman [19]many kinds of [20]songs
[21]strange, wonderful [22]everyone [23]eager [24]please them

Sounds and spellings

There is no trace of O.E. æ; *a* is regular before *-nd* (as cf. southern *o*), e.g. *hand* (7), *Ingland* (8), and also *-ng*, which is a distinctively northern feature: *strang* (5), *sanges* (23). It also occurs in *walde* 'would' (16), usually regarded as a western form. O.E. *eo* and *ēo* appear as *e*: *yhernes* (1), *lesis* (6), *bern* (7), *fel* (11) (cf. the earlier, western texts).

Consonants: the most important in northern texts are *qu-*, for a heavily aspirated initial /w/ (cf. Texts 6 and 8), i.e. /hw/ or /xw/ in *quam* (10); northern preference for *k* over *ċ* in *rike* (9; < O.E. *riċe*) and *ilkon* (25; < O.E. *ilca* + *ān*); *s* is used for the /ʃ/ sound in *Inglis* and *Frankys* (24).

Grammatical features

Nouns: there are no pl. *-en* forms here.

Pronouns: the full complement of O.N. loans is now in use – *þai* (16; < O.N. *þeir*), *þer* (6; < O.N. *þeira*), *þam* (26; < O.N. *þeim*) (see 1.7).

Verbs: northern 3pr.sgs. and pls. end in -s —sg. *yhernes* (1); pl. *lesis* (6), *likes* (26).

Vocabulary

More Fr. words are now in evidence, but few O.N. ones; but note *sere* (2, 12, 23; < O.N. *sér*) and *serekin* (21; < O.N. *sér* + O.E. *cynna*).

5. Fourteenth-century Kentish: Dan Michel's *Aȝenbite of Inwyt* [B.L. MS Arundel 57; Sis., III, p. 331.]

Michel, or Michael, of Northgate was a monk of St Augustine's, Canterbury, whose autograph copy of the *Aȝenbite* (the title means 'Remorse of Conscience', and the work is a translation from the French of Friar Lorens' *Le Somme des Vices et des Vertues*, 1279) we are fortunate enough to have. A note at the end shows conclusively that it was finished on 27 October 1340. It has been variously described as a 'long and dreary moral treatise' and 'barren of interest', the translation as 'inaccurate and sometimes unintelligible'. But as Kenneth Sisam so rightly said (p. 33), 'if its literary merit is slight, linguistically it is one of the most important works in Middle English. It provides a long prose text, exactly dated and exactly localized [the author states at the end that 'þis boc is ywrite/Mid Engliss of Kent']; we have the author's autograph copy to work from; and the dialect is well distinguished. These circumstances, unique in Middle English, make it possible to study the Kentish dialect of the mid-fourteenth century under ideal conditions.'

1   How *Merci multiplieþ* þe timliche[1] guodes, hyerof[2] we
    habbeþ uele[3] uayre uorbisnen[4], huerof ich wille hier
    zome telle. Me ret[5] of *Saint* Germain of Aucerre þet,
    þo[6] he com uram Rome, ate outguoinge[7] of Malane, he
5   acsede[8] at onen of his diaknen[9] yef he hedde eny zeluer,
    and he ansuerede þet he ne hedde bote þri pans[10], uor
    Saynt Germayn hit hedde al yeue to *pouren*[11]. Þanne he
    him het[12] þet he his ssolde yeue to þe *poure*, uor God
    hedde ynoȝ of guode[13], huerof he hise uedde[14] uor þane
10 day. Þe dyacne mid greate pine[15] and mid greate
    grochinge[16] yeaf þe tuaye pans, and ofhild[17] þane þridde.
    Þe *sergont* of ane riche kniȝte him broȝte ane his
    lhordes haf[18] tuo hondred pans. Þo clepede[19] he his dyacne,
    and him zede[20] þet he hedde benome[21] þe *poure* ane peny,
15 and yef he hedde yeue þane þridde peny to þe *poure*,
    þe kniȝt him hedde yzent þri hondred pans.

[1]temporal [2]of this [3]many [4]excellent examples [5]one reads [6]when [7]on departing from [8]asked [9]deacons [10]had only three pence [11]given to the poor

[12]ordered [13]enough wealth [14]he fed him [15]anguish [16]grudging [17]kept back [18]behalf [19]called [20]said [21]deprived ... of

Sounds and spellings

O.E. *æ* is typically seen as *e* in Kt Middle English: *þet* (3, 6), *hedde* (5, 6, etc.). A special feature of such texts is the spelling *uo*, indicating some sort of a diphthong, for words whose root vowel derives from O.E. *ǭ*, as in *guodes* pl. (1; < O.E. *gōd*), *guode* (9; ibid.). Parallel to this is the spelling *ye/ie* for O.E. *ē̜* as in *hyerof* (1; < O.E. *hēr* + *of*), *hier* (2).

Consonants: *y* is used for /j/ in, e.g., *yeue* (7), *yeaf* (11); it also remains in *yef* 'if' (5, 15; < O.E. *ġif*); *ss* represents /ʃ/ in *ssolde* (8). But the most distinctive feature of both SE and SW M.E. texts is the use of *z* to represent initial voiced /s/ in, e.g., *zome* (3), *zeluer* (5), *zede* (14), *yzent* (16), and *v* or *u* to represent intial voiced /f/ in, e.g., *uele* (2; < O.E. *fela*), *uor* (6), *uedde* (9), as these remain in some SW dialects to the present day. The overall impression is one of a conservative use of traditional conventions in spelling, combined with an effort to convey the true sounds of the Kt dialect of Middle English as it was spoken in the mid-fourteenth century.

Grammatical features

These are well preserved from O.E. times, and are similar to those found in contemporary SW texts.

Nouns: *-en* pls. in *uorbisnen* (2), *diaknen* (5), *pouren* (7; < the adj., which is French in origin).

Pronouns: in this passage, those that occur (e.g. *we*, *he*) are as in Pr.E., but elsewhere in *Aȝenbite* the old forms for 'she' and the 3pl. personal pronouns are used, not the new ones (see 1.7).

Verbs: 3pr.sg. and pl. both end in southern and conservative *-(e)þ* (cf. Text 6): sg. – *multiplieth* (of Fr. origin; 1); pl. – *habbeþ* (2); *ret* (3) is a contracted version of *redeþ* 'reads'.

Vocabulary

Dyacne(n) (*passim*) is < Lat. *diaconus*. Most of the vocabulary in this extract is native in origin, but there are a number of Fr. loan-words.

6. Fourteenth-century NW Midland: *Sir Gawayne and the Grene Knight*
[B.L. MS Nero A X; Sis., V, p. 46.]

This is yet another unique M.E. manuscript (*c.* 1400) containing four poems, all probably written *c.* 1350–75: *Sir Gawayne* plus *Pearl*, *Patience* and *Purity*, the last three all editorially named from their first words. All are in the same handwriting and in the same NW Midland dialect. All are of high literary merit.

The language, which has northern affinities with Barbour's *Bruce*

(Text 8) and other northern texts, as well with SW Midland texts such as *Piers Plowman* (not represented here), forms an interesting contrast with that of the previous text, especially since the two are virtually contemporaneous.

1   The brygge¹ watz brayde doun², and þe brode ȝatez
Unbarred and born open³ vpon boþe halue⁴.
Þe burne blessed hym bilyue, and þe bredez *passed*;
Prayses þe *porter* bifore þe *prynce* kneled,
5   Gef hym God and goud day, þat Gawayn He *saue*,
And went on his way with his wyȝe one,
Þat schulde teche hym to *tourne* to þat tene *place*
Þer þe ruful *race* he schulde *resayue*.
Þay boȝen⁵ bi bonkkez þer boȝez⁶ ar bare:
10   Þay clomben⁷ bi clyffez þer clengez⁸ þe colde.
þe heuen watz vp halt, bot vgly þer vnder-
Mist muged⁹ on þe mor, malt¹⁰ on þe *mountez*,
Vch hille hade a hatte, a myst-hakel¹¹ *huge*.
Brokez *byled*¹² and breke bi bonkkez aboute,
15   Schyre schaterande on schorez, þer þay doun schowued.
Wela wylle¹³ watz þe way þer þay bi wod schulden¹⁴,
Til hit watz sone *sesoun*¹⁵ þat þe sunne ryses
                    þat tyde¹⁶.
     Þay were on a hille ful hyȝe,
20   Þe quyte snaw lay bisyde;
     Þe burne þat rod hym by
     Bede¹⁷ his mayster abide¹⁸.

¹drawbridge ²lowered ³laid open ⁴sides ⁵passed ⁶boughs ⁷climbed ⁸clings ⁹drizzled ¹⁰melted ¹¹cloak of mist ¹²boiled ¹³very wild ¹⁴where they must (go) through the wood ¹⁵time ¹⁶then ¹⁷bade ¹⁸stop

3–5   The man crossed himself hastily, and crossed over the planks (of the drawbridge). He praises the porter (who) knelt before the prince, wished him 'God and good day', praying God to keep Gawain safe

7–8   Who was to show him how to get to that perilous place where he had to receive the grievous blow

11   The clouds were high up, but it was threatening below them

15   Dashing brightly against their banks as they forced their way down

Sounds and spellings

O.E. æ is now, at this late stage, regularly represented by *a*, though before -*ng* the western spelling and sound is *o* /ɔ/, as in *bonkkez* (9, 14); *u* for O.E. *eo* is another western feature, as in *burne* (3, 21; < O.E. *beorn*), and it also represents O.E. *y* /y/, as in *vch* (13; < O.E. *ylċ*), a feature we have already seen in the earlier western texts.

Consonants: initial *g* /g/ occurs in *gef* (5; = O.E. *ġēaf*) – cf. *y* /j/ in

Text 5; *gg* probably = /g/ in *brygge* (1; = O.E. *bryeɳg»*, with final /dʒ/), probably both under O.N. influence; *qu* in *quyte* (20; < O.E. *hwīt*) again represents /hw/ or /xw/, as in Text 4. Finally, the letter ʒ is used to mean three different sounds: /j/ in, e.g., *hyʒe* (19), /ɤ/ in, e.g., *boʒen* (9), and, commonly, final /s/ or /z/ in, e.g., *bredeʒ* (3; but I have substituted *z* for it in the text, to avoid confusion); it also occurs, under A.Fr. influence, with *t* in monosyllabic words, as in *watʒ* (1, 11, etc.). Confusingly, the letter sometimes occurs in the same word to express two different sounds, e.g. *ʒateʒ* (1; i.e. /ja:təz/), *boʒeʒ* (9; i.e. /bo:ɤəz/).

Grammatical features

Nouns: these uniformly end in *-eʒ*, *-es*, etc., and there are no *-en* endings.

Pronouns: in the poem overall, these show a typical fourteenth-century mixture of old O.E. personal pronouns and the newer loans from Old Norse, so that we find *þay* (< O.N. *þeir*) 'they' beside *hor, her* (< O.E. *heora, hiera*) 'their' and *hem* 'them'; only *þay*, however, occurs in this extract.

Verbs: the 3pr.sg. always ends in *-eʒ*, *-es*, etc. (e.g. *prayses* (4), *clengeʒ* (10), as cf. southern texts where *-(e)þ* is the norm; the 3pr.pl. is usually the Midland *-en*, though some occur in *-e*, *-es* (northern) or have no ending; *ar* (9) occurs here in contrast to southern 'be' forms, but the pr.p. is *-ande* (15) – and usually in the poem – though *-yng* occasionally appears.

Vocabulary

A wide variety of loan-words are used beside ancient native stock, e.g. *burne* (3), *wyʒe* (6; < O.E. *wiga* 'warrior'), *schyre* (15; < O.E. *scīr*)) for poetic, especially alliterative, purposes; *tourne* (7) is < O.E. *tȳrnan, tūrnian* combined with O.Fr. *to(u)rner*, both < Lat. *tornare*; *mounteʒ* (12) is < O.E. *munt* and O.Fr. *mo(u)nt*, both < Lat. *mont-*; *vgly* (11) < O.N. *uggligr*; *muged* (12) is probably < O.N., cf. Norw. *mugga* 'a drizzle'; and *wylle* (16) is < O.N. *villr*.

7. Late fourteenth-century London: Geoffrey Chaucer's *Prologue* to the *Canterbury Tales*
[Ed. F.N. Robinson, *The Works of Geoffrey Chaucer* (2nd ed., OUP, 1957), p. 17.]

The composition of the *General Prologue* is dated in the late 1380s: Robinson (p. 1) suggests 1387 on grounds external to the work. There are some 90 manuscripts of the *Tales*, together with early prints, but Robinson's text, used here, is based on the famous Ellesmere manuscript. Note that the text is slightly modernized by the substitution of *th* for *þ*, and adjusting *u* and *v* to modern practice (e.g. *vertu* and *every* for *uertu, euery*). The dialect shows typical Chaucerian features, but is clearly closer to Pr.E. than the texts so far presented in this chapter (but see 4.5, below).

1   Whan that Aprill with his shoures soote[1]
      The droghte of *March* hath *perced* to the roote,
      And bathed every *veyne* in swich *licour*[2]
      Of which *vertu*[3] *engendred*[4] is the *flour*;
5   Whan Zephirus eek[5] with his sweete breeth
      Inspired[6] hath in every holt[7] and heeth
      The *tendre* croppes, and the yonge sonne
      Hath in the Ram his halve *cours*[8] yronne,
      And smale foweles[9] maken melodye,
10   That slepen al the nyght with open ye[10]
      (So priketh hem *nature* in hir *corages*[11]);
      Thanne longen folk to goon on *pilgrimages*,
      And *palmeres*[12] for to seken *straunge* strondes[13],
      To ferne halwes[14], kowthe[15] in sondry londes;
15   And *specially* from every shires ende
      Of Engelond to Caunterbury they wende,
      The hooly blisful *martir* for to seke,
      That hem hath holpen[16] whan that they were seeke[17].

[1]sweet [2]moisture [3]potency [4]born [5]also [6]quickened [7]plantation [8]half his course [9]birds [10]eye [11]hearts [12]'palmers' (pilgrims to Compostella) [13]foreign shores [14]far-off saints [15]known [16]helped; [17]sick

Sounds and spellings (a phonemic transcription is given at 4.4,below)
These are typically Chaucerian and fourteenth-century southern, e.g. *swich* 'such' (3); the common use of *o* before *-nd* in *strondes* (13), *londes* (14), *Engelond* (16)

Grammatical features
    Pronouns: as with the *Gawain*-poet, there is a typical syncretism of O.E. and O.N. forms—note *hir* 'their' (11), *hem* 'them' (18), which Chaucer uses together with *they* (not in this passage).
    Verbs: the 3pr.sg. ends in -(e)*th*, as in *hath* (2, 6, etc.), *priketh* (11); the 3pl. has *-en* (see Text 6), as in *maken* (9), *slepen* (10), *longen* (12); the p.p. has prefixed *-y* in *yronne* (8).

Vocabulary
Fr. loan-words are numerous.

8. Fourteenth/fifteenth-century Scots: John Barbour's *Bruce*
[St John's College Cambridge MS G 23; Sis., X, p. 109.]

Our final illustration is a Middle Scots text. Middle Scots is, in fact, simply a dialect of northern Middle English, though written in a special system of spelling of a very distinctive kind.

Barbour, an archdeacon of Aberdeen, an auditor of the Scottish exchequer, and a royal pensioner, is our first identifiable Scots poet. His poem, *The Actes and Life of the most Victorious Conquerour, Robert Bruce, King of Scotland*, was written in 1375, but the two surviving manuscripts date from 1487 (that given here) and 1489. The extract below describes an incident in the unsuccessful siege of Berwick in 1319.

1 And quhen thai into sic *degre*
 Had maid thame for thair *assaling*,
 On the Rude-evyn in the dawing,
 The Inglis *host* blew till *assale*.
5 Than mycht men with ser *apparale*
 Se that gret *host* cum *sturdely*.
 The toune *enveremyt* thai in hy,
 And assalit with sa gud will –
 For all thair mycht thai set thartill –
10 That thai thame *pressit* fast of the toune.
 Bot thai that can thame *abandoune*
 Till ded, or than till woundis sare,
 So weill has thame *defendit* thare
 That ledderis to the ground thai slang,
15 And vith stanys so fast thai dang
 Thair fais, that feill thai felt lyand,
 Sum ded, sum *hurt*, and sum swavnand.

[And when they had got themselves
Into such a state [of preparedness] for their attack,
On the 'Rood-eve' at daybreak,
The English host sounded the trumpet for the attack,
Then might people see that great host
Coming resolutely in various apparel.
They swiftly surrounded the town,
And assailed it with such firm intent –
For they devoted all their might to it –
That they hard-pressed those of the town.
But those who abandoned themselves
To death, or else to grievous wounds,
So well defended themselves there
That they flung ladders to the ground,
And they struck their foes so hard with stones
That they left many lying,
Some dead, some hurt, and some swooning.]

Sounds and spellings
More than any other, this text shows evidence of O.E. *ā* remaining, instead of becoming *ǭ* (/ɔ:/) as in, e.g., Chaucer (compare similar

examples in Text 4), as in *sa* (8; < O.E. *swā*), *sare* (12; < O.E. *sāre*), *stanys* (15; < O.E. *stānas*), *fais* (16; < O.E. *fā* sg.); this is a feature which will recur in various forms in later texts. O.E. *ō* appears in its typical northern M.E. form represented by *u* (= /y:/ or /y/) in *Rude-* (3; < O.E. *rōd*) and *gud* (8; < O.E. *gōd*); again, this will appear in later texts. Typically M.E. Scots is the use of *i* to indicate a long vowel (i.e. /æ/) as in *maid* (2).

Consonants: *sic* (1; < O.E. *swylč*) shows northern /k/ as cf. southern /tʃ/; *quh* in *quhen* (1) shows the strong northern initial aspiration noted in previous texts; *Inglis* (4), with final *s* < O.E. *sc* /ʃ/ is a typical northern feature; *v* represents /w/ in *vith* (15); final /d/ is typically unvoiced in p.t.pl. *pressit* (10).

Grammatical forms

Pronouns: the full 'northern' pattern is naturally seen here – *thai* (1, 7, etc.), *thair* (2, 9, etc.), *thame* (2, 10, etc.)

Verbs: the 3pr.pl. has northern -*s* ending in *has* (13); the pr.p. ends in the usual northern -*and* in *lyand* (16) and *swavnand* (17).

Vocabulary

Note (-)*till* (4, 9; < O.N. *til*), *ser* (5; < O.N. *sér*), and *dang* p.t.pl. (15; < O.N. *dengja*, inf.).

4.4 Summary

We have now looked at the characteristics typical of some early and later M.E. texts, in an attempt to show the sort of information that can be gleaned from such works. The following brief summary is intended to give some coherence to the survey above.

In the first two texts, both of SW Midlands origin, we see typical features of this area, descended from O.E. times (e.g. *u* representing O.E. long and short *y*, *eo* representing O.E. long and short *eo*), and some of the O.E. spelling symbols still in use, e.g. (Text 1) the retention of O.E. *æ*; *sc* for later *sch*, *sh*, etc. and *þ* lingering on beside *th*. Again, grammatical features suggest a state of affairs little removed from late Old English, conservative and southern, without trace yet of, e.g., *sche* 'she' (which later replaced O.E. *hēo*) or the Scandinavian-derived pronouns *þei*, *þeir* and *þeim*. Vocabulary is virtually all of native origin.

Texts 3 and 4 are from opposite ends of the country, and between them span the thirteenth century. Early SW Midland features like those above have disappeared but *æ* (= O.E. long *æ*) remains in Orrm (though not in Text 4), as does the old O.E. dual form of the personal pronoun. One or two O.N. loans now appear in both texts. Northern features now begin to appear in Text 4, most prominently *a* (as cf. southern *o*) before -*ng*, and *qu-* for southern initial *wh-*, *k* /k/ instead of *c*, and *s* representing /ʃ/. The latter text also shows a significant increase in Fr. loans.

Turning to the fourteenth century, Text 5 shows very distinctive Kt features, such as *e* for O.E. *æ*, the unique diphthongs spelled *uo* and *ye/ie*, typical of texts from this area, and the 'voicing' of *f* and *s* to *v* and *z*. Again, grammatical forms are southern and conservative; there are a number of Fr. loans.

The language of this text contrasts sharply with that of the *Gawain*-poet, who uses typically Midland forms, e.g. *o* before -*nk* and *u* for earlier *eo* and *y* (cf. Texts 1 and 2); northern forms such as *qu*- are evidenced. In grammar, the -*(e)s* 3pr.sg. and pl. of the verb appears (beside pl. -*en*), in contrast to southern -*(e)th*, and the beginnings of the 'O.N.' system of 3pl. personal pronouns can be seen; the northern pr.p. -*ande* occurs beside occasional -*yng*. A considerable number of O.N. and Fr. loans now make their appearance.

Of all the texts, Chaucer's is more recognizably like the English of our own day, though it is not, in fact, its direct ancestor – to which we shall shortly come. The phonology is the typically SE one of his day; in grammar the originally northern form *þei* has now penetrated even London English, though the O.E. forms remain in use for 'their' and 'them'; the southern 3pr.sg. of verbs ends in -*(e)th*, but typically Chaucerian (and originally Midland) -*(e)n* occurs for the 3pr.pl. There is a plethora of Fr. loan-words.

Finally, in the decisively northern poet Barbour, we see the features of late literary Scots distinctively exemplified: some, e.g. *qu*-, and *s* (for /ʃ/), we have seen in other texts, but to these we may add *a*/*ai* representing O.E. *ā*, O.N. *á* (= southern M.E. *ǭ*) and *u* (= /y:/) < O.E. *ō*. In grammar, all 3pl. personal pronouns are Norse-derived, the 3pr.pl. of verbs ends in -*s*, and the pr.p. in -*ande*. One or two O.N. words occur in this passage.

The rich variety of the English language in M.E. times may thus be seen as spread across both the whole age and the whole country. Regrettably, there has not been space to exemplify medieval Anglo-Irish, for which I must refer the reader to the Bibliography.

I conclude this section with a phonemic transcription of the first twelve lines of the *Canterbury Tales* (Text 7, above), to give an idea of late M.E. pronunciation:

1   hwan θət april wið iz ʃu:rəz so:tə
    θə dru:xt əf martʃ həθ pe:rsəd tə θə ro:tə
    ənd ba:ðəd ɛvri vain in switʃ liku:r
    əf hwitʃ vɛrtiu ɛndʒɛndrəd iz θə flu:r
5   hwan zɛfirus ɛ:k wið iz swe:tə brɛ:θ
    inspi:rəd haθ in ɛvri hɔlt ənd he:θ

13. Localization of the homes of some of the most important M.E. works, and

θə tɛndrə krɔpəz ənd θə jungə sunnə
haθ in θə ram hiz halvə ku:rs irunnə
ənd sma:lə fu:ləz ma:kən mɛlodiə
10 θət slɛ:pən a:l θə niçt wið ɔ:pən i:ə
sɔ: prikəθ hɛm natiur in hir kɔra:dʒəz
θan lɔngən fɔlk tə gɔ:n ɔn pilgrima:dʒəz

4.5 Late M.E. dialects and the rise of a written standard

That a written dialectal diversity was the norm for the M.E. period *par
excellence* has already been emphasized, and it is out of this diversity of
local 'standards' that a national standard emerged in the fifteenth century.
This was not Chaucer's English, as seen in Text 7, nor was it similar to
two other types of Middle English previous to Chaucer which may lay
some claim to being earlier forms of a national standard in some way
(see M.L. Samuels in the Bibliography). Its rise to prominence was due
to the permanent establishment, by the middle of the fourteenth century,
of the 'Chancery' at Westminster. This institution grew out of the little
office connected with the chapel, where the Court chaplains wrote the
king's letters between conducting divine service (previously it had moved
around with the king on his royal travels). The Chancery type of English
is distinguished from the other, earlier 'standards' we have mentioned by
the presence in it of features of more central Midland origin than those
found in the language of Chaucer, which may be taken as a representative
of London English *c.* 1400. Unsurprisingly, the 'Chancery Standard' was
at first primarily the language of official documents rather than of literary
works.

I close the present chapter with an example of this type of late medieval
English, as a prelude to the well-established written/printed English to
be explored in the next chapter. But first –

> The Chancery clerks fairly consistently preferred the spellings which
> have since become standard. The documents ... show the clerks
> trying to eliminate the kind of orthographic eccentricity found in
> the Privy Seal minutes, the petitions passed on to them for entering
> in the rolls. ... At the very least, we can say that they were trying
> to limit choices among spellings, and that by the 1440's and 1450's
> they had achieved a comparative regularization.

So say John Fisher and his collaborators in their very useful *Anthology
of Chancery English* (p. 27), and the following passage taken from this
volume (pp. 288–9) – although still containing words in forms which
may look old-fashioned as compared with their Pr.E. counterparts – bears
them out.

Reproduction of the beginning of the homily for Whitsunday in John Mirk's *Festial* of English homilies, composed *c.* 1400. This manuscript, MS Cotton Claudius II, in the British Library, is dated *c.* 1425–50, and is the fullest of the 30 or so extant, written mainly in the Midlands. The first few lines (with expansions of abbreviations italicized here) read: 'Gode men, ȝe knoweth wel þat þis day is callyd Wytsonday, for encheson [= 'because'] þat þe Holy Goste as þis day broght wytte [= 'understanding'] and wysdam into alle Crystes dysciplus, and so by here prechyng aftur into alle Cristys pepul.'

9. Petition of Thomas Yong for restitution after his arrest for speaking out in Parliament [1455 SC8/28/1387]

1   To the right wise and discret Comons in this present
     parlement assembled

Besecheth humbly Tomas yong that where as he late beyng
oon of the knyghtes for the shire and towne of Bristowe in
5   dyuers parlementes holden afore this demened him in his
saiyng in the same as wele faithfully and with alle suche
trewe diligent labour as his symplenesse couthe or might
for the wele of the kyng oure souerain lorde and this his
noble Realme and notwithstonding that by the olde liberte
10 and fredom of the Comyns of this londe had enIoyed and
prescribed fro the tyme that no mynde is alle such
persones as for the tyme been assembled in eny parlement
for the same Comyns ought to haue theire fredom to speke
and sey in the hous of there assemble as to theym is
15 thought conuenyent or resonable withoute eny maner
chalange charge or punycion therefore to be leyde to theym
in eny wise Neuertheless by vntrewe sinistre reportes
made to the kinges highnesse of your said bisecher for
matiers by him shewed in the hous accustumed for the
20 Comyns in the said parlementes He was therefore taken
arrested and rigorously in open wise led to the Toure
of London and there greuously in grete duresse long
tyme emprisoned ayenst the said fredom and liberte
and was there put in grete fere of ymportable
25 punycion of his body and drede of losse of his
lif withoute eny enditement presentement appele
due originall accusement or cause laufull had or
sued ayenst him as it is openly knowen: the not
mowyng come to eny answere or declaracion in
30 that partie whereby he not oonly suffered grete
hurt payn and disese in his body but was by the
occasion therof put to ouer grete excessyue
losses and expenses of his good amountyng to the
somme of M*l* mark and muche more Please hit your
35 grete wisedoms tenderly to consider the premisses
And thervpon to pray the kyng our souerain lorde
that hit like his highness of his moost noble
grace to graunte and prouide by thavice of the
lordes spirituell and temporell in this present
40 parlement assembled that for the said losses
costes damages and imprisonment your said
bisecher haue sufficient and resonable recompense
as good feith trouthe and conscience requiren

The following may be noted: *e* (as cf., e.g., *i/y*, in unaccented syllables
(*knyghtes* 4, *parlementes* 5, *holden* 5, *assembled* 12, *arrested* 21, etc.);

suche (6; other M.E. forms – *sich*, *swich*, etc. – are in a minority in the Chancery documents); -and- spellings (*notwithstonding* 9, *londe* 10; this becomes the preferred spelling as the period progresses, although -*and*- is still frequent); *eny* (12, 15, 17, etc.; but *any* is usually preferred); pronouns *theire* (13) and *theym* (14, 16, but the older forms *here* (etc.) and *hem* (etc.) still appear – the 3pl. subject, however, is always *they*); *ayenst* (23; -*y*- forms are still preponderant in these documents: see Fisher's Glossary Ayenst, and cf. Again); *muche* (34; *moch(e)* is slightly preponderant, however); *h*- remains in 'it' (*hit* 34, 37) by the side of non-*h*- forms; 3pr.pl. -*en* in verbs: (*requiren* 43; these are sporadic occurrences of a conservative tendency (see Fisher, p. 46). Clearly there is still some heterogeneity in spelling (albeit minor) and some retention of older forms, but these were to be ironed out in the succeeding decades.

4.6 Addendum: the Latin manuscripts

As might be expected, these manuscripts are mainly useful as material evidence for changes in spelling, especially with regard to place-names. The A.S. evidence for place-names, both Old English and Latin, was mentioned in Chap. 3 (3.8) where it was observed that the majority of A.S. names are not recorded until *DB*.

The other Latin sources for the medieval period (place-names, of course, also occur in M.E. works) are listed in Cameron's *English Place-Names* (pp. 21–22), to which the following summary is indebted. These are mainly official documents in the Public Record Office, but also in other locations. Those in the PRO include the Pipe Rolls, from the twelfth century onwards, dealing with payments due to the king from shires, towns and cities. These are specially important, since they record annually many town, village and parish names.

Other sources include Charter Rolls, dealing with royal grants and confirmation of grants of various kinds; Close Rolls, concerning royal business addressed to individuals; and Patent Rolls, containing royal documents of a public nature. Assize Rolls record the causes heard by the travelling justices, and Coroners' Rolls deal with judicial cases of interest to the Crown, pending action by the king's justices.

Sources of a more local character, probably mainly written down by local scribes and therefore representing more accurately the actual pronunciation of names, include collections of land charters relating to ecclesiastical and private estates, manorial court rolls, rentals and surveys of various lands. Again, much of this unpublished material is preserved in the P.R.O. and the British Library. Some is also to be found in County Record Offices, in the national, local, university and college libraries, in the libraries of the great English houses, in the possession of the Deans and Chapters of cathedrals, and also in private hands.

Although maps do not appear in any quantity before the time of

Elizabeth I, a number do survive from the medieval period, the earliest-known detailed ones being those compiled *c.* 1250 by, or for, Matthew Paris of St Albans, for his *Chronica Maiora* and *Historia Anglorum*, and those in John of Hungerford's *Chronicle.* The fullest of these contains 280 place-names, and is thus a source of some importance. Another very well-known map is the so-called Gough map of *c.* 1335, showing a great advance on Paris's maps, both in cartographical accuracy and in the number of place-names.

Some of these types of documents are found in increasing numbers during the early modern period, especially in the form of plans and maps. Meanwhile, since the medieval period is central to the study of place-names, and also a time when they assume crucial importance as evidence of language development, I conclude by giving one or two examples. The following place-names, recorded in A.S. and later medieval documents, are simplified from Ekwall's treatment (in his *Dictionary*) and omit the names of sources except for *ASC* and *DB*.

Kippax (West Yks): *Chipesch* (*DB*), *Kippeys* 1155–8, *Kipais* 1190, *Kypask, -ax* 1293; possibly < personal name O.E. **Cyppa* + O.E. *æsc* 'ash-tree', partly Scandinavianized to *-ask*, which then > *-ax*. [Note: *DB ch* spelling of initial /k/; fluctuation between non-W.S. *e* and (W.S. *æ* >) *a* < O.E. *æsc*; final /ʃ/ > sk/ under O.N. influence (cf. O.N. *askr*); /sk/ frequently > /ks/ in dialect, cf. common *ax* 'ask'.]

Pangbourne (Berkshire): (at) *Peginga burnan, Pægeinga burnan* 843, *Pangeborne* (*DB*), *Pangeburne* 1166; < river *Pang* + O.E. *burna*, etc., 'the "bourn" or stream of Pǣga's people'. [Note: early fluctuation between O.E. provincial *e* and W.S. *æ*, with ultimate triumph of *æ* > M.E. *a*; *-an* dat. (843) after prep. *at*.]

Repton (Derbyshire): *Hrypadun c.* 745, 848, (on) *Hreopandune* 755 (*ASC*), *Rapendune* (*DB*), *Rependon* 1197, *Repedon* 1236; 'the hill [O.E. *dūn*] of the Hrype tribe' (also in *Ripon* and nearby places *Ribston, Ripley*). [Note: O.E. initial aspirated *r*, i.e. /hr/, the aspiration lost in Middle English; uncertainty in western Old English as how to express /y/, by *y* or *eo* (*a* in *DB* is a curiosity), but eventual triumph of *e*.]

Tintinhull (Soms): *Tintehalle, Tintenella* (*DB*), *Tintenhille* 1168, *Tintehull* 1219; obscure first element (probably personal name) + O.E. *hyll* 'hill'. [Note: *DB* uncertainty as to how to express the vowel in the second element, by either *a* or *e*, which is actually O.E. *y* /y/, and emerges eventually in its western form as *u*, which > Pr.E. /ʌ/.]

5 *Early Modern English*

(to c. 1700)

5.1 Introductory

In this period (*c.* 1475–*c.* 1700) there is an abundance of evidence for the history of English in both its written and its spoken forms, and some of a hitherto almost unknown kind. It occurs in both relatively informal and more formal letters and other writings from the late fifteenth century onwards; in literary texts like those of, say, Caxton, Shakespeare and Milton; and now also in the stated opinions of writers on the English language, particularly those who are known as 'orthoepists' – writers on pronunciation. Early and later dictionaries provide information on the vocabulary of English, and there is also evidence for dialectal speech during this period.

5.1.1 *Informal texts*

From the texts below it will be clear that, in the sixteenth and seventeenth centuries, there was no set of universally accepted spellings. There were many widely accepted spelling conventions, but within those considerable variation was possible. Further, not only did one writer differ from another, but the same writer could use different spellings for the same word, even sometimes in the same sentence (cf. *bond* and *bounde, don* and *doon* p.p. in Text 1, below). Even in the late seventeenth century, when something like a standard set of spellings was reached, it was confined to books, and people continued to spell idiosyncratically in their private writing – as, indeed, some people do even today.

[Note: In the following passages, punctuation is modernised, but spelling and capitalization are retained as in the original. Abbreviations are silently expanded.]

1. *The Paston Letters* (*c.* 1420–post 1500)
   [Ed. N. Davis, Parts 1 and 2, Clarendon Press, 1971–6 (no. 386; in the shorter ed., Clarendon Medieval and Tudor Series, no. 95)]

John Paston III to Margaret Paston (between 1482 and 1484):

1   *Address*: to my ryght worchepfull modyr Margaret Paston
     RYGHT worchepfull modyr, in my most humble wyse I recomand
     me to yow, besechyng yow of your dayly blyssyng; and
     when I may, I wyll with as good wyll be redy to recompence

5   yow for the cost that my huswyff and I haue put yow to as
I am now bond to thank yow for it, whyche I do in the best
wyse I can.
   And modyr, it pleasyd yow to haue serteyn woordys to
my wyff at hyr departyng towchyng your remembrance of the
10 shortness that ye thynk your dayes of, and also of the mynd
that ye have towardys my brethryn and systyr, your chyldyr,
and also of your seruauntys, wherin ye wyllyd hyr to be a
meane to me that I wold tendyr and favore the same. Modyr,
savyng your pleasure, ther nedyth non enbasatours nor meanys
15 betwyx yow and me; for ther is neyther wyff nor other frend
shall make me to do that that your comandment shall make me
to do, if I may have knowlage of it. And if I haue no knowlage,
in good feyth I am excuseabyll bothe to God and yow. And well
remembred, I wot well ye ought not to haue me in jelusye for
20 on thyng nor other that ye wold haue me to accomplyshe if I
overleve yow, for I wot well non oo man alyve hathe callyd so
oft vpon yow as I to make your wylle and put iche thyng in
serteynté that ye wold have don for your sylff and to your
chyldre and seruauntys. Also, at the makyng of your wylle,
25 and at every comunycacyon that I haue ben at wyth yow
towchyng the same, I nevyr contraryed thyng that ye wold
have doon and parformyd, but alweys offyrd my sylff to
be bownde to the same.

Spellings

Most notable in Texts 1–3 is the use of *u* and *v* and of *i* and *y*: *u* can represent both vowel and consonant. Originally, and, indeed, as seen here, *u* and *v* were merely variant ways of spelling the same letter and could be used interchangeably, but in late Middle English it became common to use *v* initially and *u* elsewhere, and this practice was continued, fairly strictly, by the early printers. The convention of Pr.E. *u* for a vowel and *v* for a consonant arose in about 1630 under Continental influence.

In this passage, *y* (interchangeable in Middle English with *i*, though used especially in the context of 'minim' letters like *m* and *n* for the purpose of clarity) is preferred to *i*, which, however, occurs in *iche*, *in*, *it*, etc. It is also used, of course, for the consonant /j/: *yow*, *your*, *ye*.

Final unstressed *-e* had ceased to be pronounced in the fourteenth century, so the *-e* we find here was silent, and this accounts for its apparent indiscriminate usage, being found in words where we would not use it in Pr.E. and vice-versa. In Pr.E., usages have become fossilized, *-e* appearing, e.g., in *there* but not in *each* (cf. *ther*, *on* 'one', *don*, with *iche, favore, jelusye* in the passage above). In the Fr. word *serteynté* (23), however, the *-e* (= Pr.E. *-y*) is to be pronounced (as /e:/).

Other idiosyncratic spellings include: *worchepfull* (1, 2), *recompence* (4), *serteyn* (8) and *alweys* (27; *ey* for late M.E. *ai/ay*), *woordys* (8), *towchyng* (9), *frend* (15), *knowlage* (17), *wold* 'would' (20; the /l/ would still be pronounced at this stage).

Sounds
One or two spellings indicate sounds different from those of Pr.E.: *modyr* (1, 2; with /d/; < O.E. *mōdor*—as with *father*, substitution of *th* for *d* occurs only from the early sixteenth century, though the pronunciation with /ð/ may have existed earlier); *enbasatours* (14; < Fr. *ambassadeur*) shows the common M.E. variant with medial /t/ for Pr.E. /d/, while *huswyff* (5) and *wyff* (9) probably had short /i/—roughly *hussif, wiff*— before final /f/; *depertyng* (9; < Fr. *departir*) with *er* shows late M.E./early Mod.E. variation with *ar* (/ar/), cf. Pr.E. *certain, serve* as cf. *farm, marvel; Derby, sergeant* (with /a:/ pronunciation, but old *er* spelling); *oo* 'one' (21; < O.E. *ān*) is a traditional M.E. variant with loss of /n/.

Unstressed syllables apart from *-e* were apparently still being pronounced in full, as is shown by the endings *-yd, -ys: pleasyd* (8), *wyllyd* (12), *callyd* (21), *woordys* (8), *towardys* (11), *seruauntys* (12), etc.

Grammatical features
The older form *brethryn* (11) is in use for Pr.E. 'brothers', and *chyldyr* (11), *chyldre* (24) lack the *-n* of the Pr.E. double pl. form; in the pronouns, *ye, yow* and *your*, the 'polite' forms (as cf. *thou, thee, thy*) are naturally used by a son to his 'ryght worchepfull modyr' (see 1.18); *nedyth* (14), the 3pr.sg. of the verb, retains its *-th* ending. In syntax, note the use of *to*: 'ye wold haue me to accomplyshe' (20).

Vocabulary
One or two now archaic words are found: *non* 'no' (14; < O.E. *nān*), 'not' (21), *betwyx* 'between' (15), *overleve*? 'neglect' (21; n.r. *OED*), *wot* 'know' (21); *contraryed* 'acted contrary to' (26).

2. *Letters of Queen Elizabeth and King James VI of Scotland* (1582–90)
[Ed. J. Bruce (Camden Society, 46, 1849), pp. 12–13.]

1   I haue, right deare brother, receaued your frendly and
     affectionat letters, in wiche I perceaue the mastar Grayes
     halfe, limping answer, wiche is lame in thes respectz: the
     one, for that I se not that he told you who bade him talke
5   with Morgan of the price of my bloude, wiche he knowes, I

am assured, right wel; nor yet hathe named the man that
shuld be the murtherar of my life. You wel perceaue that nothing
may nearelar touche me than this cause, and therfor, accordinge
to the bond of nature and the promes of strikte frindeship,
10   let me coniure you that this vilanye may be confest. I hope
I may stand you in bettar sted than that you wyl shew you
uncareful of suche a treason.

Spellings

The use of *u* and *v* continue in the same way as before: *haue* (1), *receaued*
(1), *perceaue* (2), with *v* initially in *vilanye* (10). Only *i* is used for the
vowel (as cf. mainly *y* in Text 1), *y* being used, as in Pr.E., for /j/: *you*.
Final *-e* is still not firmly settled, e.g.: *deare* (1), *wiche* (2), *talke* (4),
strikte (9), cf. *affectionat* (2), *thes* (3), etc.

Other idiosyncratic spellings include: *-z* for the pl. in *respectz* (3); *ar*
for Pr.E. *er* in *mastar* (2), *murtherar* (7), *bettar* (11), etc.; *se* 'see' (4), *wel*
(6), *promes* (9) *shuld* (7) (the /l/ was probably still pronounced).

Sounds

Some of the spellings in the text may represent the sounds of spoken
English: there appears to be a variation between /ɛ/ and /i/ before /n/ in
frendly (1) as cf. *frindeship* (9); *wiche* (2; < O.E. *hwylc*) suggests that
the initial /h/ was no longer sounded (it was being lost in the south from
the twelfth century onwards, possibly first in vulgar speech but only very
much later (eighteenth century) regularly in 'good' speech); *murtherar*
(7) retains the old /ð/ of O.E. *morþor* 'murder' (the *d* which emerges
first in the fourteenth century is due to Fr. influence: cf. A.Fr. *murdre*,
moerdre, etc.); *bloude* (5) is not an uncommon spelling at this period,
evidently showing a shortened sound /u/. Noun and verb forms, since
they end in *-ed*, *-es*, often, as in Pr.E., do not certainly tell us whether
unstressed vowels were still being pronounced in full in the writer's
speech: *receaued* (1), *knowes* (5), *assured* (6), *named* (6), though *confest*
(10) clearly expresses a reduced ending, with /d/ > /t/ after /s/; *ar*
presumably reflects /ar/ < earlier /ɛr/ (see Text 1, above).

Grammatical features

In the verb, the 3pr.sg. *-th* occurs in *hathe* (6), but otherwise an *-s* sg. is
found (e.g. *knowes* (5) (-*th* seems to have lasted longest in *hath* and *doth*,
but by the 1590s *-(e)s* was probably normal in educated speech (see 1.18));
the pronouns *you* and *your* are used naturally to an equal (1.18).

In syntax, note: *for* (4) preceding *that*, the whole phrase meaning
'because', *I se not* (4; cf. Pr.E. *I do not see*—the use of *do* in such
constructions was becoming increasingly normal from the middle of the
sixteenth century, but the older construction continues side by side for
some time); *you* is used in *shew you* (11), where Pr.E. would use *yourself*.

Vocabulary

Nearelar (8) –? a form of 'nevertheless' (not recorded in this form by *OED*); *uncareful* (12) 'neglectful' looks slightly archaic, and is in rare usage in Pr.E. Nothing else distinctive appears in this passage.

3. *Wentworth Papers* (1597–1628)

[Ed. J.P. Cooper, Camden Society, Fourth Series, vol. 12, 1973, p. 224.]

To Elizabeth Danby, Fetter Lane, 7 Dec., 1624

1   My good Annt, I am very sorry that my occasions enforce
mee to bee soe longe absent from yow, when it is so fittinge
I should attend yow, which yow wilbee pleased for a season
to excuse mee for and by God's goodnes, I will make yow amends
5   upon the first oportunity. As concerninge our proceedings
here, Michaell Hopwood will giue yow a perticuler accompt for
your affaires and those of your grandchild, my cosen, in the
Cuntry. I haue writt at large to my cosen Wentworth of Woolley,
whome I haue desired to take the paines to visitt yow and both
10 to make yow acquainted and take your aduise therin. My best
Annt, let nothinge eyther concerning your selfe, your sonne's
children, or estate trouble yow, for I doubte not but God will
giue such blessinges to our endeauores, as that all will succeed
to your owne hart's desire and bee happily ouercome with a little
15 tyme and pacience, wherin I assure yow I shall trauaile with the
same care, as if it did concerne mee euen the most importantly in my
owne fortune, as indeed it cannot chuse but doe, when it
doth soe nearly touch persons soe neare unto mee in blood.

Spellings

These continue to look idiosyncratic to modern eyes. The use of *u* and *v* continues in the same way as before: *giue* (6), *aduise* (10), *endeauores* (13), *trauaile* (15), but *very* (1), *visitt* (9); *i* is used for the vowel, except in *tyme* (15), *y* now being in regular consonantal use – *yow, your*. Words with final *-e* have still not assumed their Pr.E. forms: *soe, longe, doubte, concerne*, etc., but no words occur in this passage which omit *-e* where Pr.E. has it. *Mee* (2), *bee* (2), etc. are given an extra *-e*, perhaps for reinforcement.

    Other idiosyncratic spellings include: *goodnes* (4), *oportunity* (5), *cosen* (7), *cuntry* (8), *visitt* (9), *chuse* (17). *Accompt* (6; < O.Fr. *acconter*) is remodelled on the basis of Lat. *ad + computāre*, and *doubte* (12; < O.Fr. *douter*) shows the restoration of *b* on the model of Lat. *dubitāre* (cf. the *Love's Labour's Lost* passage, pp. 124–5, below).

Sounds

Antt (1, 11) appears to show the short vowel /a/ (St.E. /a:/ in this word-class – *aunt, branch, dance,* etc. – did not emerge until after the early Mod.E. period); *hart* (14; < M.E. *herte*) presumably shows /ar/, the ancestor of Pr.E. /a:/.

Grammatical features

Note 3pr.sg. of the verb as *-th* in *doth* (18); *writt* (8) is the p.p. 'written'. In syntax, again *do* is of special interest; it is not used in the negative construction *I doubte not* (12; cf. *I se not* in Text 2), but it appears unemphatically in *if it did concerne mee* (16) and *when it doth soe nearly touch* (17–18), a construction which was dying during the seventeenth century (cf. Pr.E. *if it concerned me; when it so nearly touches*).

Vocabulary

There is nothing here different from Pr.E., except *persons* (18), where colloquial modern usage would have *people*.

4. *The Letters of Henry St John to the Earl of Orrery* (1709–11)
   [Ed. H.T. Dickinson (Camden Society, Fourth Series, Vol. 14, 1975), pp. 151–2.]

Whitehall. 9 March 1710/11

1 My Lord,
   I was extreamly glad to find by the honour of your letter of
   the 6th N.S. that your Lordship was safely arrived at the Hague,
   and had begun to enter upon business with the Pensioner. I do not
5 doubt but in a little time we shall see the good effect of your
   Lordship's negociations, particularly in contributing towards a
   proper regulation of the government of the Spanish Low Countries;
   which, as your Lordship observes, is in a very distracted condition
   at present; and therefore no time should be lost in putting it upon
10 a better foot.
     Your Lordship will find in the newspaper from my office a
   short account of a villanous action which I think is not to be
   parallelled in history. Monsieur de Guiscard has four wounds; but
   none mortal, as we hope. The chirurgeons beleive that he will
15 recover, there being no bad symptoms as yet: and it is pity he
   should dye any other death, than the most ignominious which such
   an attempt deserves. Mr Harley is in a very good way at present
   and I hope not in the least danger of his life.
     I must deferr writing till next post particularly and fully
20 to your Lordship, the hurry I am now in making it impossible to
   do it by this post.
         I am ever, my Lord,
             your Lordship's ever faithful and most humble servant
                                                         H. St. John

Spellings
There is now little to distinguish this text from a Pr.E. one: *u*/*v* and *i*/*y*
have more or less settled down (though note *dye* 16), as has final *-e*:
time, there, doubt, wounds, etc. The last of these (13) shows that the
-es ending has now been reduced to /-z/ (after voiced consonants) or
/-s/ (after voiceless consonants – no examples in this passage). Indeed, the
very few older spellings which do occur stand out because of their very
paucity: *extreamly* (1), *negociations* (6), *beleive* (14), *deferr* (19). The
spellings now do not indicate any pronunciations, having settled down
into an early Mod.E. system remarkably similar to that of Pr.E.

Grammatical features
Note 3pr.sg. of the verb *has, deserves* (17), i.e. ending in *-(e)s*, as distinct
from earlier *-(e)th*. We may also note *was safely arrived* (2; Pr.E. *had* . . .;
the auxiliary 'be' is especially used with verbs of motion in the early
Mod.E. period, and is commoner in these contexts than 'have'; it denotes
a state which has arisen as a result of the action of the verb). With *I do
not doubt* (4–5) cf. Text 3 *I doubte not*.

Vocabulary
Only *chirurgeons* 'surgeons' (14; < O.Fr. *cirurgien*, etc.), in use, side by
side with *surgeon* (contracted form of *serurgien*), and in regular use until
the eighteenth century.

5.1.2 *Literary texts*

5. Sir Thomas Malory, *Morte d'Arthur* (1469–70)
[Taken from the Winchester manuscript, c. 1480, folio 324: see *The Winchester Malory:
a Facsimile*, with an Introduction by N.R. Ker, EETS, 1976. The text is printed in
The Works of Sir Thomas Malory, ed. E. Vinaver, 3 vols., 2nd ed., Clarendon Press,
1967 where, however, archaic letters are modernized. It was first printed by Caxton
in 1485, and reprinted by his successors.]

1   Than sir Launcelot ayenst nyght rode vnto the castell, and
    there anone he was receyved worshypfully wyth suche people,
    to his semynge, as were aboute quene Gwenyuer secrete.
    So whan sir Launcelot was alyght he asked where the quene
5   was. So dame Brusen seyde she was in her bed.
       And than people were avoyded and sir Launcelot was
    lad into her chambir. And þan dame Brusen brought sir
    Launcelot a kuppe of wyne, and anone as he had drunken
    that wyne he was so asoted and madde that he myght make no
10   delay but wythoute ony let he wente to bedde. And so he
    wente that mayden Elayne had bene quene Gwenyuer. And
    wyte you well that sir Launcelot was glad, and so was

that lady Eleyne that she had gotyn sir Launcelot in her
armys, for well she knew that þat same nyght sholde be
15 bygotyn sir Galahad uppon her, that sholde preve the beste
knyght of the worlde.
      And so they lay togydir untyll underne of the morne;
and all the wyndowys and holys of that chambir were stopped,
that no maner of day my3t be seyne. And anone sir Launcelot
20 remembryd hym and arose vp and wente to the wyndow, and anone
as he had unshutte the wyndow the enchauntemente was paste.
Than he knew hymselff that he had done amysse.

Spellings

The same conventions emerge with regard to *u*/*v* as were found in Texts
1–3, above, except that here *v* is occasionally used where the Pastons,
e.g., might have used *u* (*avoyded* 6); *y* is preferred to *i* (*nyght* 1,
wyndowys 18, *hymselff* 22), which, however, occasionally occurs in
unstressed syllables (*chambir* 18, *togydir* 17, also *sir* passim); final -*e* often
remains (*anone* 2, *kuppe* 8, *seyne* 19, *wente* 20). In this passage the old
symbol þ (side by side with *th*) occurs twice, and 3 once.
      Other idiosyncratic spellings include: *castell* (1), *quene* (3), *kuppe* (8),
maner (19), *sholde* (14; the /l/ was still pronounced).

Sounds

A number of spellings suggest the sounds which lie behind them: *ayenst*
(1; < O.E. *on-ġēanes*) retains *y* /j/ (the *g* in the Pr.E. form may be of
northern origin); *whan* (4; < O.E. *hwænne*) and *than* (< O.E. *þænne*) are
the normally-derived forms with *a* instead of Pr.E. *e* (which were
probably unstressed forms at first): *lad* (7) is < O.E. *lǽdde*, which could
give either *lad* or *led*, and there is fluctuation in M.E. texts; *ony* (10;
presumably /ɔni/ < M.E. *anie* /ani/); *preve* 'prove' (15) is < an O.Fr.
form with *ue*, later *eu*, giving, in Middle English, *preove* and *preve*,
beside *prove* (< O.Fr. *prover*); *togydir* (17) is < O.E. *tōgædere* (though
the /d/ had started to change to /ð/ as early as the fourteenth century),
with progressive raising of /æ/ to /ɛ/ and then to /i/; *enchauntemente* (21)
shows /au/ normally developed from A.Fr. *au*.

Grammatical features

Was is used with the p.p. (?; see Text 4, above; note on line 2); *alyght*
(4; < O.E. *ālīhtan* inf.): the normal M.E. p.t.sg. would be *alighted(e)*,
but the final unstressed syllable has been assimilated to the preceding -*t*;
gotyn (13; modern American English *gotten*) is the older M.E. p.p. before
it was later replaced (in the sixteenth century and subsequently) by the
p.t. form *got*. Unstressed endings in nouns were still in their full form
at least in *armys* (14), *wyndowys* (18) and *holys* (18); but in the verbs,

paste 'passed' (21) shows that the unstressed syllable was no longer /-id/ but had been reduced to simple /t/.

Vocabulary

The following are archaic in Pr.E., or have disappeared altogether: *avoyded* 'dismissed' (6), *asoted* 'foolish' (9), *let* 'delay' (10), *wente* 'thoughte' (11; < O.E. *wēnan* inf.), *wyte* 'know' (12; < O.E. *witan* inf.), *bygotyn* (15), *underne* 'noontide' (17; < O.E. *undern*), *morne* (17), *unshutte* 'opened' (21).

6. Christopher Marlowe, *Doctor Faustus* (1588/9)
[Oldest known printed ed. 1604 (ed. W.W. Greg, Clarendon Press, 1950), lines 1358–69, p. 278.]

Enter Helen

1   Fau: Was this the face that lancht a thousand shippes ?
    And burnt the toplesse Towres of Ilium ?
    Sweete Helen, make me immortall with a kisse:
    Her lips suckes forth my soule, see where it flies:
5   Come Helen, come giue mee my soule againe,
    Here wil I dwel, for heauen be in these lips,
    And all is drosse that is not Helena:
    I wil be Paris, and for loue of thee,
    Insteede of Troy shal Wertenberge be sackt,
10 And I wil combate with weake Menelaus,
    And weare thy colours on my plumèd Crest:
    Yea I will wound Achillis in the heele,
    And then returne to Helen for a kisse.

[Readings from the six quarto eds. 1616–63: 4 *suckes* > *sucke.* 6 *be* > *is*]

Spellings

u is used for Pr.E. *v* in *giue* (5), *heauen* (6) and *loue* (8), but *i* has now displaced *y* as a vowel, the latter being used as a consonant only; final *-e* often remains (*sweete* 3, *soule* 4, 5, *weake* 10), but seems to mean nothing metrically, and was clearly not being used for this purpose – not, at least, in this passage; other spellings different from those of Pr.E. include *dwel* (6), *shal* (9) and *wil* (8, 10) with single *l*, *immortall* (3) with double *l*, *mee* (5; double *ee* perhaps for emphasis), and *insteede* (9).

Sounds

Note *lancht* 'launched' (1; and cf. *enchauntemente* in Text 5); A.Fr. *an* in the *haunch, haunt, launch, laundry, lawn, staunch, vaunt* group usually > M.E. /au/, then Pr.E. /ɔ:/, but many show side-forms in ?/a:/ in early texts.

Doctor Faustus.

Come Helen, come giue mée my foule againe.
Here wil J dwel, for heauen be in thefe lips,
And all is droffe that is not Helena: *enter old man*
J wil be Pacis, and for loue of thée,
Inftéede of *Troy* fhal *Wertenberge* be fackt,
And J wil combate with weake Menelaus,
And weare thy colours on my plumed Creft:
Yea J wil wound Achillis in the héele,
And then returne to Helen for a kiffe.
O thou art fairer then the euening aire,
Clad in the beauty of a thoufand ftarres,
Brighter art thou then flaming Iupiter,
when he appeard to haplefle Semele,
More louely then the monarke of the fkie
In wanton Arethufaes azurde armes,
And none but thou fhalt be my paramour.   *Exeunt.*
   Old man Accurfed Fauftus, miferable man,
That from thy foule excludft the grace of heauen,
And flieft the throne of his tribunall feate,
       Enter the Diuelles.
Sathan begins to fift me with his pride,
As in this furnace God fhal try my faith,
My faith, vile hel, fhal triumph ouer thée,
Ambitious fiends, fée how the heauens fmiles
At your repulfe, and laughs your ftate to fcorne,
Hence hel, for hence J flie vnto my God.   *Exeunt.*

     Enter Fauftus with the Schollers.

  Fau: Ah Gentlemen!
  1. Schr what ailes Fauftus?
  Fau: Ah my fwéete chamber-fellow! had J liued with
thée, then had J liued ftil, but now J die eternally: looke,
comes he not? comes he not?
  2. Sch: what meanes Fauftus?
  3. Scholler Belike he is growne into fome fickeneffe, by
                F   being

Doctor Faustus, 1604 edn.

Grammatical features

Note 3pr.pl. *suckes* (4; altered later to *sucke*): this was not uncommon, appearing, e.g. in the Shakespeare First Folio (1623); and 3pr.sg. *be* (6; later *is*) – an oddity, since the element of doubt which would warrant a subjunctive is not implied here.

Lancht (1), *burnt* (2), *sackt* (9) show a reduced ending, as cf. *plumèd* (11), p.p. adj., in both cases for the exigencies of the metre.

Vocabulary

Only the now archaic *yea*.

7. Sir Thomas Browne, Dedication to *Hydriotaphia*, or *Urne-Buriall* (1658)

[Ed. C.A. Patrides (Penguin Books, 1977), p. 265.]

1   'Tis opportune to look back upon old times, and contemplate
    our Forefathers. Great examples grow thin, and to be fetched
    from the passed world. Simplicity flies away, and iniquity
    comes at long strides upon us. We have enough to do to make
5   up our selves from present and passed times, and the whole
    stage of things scarce serveth for our instruction. A compleat
    peece of vertue must be made up from the Centos of all ages,
    as all the beauties of Greece could make but one handsome
    Venus.
10 When the bones of King Arthur were digged up, the old Race
    might think, they beheld therein some Originals of themselves;
    Unto these of our Urnes none here can pretend relation, and
    can only behold the Reliques of those persons, who in their
15 life giving the Laws unto their predecessors, after long
    obscurity, now lye at their mercies. But remembring the
    early civility they brought upon these Countreys, and
    forgetting long passed mischiefs; We mercifully preserve
    their bones, and pisse not upon their ashes.

Spellings

These now become more and more like those of Pr.E., exceptions being the occasional use of capital letters for unusual or emphatic words (a traditional foible of early printers, probably adopted from Germany and the Netherlands); and the words *compleat* (6), *peece* (7), *vertue* (7), *reliques* (14), *lye* (16), *remembring* (16), *countreys* (17), still acceptable forms at this time. Final *-e* has more or less stabilized in its Pr.E. form. The spelling system has now reached a stage where its conventions preclude inferences about the sounds which lie behind it.

Grammatical features

Note p.t. *digged* (10: < O.Fr. *diguer*), the normal form up to the seventeenth and eighteenth centuries. *Passed* adj. (3) = Pr.E. *past*, showing that the *-ed* ending was reduced to /-t/ despite the spelling, producing confusion in the spelling between the p.p. and the adj. The prose being couched in a somewhat conservative and formal style has the 3pr.sg. of the verb *-eth* ending, not *-es*.

Vocabulary
Note only *pisse*, not 'polite' in Pr.E.

5.2 Grammarians, writers, orthographers and orthoepists

A new class of evidence for the history of the English of this time, both standard and dialectal, is provided by the contemporary scholars of the language. These men were occupied in a variety of activities (the dates given below are those of their main works (see, further, the Bibliography)): reviving an interest in Old English (e.g. Dean Laurence Nowell (*c.* 1565), William Somner (1659), George Hickes (1703–5)); writing about the contemporary state of the English language (e.g. headmaster Edmund Coote (1597); Alexander Gil (1619, 1621), High Master of St Paul's School; Suffolk schoolmaster Simon Daines (1640); the notable dramatist Ben Jonson (1640–41); and schoolmaster and cleric Christopher Cooper (1685, 1687)); and making dictionaries (e.g. Peter Levins (1570); Robert Cawdrey (1604); Stephen Skinner (1671); and, later, Elisha Coles (1676); John Kersey (1708, etc.); Nathan Bailey (1721, 1727) and, of course, the redoubtable Dr Samuel Johnson (1755)).

The work of such men allows us to make reasonably definite assertions about the pronunciation, grammar and vocabulary of the time. First, however, what information is available about the overall state of the language at this time, in its different forms?

5.3 Different types of English

From the statements of a number of writers it is clear that from the early 1530s there *was* more than one type of English in existence – including some form of standard in speech to which it was desirable to conform. Evidence for this is to be found in, e.g., Elyot's *Governour* (1531), which advises women who attend a nobleman's son in infancy to 'speke none englisshe but that which is cleane, polite, perfectly and articulately pronounced ...'; while the spelling reformer Hart's standard of speech as announced in his *Orthographie* (1569) is that of the 'learned and literate', the 'best and moste perfite English'. This appears (according to his *Methode*, 1570) to be the equivalent of that of the Court and London, where 'the generall flower of all Englishe countrie speaches, are chosen and used'. For the first time, therefore, a writer is specifying what in fact *was* the 'best speech', and his *Orthographie* was indeed intended to be a guide to this 'flower', Court English.

A Table Alphabeticall,

contayning and teaching the true writing, and vnderſtanding of hard *vſuall Engliſh words. &c.*

(·.·)

(k) ſtandeth for a kind of.
(g. or gr.) ſtandeth for Greeke.
The French words haue this (§) before them.

A

§ **A** Bandon, **caſt away, o₂ yælde vp, to leaue, o₂ fo₂ſake.**

Abaſh, **bluſh.**

abba, **father.**

§ abbeſſe, abbateſſe, **Miſtris of a Nunne₂rie, comfo₂ters of others.**

§ abbettors, **counſello₂s.**

aberration, **a going a ſtray, o₂ wande₂ring.**

abbreuiat, ⎱ **to ſho₂ten, o₂ make**
§ abbridge, ⎰ **ſho₂t.**

§ abbut, **to lie vnto, o₂ bo₂der vpon, as one lands end mæts with another.**

abecédarie, **the o₂der of the Letters, o₂ hee that vſeth them.**

aberration, **a going aſtray, o₂ wandering.**

§ abet, **to maintaine.**

B.   § abdi-

A page from Cawdrey's *Table Alphabeticall of Hard English Words* (1604)

Most famous of all—though marginally, and less precisely, preceded by William Harrison's bold statement (1587) that the 'excellencie of the English tong is found in one, and the south part of the Iland'—is Puttenham's dictum (1589) that the best English is 'the vsual speech of the Court, and that of London and the shires lying about London within lx. miles and not much above'. (The rest of his remarks about provincial English, and who used it and how, are open to argument: I agree with Dobson that Puttenham may mean that, outside the 60-mile radius, even the country gentry spoke 'modified standard', but not necessarily that in the far west and north the standard did not apply at all. On this, Puttenham is unclear.)

The idea of a Standard English persists into the seventeenth century, being variously defined as the speech of those with education (Gil), of those from 'the Universities and Citties' (Butler, 1633), of 'London and our universities, where the language is purely spoken' (Owen Price, 1665), as that 'most in use among the generality of scholars', 'the present proper pronunciation . . . in Oxford and London' (Coles, 1674), and that of educated southerners (Cooper, 1685). The picture, though differing in detail from writer to writer, is clear: 'Standard' is southern, upper-class and educated. The obverse of this may, of course, clearly be inferred to be non-southern, non-upper-class and non-educated, i.e. 'vulgar' or 'barbaric' speech—two over-used epithets of the period.

5.4 Vocabulary and the 'Ink-horn' controversy

The early dictionaries naturally enable us to say a great deal about the lexical stock of the language at this time as, of course, do Spenser, Shakespeare, Milton, and other writers. It is evident what a very rich period it was for the composition and adoption of new words, an activity which often reached astounding and ridiculous lengths. Mercifully for posterity, not all of these words survived.

There consequently arose a lively controversy between men of letters about what were by some scornfully referred to as 'inkhorn' terms, on the grounds that such words smelled of the inkhorn—learned compositions or foreign loans. Should they or should they not have a place in the English language? The battle between the two sides raged fast and furious, with some who inevitably wanted it both ways, counselling caution and moderation. As William Camden sensibly observed in his *Remaines Concerning Britain* (1605), 'Whereas our tongue is mixed, it is no disgrace, whenas all the tongues of Europe doe participate interchangeably the one of the other.' It is false, he says, 'that our tongue is the most mixt and corrupt of all the other'. At the other end of the century, Dryden sententiously disapproved of those 'who corrupt our English idiom by mixing it too much with French'.

The evidence for all this is extensive: quite apart from the dictionaries—

To the Reader.

SVch as by their place and calling, (but efpecially Preachers) as haue occafion to fpeak publiquely before the ignorant people , are to bee admonifhed , that they neuer affect any ftrange ynckhorne termes, but labour to fpeake fo as is commonly receiued, and fo as the moft ignorant may well vnderftand them : neyther feeking to be ouer fine or curious, nor yet liuing ouer carelefie, vfing their fpeech, as moft men doe, & ordering their wits, as the feweft haue done. Some men feek fo far for outlandifh Englifh , that they forget altogether their mothers language , fo that if fome of their mothers were aliue, they were not able to tell,or vnderftand what they fay, and yet thefe fine Englifh Clearks, will fay they fpeak in their mother tongue ; but one might well charge them, for counterfeyting the Kings Englifh. Alfo, fome far iournied gentlemē,at their returne home, like as they loue to go in forraine apparrell, fo they will pouder their talke with ouer-fea language. He that commeth lately out of France, will talk French Englifh, and neuer blufh at the matter.

The opening of the Introduction to Cawdrey's *Table Alphabeticall* the earliest compiled to explain these 'hard words' – there are, as we have seen, a great many learned opinions expressed in print on both sides. As specimens of the sort of evidence we have for inkhorn terms, I give two extreme examples, specifically intended to make fun of the practice of inventing or adapting and using them.

The first is a small part of a spoof letter containing as many of such words as possible in order to make the practice look ridiculous, while the second is Shakespeare's illustration of the same notion in theatrical terms, as he satirises the pedant Holofernes.

1. Thomas Wilson, 'Plaines What it is', in *The Arte of Rhetorique* (1553)
[Printed in J.L. Moore, pp. 91–3.]

An ynkehorne letter

Ponderyng, expẽdyng, and reuolutyng with my self your ingent affabilitie, and ingenious capacitee, for mundane affaires: I cannot but celebrate and extolle your magnificall dexteritee, aboue all other. For how could you haue adepted suche illustrate prerogatiue, and dominicall superioritee, if the fecunditee of your ingenie had not been so fertile, & woũderfull pregnaunt. Now therfore beeyng accersited, to suche splendent renoume, & dignitee splendidious: I doubt not but you will adiuuate suche poore adnichilate orphanes, as whilome ware cõdisciples with you, and of antique familiaritie in Lincolne shire. Emong whom I beeyng a Scholasticall panion, obtestate your sublimitee to extoll myne infirmitee.

2. William Shakespeare, *Love's Labour's Lost* (c. 1594) Act V, Scene 1.
[The Arden Edition, 4th ed., 1956; more detailed notes will be found there.]

Enter HOLOFERNES, *Sir* NATHANIEL, *and* DULL.

Hol. Satis quid sufficit.[1]
Nath. I praise God for you, sir: your reasons[2] at dinner have been sharp and sententious; pleasant without scurrility, witty without affection[3], audacious[4] without impudency, learned without opinion[5] and strange without heresy. I did converse this quondam[6] day with a companion of the king's, who is intituled, nominated, or called, Don Adriano de Armado.
Hol. Novi hominem tanquam te:[7] his humour is lofty, his discourse peremptory, his tongue filed[8], his eye ambitious, his gait majestical, and his general behaviour vain, ridiculous, and thrasonical[9]. He is too picked[10], too spruce[11], too affected, too odd, as it were, too peregrinate[12], as I may call it.
Nath. A most singular and choice epithet.

[*Draws out his table-book*

Hol. He draweth out the thread of his verbosity finer than the staple[13] of his argument. I abhor such fanatical phantasimes, such insociable[14] and point-devise[15] companions; such rackers of orthography, as to speak dout, fine, when he should say doubt; det, when he should pronounce debt,—d, e, b, t, not d, e, t; he clepeth a calf, cauf; half, hauf; neighbour *vocatur* nebour; neigh abbreviated ne. This is abhominable, which he would call abominable, it insinuateth me of insanie:[16] *ne intelligis domine*:[17] to make frantic, lunatic.

Nath. Laus Deo, bone intelligo.[18]

Hol. Bone? Bon, fort bon,[19] Priscian a little scratched: 'twill serve.

[1]'What is adequate is enough' [2]probably = 'discourse' [3]affectation [4]spirited, animated [5]self-conceit, being opinionated [6]former, previous [7]'I know the man as well as I know you' [8]polished [9]boastful [10]elaborate, over-refined [11]over-elegant, affected [12]having the air of a traveller [13]thread [14]intolerable [15]precise, affectedly exact [16]perhaps = 'drives me frantic' [17]'Don't you understand, Master?' [18]'Praise God, I understand well' [19]'Well? Good – very good.'

[Note: the passage also illustrates the contemporary mania for what are called 'etymological spellings' – i.e. spellings reconstructed in line with their real or supposed originals, e.g. *debt* < Lat. *debitum* (though the word had really already come into English from French without the *b*); *abhominable* (with *h* inserted, wrongly regarded as < Lat. *ab + homine*, but really ultimately < Lat. *abominari* 'to deprecate as an ill omen'.]

5.5 Analyses of English: 1. Sounds

The statements of scholars, grammarians and other writers, however, are of essential interest not only for what they tell us of the state or condition of their contemporary English and matters of vocabulary, but are even more important in the field of pronunciation, in particular with regard to the Great Vowel Shift (1.14). Spellings may offer us some insight into pronunciations (see 5.7, below), but the writers of the sixteenth and seventeenth centuries present an additional and more important source of information. I shall illustrate this (and also grammar) by reference to two writers, one from the beginning and one from later on in the period.

1. John Hart's *Orthographie* (1569)
[Ed. B. Danielsson, Part I, Stockholm, 1955, p. 190.]

'John Hart', says E.J. Dobson (I, p. 62), 'deserves to rank with the greatest English phoneticians and authorities on pronunciation.' His *Orthographie*, the second of three works, is an analysis of the sounds of English (the first really systematic one, indeed) and suggests letters that might represent them better than the contemporary system, followed by a long continuous passage of phonetic writing in Hart's proposed reformed alphabet. His new spelling was based on strictly phonetic principles, and he conceived it as a means of teaching the correct pronunciation of English and of foreign languages. From his passage on the five short vowels /a, ɛ, i, ɔ, u/ and on the diphthong *ei* (< M.E. *ī*), we may select for comment *u* and *ei*. M.E. *u* /u/, as we said earlier (1.14) ultimately > / ʌ / (*come, cup, glove*) in St.E., where this latter sound is first definitely attested by Daines (1640; see Dobson, II, p. 586). It may, however, have existed in some dialects as early as the sixteenth and even the fifteenth centuries (ibid., p. 587). Hart's views on the sound are therefore of crucial importance. He writes:

> Their due and auncient soundes, may be in this wise verye
> sensibly perceyued. ... For the fift and last, by holding in lyke
> maner the tongue from touching the teeth or gummes (as is said
> of the a, and o) and bringing the lippes so neare togither, as there
> be left but space that the sounde may passe forth with the breath,
> so softly, that (by their ouer harde and close ioyning) they be not
> forced thorow the nose, and is noted thus u.

Quite clearly, this statement, about bringing the lips as close together as possible, indicates the older sound /u/, which was therefore still used in the 'best English'.

Turning to *ei*, Hart here says:

> And we our selues doe rightly sound all fiue vowels in the Gospel
> in Latine. *In principio erat verbum*, etc. vnto *sine:* where i, is
> sounded the Diphthong ei, or Greeke ɛi and in *qui*, as thou it
> were written *quei*.

How is this to be interpreted? It is the mid-sixteenth-century sound developed from M.E. *ī* /i:/ in words like *white, kind, like*, Pr.E. /ai/: it therefore represents an intermediate stage in this development. Scholarly opinion, based on statements such as Hart's, used to be that it was /ei/ (as in Pr.E. *bake, late*), but a more recent view is that it was only an approximation to this diphthong, and was really something more like /əi/, i.e. /ə/ as in *China* plus /i/ as in *bit*. Although many of the writers equate *ei* with /ei/, Gil seems to support /əi/ in his statement – more precise than some others – that the diphthong is almost *ei*, but that the first element is not the ordinary *e* but a 'thinner' (i.e. more obscure) sound, which must be /ə/ or something very close to it. Dobson (II.137) sets out the rest of the evidence in support of /əi/, from which it becomes clear that the spelling *ei* in various orthoepical writings (including those of Hart) was intended first of all to express a diphthong as distinct from M.E. ī; secondly, that it was as near as they could get to /əi/ while still retaining the conventional English alphabet.

An extract from Hart's *Orthographie* in his 'reformed' spelling [Danielsson's ed., p. 203]

(47 b) An exersīz ov ðat huitʃ iz sēd: huēr-in iz de-
clārd, hou ðe rest ov ðe konsonants ar mād
bei ðinstruments ov ðe mouþ: huitʃ
naz omĭted in ðe premĭsez, for ðat
ui did not mutʃ abiuz ðem.
Cap .vii.

In ðis tītl abuv-uritn, ei konsider ov ðe ī, in exersīz, *and* ov ðe u, in instruments: ðe leik ov ðe ī, in tītl, huitʃ ðe kŏmon man; and mani lernd, dū sound in ðe diphþongs ei, and iu: iet ei uld not þink it mīt to ureit ðem, in ðōz and leik ūrds; huēr ðe sound ov ðe voël ōnli, mē bi as uel ălouëd in our spītʃ, as ðat ov ðe diphþong iuzd ŏv ðe riud: and so fǎr ei ălou observasion for derivasions. ~ Hierbei iu mē persēv, ðat our singl sounding and ius of letters, mē in proses ov teim, bring our hōl nasion tu ōn serten, perfet and dʒeneral spēking.

2. John Wallis's *Grammatica Linguae Anglicanae* (1653, first ed.)
[Ed. J.A. Kemp, John Wallis: *Grammar of the English Language*, Longman, 1972]

John Wallis was primarily a phonetician, and his work (in Latin) was written, he says, for the benefit of foreigners. The pronunciation of English is explained in the first place, by the usual method of comparing the sounds of our language with those of others. He also includes a section on morphology and syntax. Let us now consider the same two sounds we examined in Hart, as revealed some 80 years previously. On 'obscure' u, Wallis tells us (pp. 140–41):

The French sound in the last syllable of the words: *serviteur, sacrificateur*, etc is almost the same as this. In English it is usually represented by a short *u*, as in *turn, burn, dull, cut* etc. .... The Welsh always represent the sound with *y* ...

Here, the (rough) equation with Fr. *eur* (i.e. /œ:/ and Welsh *y* (i.e. /ə/) shows conclusively that in Wallis's speech M.E. *u* had become / ʌ /.

As regards *i* (pp. 257–9), this is 'rather [N.B.] like Greek ει' again (as in Hart), with various reservations. With Dobson, who argues the case very cogently (I, pp. 233–4; II.137), we assume again that this is a mere approximation to /ei/, and that the intended sound is more like /əi/.

5.6 Analyses of English: 2. Grammar

Hart (above) was solely a phonetician, so affords no evidence of the state of the parts of speech as they existed in his day. Wallis does, however, and here is an example (Kemp's ed., pp. 281–5):

PLURAL NUMBER

Singular substantives are made plural by adding *s*; sometimes this is preceded by *e*, when the pronunciation makes it necessary, for example when *s* immediately follows *s*, *z*, *x*, *sh*, or *c*, *g*, *ch* when they have their softer sound. So, for instance, *a hand*, *a tree*, *a house*, *a fox*, *a fish*, *a maze*, *a prince*, *an age*, *a tench* have the plural forms *hands*, *trees*, *houses*, *foxes*, *fishes*, *mazes*, *princes*, *ages*, *tenches*. This is the only regular way (nowadays) of forming the plural number. At one time, however, they formed plurals with *en* or *yn* as well, and we still have a few examples of this; *an ox*, *a chick* have the plural forms *oxen*, *chicken* (some say *chicken* for the singular and *chickens* for the plural). Similarly the plural of *fere* is *fern*–though nowadays *fern* is usually used for both numbers, with *ferns* as an alternative plural form; *fere* and *feres* are almost obsolete. Occasionally, though this is less common, you hear *housen*, *eyn*, *shoon*, etc instead of *houses*, *eyes*, *shoes*, etc. Some say *a pease* and, in the plural, *peasen*, but the singular form *a pea* with plural *peas* is preferable.[1] There are some other survivals of this type of formation, but most of them are irregular for other reasons too, for example *a man* (formerly *manne*), *a woman* have the plural forms *men*, *women* (*wemen*, *weomen*) by a syncope of *manen*, *womanen*; in Anglo-Saxon they used to say *a man* (Latin *homo*), *a weaponman* (Latin *vir*) and a *wyfman* or *wombman* (Latin *mulier*). Similarly from *a brother*, *a child* we get the plural forms *brethren*, *children*,[2] and from *a cow* the plural *keen* or *kine* (as if from *cowin*), and *swine* (as if from *sowin*) from the singular *sow*[3] though *sow* is now only used of a female pig, whereas *swine* is used in singular and plural, and for either sex. However, some of these words also have a plural form by analogy from the regular formation, for example *brothers*, *cows*, *sows*.

Notes:

1. *Chicken* is not the pl. of *chick*, which is merely a shortened form of *chicken*, < O.E. *cicen*, pl. *cicenu*, both of which give Pr.E. *chicken*, though as a pl. form this survives only in dialectal English. St.E. has added -*s*, thus making a double pl. *Fearn*, which is actually < O.E. *fearn* (pl. *fearn*), is a similar case. *Kine*, *shoon*, *eyen* and *housen* are cited by other of the grammarians. *Peas* is given by Gil as both sg. and pl. (the sg. is *pise* in Old English (pl. *pisan*, but this later came to be regarded as

a pl. because of the -s, and a new sg. *pea* formed). *Peas* is still recorded as a sg. in scattered Pr.E. rural dialects.

2. *Womanen* is a sixth-edition misprint; *wombman* is a false etymology: the word *woman is < O.E. wīfman.* Brethren is < O.E. *brēþer* pl. + -*en* (thus another double pl.); likewise *children* is < O.E. *ċildru*, M.E. *childre* pl. + -*en* pl.

3. *Kine, keen* are both < O.E. pl. *cȳ* (not from *cowin!*) + pl. -*n* (another double pl.); the former was still normal in the first half of the seventeenth century – Gil, e.g., lists it as only pl. form – but a new pl. *cows* appears side by side with it at about the same time. *Swine* < O.E. *swīn* (like some other animal words: *sheep, deer,* etc.) had no distinct form in Old English.

Despite Wallis's erroneous etymologizing, his statements about nouns in the mid-seventeenth century are admirably clear, providing much valuable information about pls. then current, but now obsolete except in dialect.

An extract from Wallis's treatment of the verb (Kemp's edition, pp. 335–7):

> However, in the second person singular of both tenses the termination *est* is added, and in the third person singular, present tense, the termination *eth,* or alternatively *s* (or *es* if the pronunciation requires it): *thou burnest, he burneth* (or *burns*), *thou burned'st.* We also say (from the auxiliary verbs *will, shall*) *wilt, shalt,* by syncope, for *will'st, shall'st,* and *hast, hath* (*ha'st, ha'th*) for *hav'st, hav'th* (and *had* for *hav'd*). In the auxiliary verbs *will, shall, may, can* the termination *eth* never occurs.
>
> Both terminations are left out in commands, and after the conjunctions *if, that, although, whether,* and sometimes after other conjunctions and adverbs, namely where Latin would have the imperative or subjunctive mood.
>
> The vowel *e* in the terminations *est, eth, ed* (and *en*, which I will talk about later, and in a number of other places) may be freely omitted by syncope, except perhaps where the resulting sound is harsh. The omission is indicated, when necessary, by an apostrophe: for example, *do'st* for *doest; do'th* for *doeth; did'st, didst,* for *diddest; plac'd* for *placed; burn'd, burnd* for *burned; know'n, known* for *knowen.*

Wilt, shalt are not syncopated forms, but derive directly from M.E. *wilt, schalt,* but, again, Wallis's treatment is admirably lucid, citing the alternatives in the 3pr.sg. of the verb: -(*e*)*th* versus -(*e*)*s*, which we have already seen emerging in the texts above (cf. Text 4, and 1.18); and expanding syncope, which again we have seen in the texts. Wallis and his fellow-writers thus usefully provide us with a concrete descriptive background to the items which emerge naturally in the early written and printed material.

5.7 'Occasional spellings' as evidence for early Mod.E. sounds

An older but still useful theory concerns spellings, found in English documents, which apparently testify to changes in pronunciation. The later M.E. and early Mod.E. periods were different from earlier periods in that they produced a wealth of private documentary matter. A considerable portion of the population was now able to write, and produced in abundance letters, domestic and business accounts, diaries and journals, memoirs and family histories, most of which were not intended for publication. The theory depends on the notion that the writers of these documents, not being professional scribes (indeed, frequently they were unlearned), constantly forgot established spelling conventions, and (as H.C. Wyld, one of the early proponents of the theory, says in his *Short History*) 'therefore drifted unconsciously into a spelling which expressed, more or less faithfully, [their] pronunciation' (p. 153). Wyld made out a strong case for such spellings as at least supportive evidence to what evidence we have from, say, rhymes, or the statements of grammarians. But it was R.E. Zachrisson who, by adducing a large body of such spellings of the fifteenth and sixteenth centuries, tried to show that the chronology of the early Mod.E. sound changes needed to be re-appraised – in particular that the origin of these sound changes ought to be put a lot earlier than was previously thought. Attempts have been made to discredit the 'occasional spelling' theory on various grounds – for example, that many spellings were taken from unreliable early editions of texts produced solely for historical purposes, and not concerned with linguistic niceties, and the spellings have turned out to be errors or misreadings; that handwriting always produces ambiguities, letters like *e* and *o*, *a* and *u*, e.g., having only slight differences in appearance; and that one has to decide how to interpret these spellings, even when they are unambiguous on the written page. Nevertheless, this type of evidence seems to confirm the early beginnings of the Great Vowel Shift and the other early Mod.E. sound changes.

What, then, do we make of spellings such as *gannes* 'guns' or *neturally* 'naturally'? Now, Wyld and his school would interpret these as follows: (1) since the sounds $/\wedge/$ and $/a/$ are phonetically similar, *a* in *gannes* shows an unstudied spelling representing the 'unrounding' of M.E. $/u/$ to $/\wedge/$, as in Pr.E. *guns*; (2) *e* in *neturally* represents the raising of M.E. *a* $/a/$ to $/æ/$, which it is thought to have become in early Mod.E. times. In such cases, however, Dobson, perhaps the chief opponent of the occasional spelling notion, is unquestionably correct: no native speaker could possibly confuse $/\wedge/$ and $/a/$ or $/a/$ and $/ɛ/$, since these are different phonemes –

i.e. the structure of the language depends upon their being kept separate in spelling and pronunciation, otherwise there would be no difference between, say, *bud* and *bad*, and between *bad* and *bed*. Spellings of this sort Dobson attributes to dialect speakers – in this instance to SE or London people (II, pp. 548–52 (notes), 588 (note 2), 593 (note 6)). Similar explanations attach to the many spellings like *prist* 'priest', *grivous* 'grievous', *tri* 'tree', where the *i* represents (sometimes dialectal) short /i/ rather than /i:/ as in the Pr.E. forms. But in any case, these spellings are often valuable, as they show dialect forms (e.g. *o* in *was*, *warren* (earlier /a/)), which often made their way into St.E. and became norms.

On the other hand, there are cases where the spellings obviously do mean something for St.E., not dialect – that is, they were written for people who spoke the St.E. of the day, and unconsciously show the way certain words were pronounced, e.g. *sord* 'sword' must indicate that the /w/ in this word (O.E. *sweord*) has disappeared, *hye* 'high' (O.E. *hēah*) that the final consonant represented by Pr.E. *gh* has disappeared. It becomes clear from such instances that 'occasional spellings' are more reliable in relation to consonants than to vowels.

I conclude this section with a phonemic transcription of the first seven lines of a speech from *Doctor Faustus* (Text 6, above, p. 117), to give an idea of early Modern English pronunciation:

1 waz ðis ðə fæ:s ðət la:ntʃt ə θəuzənd ʃipəz
   ənd burnt ðə tɔpləs təurəz əv ilium
   swi:t hɛlən mæ:k mi: imɔrtəl wið ə kis
   hɛr lips suks fɔrθ mi sɔul si: hwe:r it flɔiz
5 kum hɛlən kum giv mi: məi sɔul əgein
   hi:r wil əi dwɛl fər hɛvən bi in ði:z lips
   ənd aul iz drɔs ðət iz nɔt hɛlənə

5.8 Dialectal sources

5.8.1 *Spellings*

Here I include spellings found in historical documents such as wills, inventories, various local records, early place-name records, and the like, which have been used as evidence for the development of the M.E. *sounds* in one dialect or another. (This should not, of course, be taken to mean that sounds are the only important aspects of dialect, though traditional dialect studies have often considered them in this way. Perhaps I may use them here, anyway, as an illustration). I take two examples from the north of England, one from the south-east, and one from the south-west.

In 1933, the late Harold Orton, in a study of his native dialect of Byers Green (Durham), drew extensively upon early spellings. Especially full is his illustration of forms of words which contain northern M.E. *al* (para.

400), which in the early documents appears as *au* or *aw*, in fact the traditional development of the sound in this area. Examples are: *Alnwick* (Nb; modern pronunciation /anik/) is *Awnewik* 1496 (*wīc* (= 'village') by the river Alne), *Dalton-le-Dale* (Durham) is *Dawton* 1604, 1637 (first element possibly O.E. *dāl*, as in *dāl-mǣd* 'meadow-land held in common'). Outside place-names, it occurs in northern wills and inventories in *cawffs* 'calves' 1540 and *caufes* 1583, in *haufe, hauffe* 'half' 1583, *bawkes* 'balks, beams' (O.E. *balca*) 1582, *bauke* 1585–6, etc., and *waunet-tre* 'walnut-tree' (O.E. *walh-hnutu* + *trēo*) 1596.

Over 30 years later, Bertil Hedevind was still using this type of evidence in his study of Dent in the old West Riding of Yorkshire (now in North Yorkshire). He infers (p. 91) the 'lowering' of northern M.E. *i* /i/ to /ɛ/, from local sixteenth-century wills and documents from the Lonsdale (Lancs) deanery, and from Richmond-shire wills. Examples of the first are: *Necoles* 'Nicholas' 1530, *chelder* 'children' 1574, *well n.* 'will' 1575; and of the second: *shelyngs* 'shillings' 1543, *tember* 'timber' 1556, *sekelles* 'sickles' 1556, *thembles* 'thimbles' 1577.

H. Kökeritz illustrated another dialectal sound-change in his 1932 study of the Suffolk dialect (para. 370) from spellings of M.E. initial /hw/ words with *w*, showing that in the Suffolk dialect the /h/ element had disappeared: *weche* 'which' 1479, *weytte* 'wheat' *c.* 1530, and conversely *whyth* 'with' 1535, *whee* 'we' 1547, the latter two examples with 'unhistorical' *h* showing that the *h* could be added indiscriminately in spelling, and therefore meant nothing. These are known as 'inverted' spellings.

Finally, for the south-west (Cornwall, Devon, Soms and Dorset), in 1939 W. Matthews adduced a large body of early spellings – some more reliable than others – providing examples of such dialectal features as: the 'unrounding' of M.E. *o* to something like /a/ (p. 199; still in the south-west to-day): Cornwall – *aspetall* 'hospital' 1595, *haxads* 'hogsheads' 1595; Devon – *rachyttis* 'rochets' 1526, *argons* 'orgons' 1538; Soms – *varminge* 'forming' 1508, *Jhan* 'John' 1547, and many more; and the 'voicing' of /f/ to /v/ (p. 202), a common SW feature from at least M.E. times to the present day: Devon – *vel* 'fell' 1533, *vant* (with unrounding of /ɔ/) 'font' 1685; Soms – *vetch* 'fetch' 1468, *Vorde* 'Ford' 1511; Dorset – *verken* 'firkin' 1583.

More important than any of the examples above, however, are spellings which demonstrate the progress of the Great Vowel Shift as it took place in the dialects, where it had a course different from that which it took in St.E. To give but one example: in the spoken dialects north of the river Humber, M.E. *ọ̄* /o:/ did not > early Mod.E. /u:/ (e.g. M.E. *fode* > (via early Mod.E.) Pr.E. *food*), but moved forward in the mouth to something like /y:/ (as in Fr. *lune*) or /ø:/ (as in Fr. *peu*), and has since, in those dialects, become /iə/. The intermediate stage /y:/ or /ø:/

is recorded in a number of spellings which attempt to render this sound: A. Vikar, writing on the Durham dialects in 1922, cites (pp. 93–4) *oy/oi* spellings such as *Boyth* 'Booth' (personal name), *croykks* 'crooks', *spoyns* 'spoons' in Durham documents 1530–34, and *boyth* 'booth' 1536, *boites* 'boots' 1544. *Soyne* 'soon' (1516) and *toiles* 'tools' (1578) are found in documents from Kendal (Cumbria).

5.8.2 *The observations of writers*

These are numerous. Some write in general terms, like Richard Carew, who observes in his *Excellency of the English Tongue* (published in 1614) that:

> wee haue court, and wee haue countrye Englishe, wee
> haue Northern and Southerne, grosse and ordinary,
> which differ ech from other, not only in the
> terminacions, but alsoe in many wordes, termes, and
> phrases . . . .

and, of course, George Puttenham (1589) who, holding that the 'best' English is that of London and the Home Counties, inevitably accompanies the assertion by others on the language of the more distant shires of the north and south-west. More precise examples of the 'barbarous speech of your countrie people' are given by the Suffolk schoolmaster Edmund Coote in his *English School-Master* (1596); but perhaps the most important of such sources is Alexander Gil, who, in Chap. VI of his *Logonomia Anglica*, describes the dialect features of various areas of England. In addition to well-known ones such as initial /v/ for /f/ in the south, and southern *cham* 'I am', *chill* 'I will' (notorious stage features – see below), and lexical antiquities such as western *nem/nim* 'take', *vang* 'take, accept', and northern *sark* 'shirt', *gang* 'go', he also – more valuably – describes some of the current dialect sounds and one or two grammatical items. The first, although raising a number of problems, are of intense interest for our knowledge of the chronology of the Great Vowel Shift. Thus, in the north, he says, they use *ai* for *j* (i.e. M.E. $\bar{\imath}$) and *au* for *ou* (i.e. M.E. $\bar{u}$), suggesting that northern England had already reached approximately /ai/ and /au/ stages in the development of these two sounds, whereas further south they were still /əi/ and /əu/; northerners, he tells us, also use *ea* (/ɛə/) for *ë* (/e:/) as in *meat*, and also for *o* (/ɔ:/) as in *both*, while in his native county Lincolnshire they use *oa* (? /ɔə/) in words of a similar class: he cites *toes* and *hose*.

In the east, Gil notes, e.g., /i:/ in *fir* 'fire', the equivalent of *fjer* (which probably means /fəiər/ at this stage), which is a typical SE development deriving from O.E. $\bar{y}$ (O.E. *fyr*).

Grammatical features are northern *seln* 'self' and *hez* 'has'; and SW p.p. prefix *i-* (< O.E. *ge-*), as in *ifrör* (< O.E. *ge-froren*) 'frozen' and *idü* (< O.E. *ge-dōn*) 'done', which survives in Pr.E. SW dialect as [ə] – *a-frozen*, *a-done*. He also comments on the old pl. *-(e)n* endings of nouns, e.g. *hözn* 'hosen' and *pëzn* 'peasen'.

A few references to dialect pronunciations are given by John Wallis, e.g. the SE forms *keen*, *meece*, *leece* (5.6, above), and these are repeated later by Christopher Cooper, who also mentions vulgarisms and colloquial forms such as *bushop* 'bishop', *wuts* 'oats', *shet* 'shut', *yerth* 'earth', *git* 'get', and others.

5.8.3 Dialect in literature and on the stage

After the rise of a standard form of written English, although northern, south-western and other peripheral varieties began to disappear, the spoken dialects stayed very much alive, and from now on authors and playwrights used them – even if crudely at first – to add local colour to their works. The north and the south-west were particularly popular for this purpose.

Chaucer had already set a precedent in his profile of two northern students in *The Reeve's Tale*, giving them quite well delineated northern dialects. But it is in the post-medieval period, and on the stage, that we see artificial dialect used to its greatest effect, though we may assume that the playwrights merely sketched in certain dialect features and left their actors to elaborate.

Shakespeare gave northern features to only one of his characters – the Scottish Captain Jamy in *Henry V*, who appears on stage (Act III, Scene 2) with Welsh Fluellen and Irish Macmorris:

I say gud day, Captaine Fluellen.
....
It sall be vary gud, gud faith, gud Captens
bath,[1] and I sall quit you with gud leve, as I
may pick occasion:[2] that sall I, mary.[3]
....
By the Mes,[4] ere theise eyes of mine take
themselves to slomber, ayle[5] de[6] gud service, or
I'le ligge[7] i'th' grund for it; aye, or goe to
death: and I'le pay't as valorously as I may,
that sal I suerly do, that is the breff[8] and the
long: mary, I wad full faine[9] heard some question
tween you tway.[10]

[1]both [2]find occasion (i.e. cause) [3]'marry', i.e. by (St) Mary [4]Mass [5]I'll [6]do [7]lie [8]brief [9]gladly [10]two

Ben Jonson's play *The Sad Shepherd* (first printing 1641) is 'A Tale of Robin Hood', set in Sherwood Forest in north Nottinghamshire. Jonson made extensive use of artificial northern dialect – clearly of a stage variety, since the features found in it are, geographically speaking, *too* 'northern' to be accurate for the seventeenth century. Forms such as *twa* 'two', *claithed* 'clothed', *whame* 'whom' had retreated further north by Jonson's time, and likewise *gud* 'good', *tu* 'too', *du* 'do' (where $u = /y/$ or $/y:/$) occurred only north of the Humber even in late M.E. times. The phonological scenario is supported by a variety of grammatical and lexical items.

It was, however, unquestionably SW dialect that was the most notoriously popular of all stage dialects, especially as a vehicle for ridicule and fun at the expense of lowly and rustic characters. This is classically seen in Shakespeare's *King Lear* in the altercation between Oswald the Steward and Edgar masquerading as a 'peasant', but Shakespeare had many anonymous fellows in this respect, not least in comic dialogues and masques, such as the nameless author of *The King and Queenes Entertainement at Richmond* (1636), which includes 'some Clownes' speaking in the Wiltshire dialect. An earlier example is the crude representation of supposed Devonshire dialect in *Respublica*, a morality play of *c.* 1553, while with *Gammer Gurton's Needle* (*c.* 1560) we see dialogue of a general 'southern' or 'south-western' variety being used in a play proper. Typical SW stage features of the time are used by the character Hodge and the village gossips, the effect depending chiefly on the constant use of *ich* for 'I', one or two examples of initial $/v/$ for $/f/$ (*vilthy, vast, vathers*), quantities of oaths, copious references to drinking, and perhaps by the use of antiquated vocabulary. In his comedy *A Tale of a Tub* (1596/7) Jonson does much the same sort of thing, but adds one or two other SW features such as *'un* or *hun* 'him', and the old p.p. prefix *y-* in *yvound* 'found'.

Early examples of stage Cockney are hard to find. Kökeritz (*TYDS*, pp. 20–21) deals with the characters 'that plied their business in or round the Boar's Head in East Cheap', in particular Mrs Quickly and Doll Tearsheet, but the items he cites are mainly examples of slovenly speech (*Wheeson* 'Whitsun', *vilde* 'vile', etc.), malapropisms (*canaries* 'quandaries', etc.), and popular London features (perhaps *debity* 'deputy', *pulsidge* 'pulses'). However, Mrs Quickly's hypercorrect *alligant* 'elegant' and *allicoly* 'melancholy', together with her *exion* 'action', imply that $/a/$ appears as $/\varepsilon/$ in this dialect, as is still common today.

Turning to the early novel, we may briefly look at Thomas Deloney, who, in Chaps. IV and VIII of his novel *Thomas of Reading* (1623), composed some north-country speech for Hodgekins, a clothier from Halifax (and also for a north-country smith):

With that Hodgekins unmannerly interrupted the King, saying in broad Northerne speeche, Yea, gude faith, mai Liedge, the faule eule[1] of my saule, giff[2] any thing will keepe them whiat,[3] till the

karles[4] be hanged by the cragge.[5] What the dule[6] care they for
boaring their eyne,[7] sae long as they mae gae[8] groping up and
downe the Country like fause[9] lizar[10] lownes,[11] begging and
craking[12] ?

(p. 101)

[1]evil [2]if [3]quiet [4]'carls', i.e. wretches [5]neck [6]devil [7]eyes [8]may go [9]false
[10][obscure] [11]rogues [12]croaking

In Deloney's *Jacke of Newberie* (1626), we see the same stock SW
features as before put in use to characterize a humble couple from
Aylesbury in Buckinghamshire: *v* and *z* (*i-vaith*, *zoone*, etc.), *ich*, *che*,
cham, etc., and a sprinkling of malapropisms.

It is clear from the southern/south-western extracts that the ancient
dialect of King Alfred's Wessex had, by the sixteenth century, become
so unprestigious that it could serve as a vehicle for low comedy. By this
time the capital was discarding its 'southern' characteristics for those of
a different (predominantly Midland and SE) region, with the consequent
degradation of common southernisms.

5.8.4 *Dialect literature*

From the sixteenth century onwards, writers of various sorts – especially
those who had pretensions to learning – attempted to enshrine the
moribund relics of the English dialects in a variety of different forms,
usually of a comic nature – dialogues, poems and monologues being the
most prominent – both to preserve these fragments for posterity and to
cast a perhaps somewhat sentimental backward glance at the linguistic
ruins of time. Many of these authors had an interest in Old English and/or
the roots of the language and of languages in general, and realized that
elements of the dialects which survived into the sixteenth century looked
back to these roots as much as, or probably more than, St.E. – with its
influence from the written word – did. Such writings became even more
popular in the eighteenth and nineteenth centuries.

Literature of this sort seems to have developed earliest – perhaps
predictably – in the far north and south-west, areas remotest from London,
and we have works from Westmorland and Northumberland, from Lancs
and Yks; and, on the other hand, from Cornwall and Devon. There is
also an early (1611) song from Kent. But at this early period, these works
are very few. We will glance again, first, at George Meriton's famous
Yorkshire Dialogue (see 3.9.4, Text 3), and then at Wm. Strode's
Devonshire poem 'The Wonders of Plymouth' (*c.* 1620). The following
is the beginning of the *Dialogue* (Cawley's ed., p. 14. *D.* = 'Daughter',
M. = 'Mother'. Words of Scandinavian origin are italicized, as before).

1 *D.* Mother, our Croky's[1] Cawven[2] sine't[3] grew dark,
    And Ise *flaid*[4] to come nar,[5] she macks sike wark;[6]

M. Seaun, seaun,[7] *Barn*,[8] bring my *Skeel*[9] and *late*[10] my tee[11]
Mack hast, and hye[12] Thee ore[13] to'th *Laer*[14] to me:

5   Weese[15] git a *Battin*[16] and a *Burden* Reap,[17]
Though it be mirke,[18] weese *late*[19] it out by grape;[20]
Than wee'l toth[21] Field and give the Cow some Hay,
And see her Clean,[22] before we come away;
For *flaid*[23] she git some water before she Cleen,

10   And marr[24] her Milk, Ise greet[25] out *beath*[26] my Neen.[27]

[1]The name of the cow [2]calved [3]since it [4]I is frightened [5]near [6]makes such a commotion [7]'soon', i.e. quickly [8]child [9]pail [10]look for [11]cow-tie [12]hasten [13]over [14]barn [15]we shall [16]bundle of straw [17]hempen hay-band (literally '-rope') [18]dark [19]seek [20]groping [21]to the [22]expel the afterbirth [23]fear [24]spoil [25]cry [26]both [27]my eyes (literally 'mine een')

Sounds and spellings (reference is also made to Text 3 in 3.9.4, designated '3' + line reference)

Meriton invented an ingenious and effective method of spelling, designed to demonstrate, with some degree of consistency, the sounds of the north Yks dialect as they existed towards the end of the seventeenth century. The most important of these features to be seen in the extract above (and that in Chap. 3) are:

Lines:

1. *cawven*. Meriton's *aw* probably = /ɔ:/, as it is today in north Yks. Cf. 3.14 *yawds*.

3. *seaun*, cf. 3.11, 18 *deau* 'do', 20 *steauls* 'stools', also 3.7 *-crewke* 'crook', 8 *newke* 'nook', 17 *plewgh* 'plough', 18 *aneugh* 'enough'. In all these words the diphthong is derived from M.E. ǭ /o:/. In present-day north Yks dialect this sound has > /iə/ or /iu/, and so Meriton's *-eau-* and *-ew-/-ea-* show the intermediate stage in this development, a diphthong perhaps something like /iy/.

3. *tee* (M.E. *tēȝ*, O.E. *tē(a)h*) and 10. *neen* (M.E. *ēȝen*, O.E. *ēagan*) show development of M.E. ę̄ to /i:/ before /ç/ or /x/, as it is today in Yks dialect (cf. 3.9 *neet*, with the same development).

5. *reap* (northern M.E. *rape*, O.E. *rāp*) rhyming with *grape* (northern M.E. *grape*, O.E. *grāpian*); and 10 *beath* (northern M.E. *bathe*, O.N. *báðir*), cf. 3.6 *geay* 'go', 20 *tweay* 'two'. All these words contain northern M.E. *ā* < O.E. *ā* or O.N. *á*, which is /iə/ or /ia/ in Pr.E. north Yks dialect. The intermediate sound shown here by Meriton (he uses various other spellings, especially *a*) may be /æə/, /ɛə/ (cf. Gil, 5.9.2, above), and Meriton seems to regard both *ea* and *a* as suitable symbols for this sound.

Other northern features of pronunciation seen here are, briefly; line 2 – short vowel in *macks* (cf. 3.1 *tack* 'take', 17 *mack*) *k* in *sike* < O.E.

swylč, wark literally 'work', with typical northern *ar* (modern north Yks /aː/).

Meriton's interest in grammar is slight, but we may note: 1. *cawven*, with old p.p. *-en* ending (Pr.E. *calved*), and 4 *hye thee*, with the northern use of the personal pronoun as a sort of reflexive 'hurry yourself'. In vocabulary, there is a good sprinkling of O.N. loan-words.

The following is the beginning of Strode's *The Wonders of Plymouth* (ed. J. Simmons, *A Devon Anthology*, Macmillan, 1971, p. 139). There are six verses in all.

> Thou ne're wutt[1] riddle, neighbour Jan,
>   Where Ich a late ha been-a ?
> Why ich ha been at Plymoth, Man,
>   The leeke[2] was yet ne're zeen-a.
>
> Zutch streetes, zutch men, zutch hugeous zeas,
>   Zutch things with guns there tumbling,
> Thy zelfe leeke me thoudst blesse to see,
>   Zutch overmonstrous grumbling.[3]
>
> The towne orelaid with shindle[4] stone
>   Doth glissen like the skee-a:[5]
> Brave shopps stand ope, and all yeare long
>   I think a Faire there bee-a:
> A many gallant man there goth
>   In gold that zaw the King-a;
> The King zome zweare himzelfe was there,
>   A man or zome zutch thing-a.[6]
>
> Voole thou that hast noe water past,
>   But thicka[7] in the Moore-a,[8]
> To zee the zea would be agast,
>   It doth zoe rage and roar-a.

[1]wilt [2]like [3]? making of noise [4]shingle (a thin stone) [5]sky [6][obscure] [7]that [8][? a local reference]

We may dispose of the predictable conventional features at once—*ich* 'I', and the voicing of initial /s/ to /z/ and /f/ to/v/: the one matter of outstanding interest is the apparent retention of M.E. *ī* pronounced as /iː/ (*leeke* and *skee*; possibly (later in the poem) *vier* 'fire') instead of going on to a later stage of development. There are a number of further examples of this in other SW dialect texts. The only matter of grammatical interest is SW *thicka* (< M.E. *þilke*), Pr.E. SW dialect *thick(y)*. No dialect words appear.

Even the most cursory reading of the above two passages will demonstrate the obvious difference between Meriton's attempt to portray the north Yks dialect with accuracy and Strode's conventional treatment of Devonshire dialect, but both are of value in building a picture of the characteristics of the English dialects as they existed in the seventeenth century.

5.8.5 Dialect in dictionaries and glossaries

We can glean information about dialect usages both from early dictionaries and from the dialect glossaries. The earliest dictionaries may also unwittingly reveal the compilers' own language: this is the case, for example, with Peter Levins's *Manipulus Vocabulorum* (1570), the first English rhyming dictionary, who betrays his East Riding origin by recording forms like *gayt* 'goat' and *toyle* 'tool'. He thus provides useful information about northern pronunciations (and also vocabulary) in the late sixteenth century. But a hundred years later, the lexicographers – although they may not tell us the difference they assume between 'colloquial', 'vulgar', 'low', 'dialect' (or 'country') – actually start to include words which are obviously regional. Elisha Coles is usually credited with being the first dictionary-maker to include dialect words (1676), but the honour actually goes to Stephen Skinner, who practised medicine at Lincoln, and includes dialect words mainly from that area in his *Etymologicon Linguae Anglicanae* (1671), e.g. (I have translated Skinner's Lat. definitions): *beck* 'stream' (Lincs); *kirk* 'church' (northern England and Scotland); *nesh* 'delicate' (Worcestershire and neighbourhood); *vang* (west England, especially Soms, as in 'he vang'd for me at the vant' – 'he sponsored me at baptism' (Gil has the same phrase: see the reference at 5.8.2)).

Five years later, Elisha Coles's *English Dictionary* included 'a large addition of many words and phrases that belong to our English Dialects in the several Counties', e.g. *fraine* (Scots) 'to ask'; *loppe* ('old') 'spider' (or, rather, as in Lincolnshire, 'a flea'); *stut* (Soms) 'a gnat'; *weel* (Lancs) 'a whirlpool'. The next work of interest in this respect is the *Gazophylacium Anglicanum* ['English Treasury']: *Containing the Derivation of English Words, Proper and Common* (1689). The author was a fervent etymologizer, and was deeply indebted to Skinner both on this front and for his dialect words. We need only compare, e.g., his *Barken* 'a word very common in the County of Wilts: a Yard of an house', with Skinner's *Barken* 'vox in comitatu Wilts usitatissima: *Atrium*, a Yard of a House'.

For this period, we may finally mention 'J.K.', who, if he is the same as John Kersey, produced three works, his *New English Dictionary* in 1702, his revision of Edward Phillips' *New World of Words* (first published in 1658) in 1706, and his *Dictionarium Anglo-Britannicum* in 1708. In the first, all obsolete, 'barbarous' and dialect words are omitted, but in the second he states that he will be including 'many Country-

Words'. These were borrowed from various sources, including the dialect glossarist John Ray. Here is an example of his method:

> Gawn or Goan, a Country Word for a Gallon.

Or, more precisely,

> Kit-floor, a particular Bed or Lay in a Coal-Mine; as at Wednesbury in Stafford-shire.

Kersey's final work, its material taken directly from the Kersey-Phillips revision, uses a more elaborate system of designation:

> Karl-Cat, (in Lincolnshire) a Male or Boar-Cat.
> Mauther, (in Norfolk) a little Girl.
> Snag, a Knot, Knob, or Bunch: in Sussex, a Snail.

From these very few examples it will be clear that we can 'excavate' the regional vocabulary of the early Mod.E. period to some extent.

We now turn to look at the early glossarists. Among these we may number the antiquary Dean Laurence Nowell (c. 1514–76), whose *Vocabularium Saxonicum* includes 173 Lancs words plus 17 from other areas which had survived in dialect as relics of Anglo-Saxon, and, once again, George Meriton who to the second and third editions of his *Yorkshire Dialogue* added a glossary or *Clavis*. In 1685 he also wrote a *Nomenclatura Clericalis* or *Young Clerk's Vocabulary*, which contains many northern words which were also in the *Clavis*.

However, undoubtedly the most important dialect glossarist of this period was the naturalist John Ray (1627–1705), famous for his systems of classification and a member of the Royal Society, whose *Collection of English Words not Generally Used* (1674; considerably revised and augmented in 1691) was the first real English dialect dictionary. Ray added to his own material words from various other sources and contributors (including Skinner, and the noted scholar Ralph Thoresby), and divided his book into 'North Country Words' and 'South and East Country Words', within which there is sometimes a rough indication (usually by county) of the area where the words were to be found. Ray's collection was used, directly or indirectly, not only by Kersey, but by eighteenth-century lexicographers, and later by *OED*. It is thus a most significant landmark in both the early history of dialectology and the process of dictionary making more generally.

With Ray, we take leave of the early Mod.E. dialectal side of the language, and go on to something closely related to it – the spread of English overseas; 'closely related' because the earliest voyagers to the New World were, to some extent at least, dialect speakers, and it is their varied form of speech which formed the basis of present-day American English.

5.9 The origins of English in America

Settlement from England in America began with the early seventeenth-century voyages; and the term 'archaeology', as applied to the study of American English, signifies here the 'digging up' of its roots with a view to discovering its origins and subsequent early development. What materials are available, then, for reconstructing the English of the first settlers?

5.9.1 *Historical background*

Although North America had been 'discovered' from a very early period – notably by the Vikings in the tenth and eleventh centuries, and some 500 years later by Christopher Columbus – the first permanent settlement was made in the seventeenth century by a few hundred pilgrims, mainly (though not all) of Puritan persuasion. These sought liberty of belief and religious practice on the coasts of New England, and there established a colony at Plymouth, Massachusetts in 1620, from which independent settlements were established after 1627 by expansion into the surrounding areas (see map 14).

5.9.2 *Origin of the settlers*

The first hundred or so pilgrims, although they left from the SW coast of England, actually came in the main from the eastern shires (notably from Lincs, Nottinghamshire, Essex, Kent and London), although there were some from as far afield as Soms and Lancs. In this first group there were apparently none from north of the Humber or south-west of the Plym. Landing at Plymouth Rock in November 1620, after a hazardous and uncomfortable voyage, they were soon to be joined by other groups of refugees from the fatherland.

It was thus a very mixed group linguistically that was to lay the foundations of American English, speaking a variety of types of regional English. They were people with varying trades and skills – weavers, servants, carpenters, shoemakers, soldiers, merchants, salt-makers, tailors – and their ages in 1620 ranged from under three years old to 55. In the main, however, it may be assumed that the main linguistic thrust would have come from people from between 20 and 40, since the majority appear to have been born between 1580 and 1600. The speech trends of the young community would therefore range from those of a few well-established 50-year-olds, through the solid basis of 40- and 30-year-olds, through perhaps less conservative 20-year-olds, to under-20s who might be in the van of new trends in speech habits. They would mainly have learned to speak between, let us say, about 1585 and 1605. Naturally – besides age, education and social class – we have to take into account possible influence from a marriage partner and from the group as a whole, whose speech habits were not static and unchanging, and certainly not homogeneous. One thing is certain, however: the members of such a

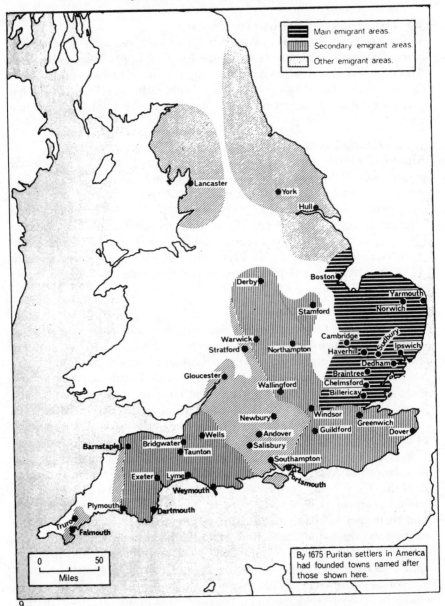

Main emigrant areas.
Secondary emigrant areas.
Other emigrant areas.

By 1675 Puritan settlers in America had founded towns named after those shown here.

14. The English origins of the Puritans 1620–75

mixed group would have listened to each other's voices with considerable interest, both in the claustrophobic conditions of the voyage and during the subsequent process of settlement. And doubtless, as today, there would have been a certain degree of ribaldry at the expense of any with gross dialectal traits.

5.9.3 *Pr.E. dialects and present-day American English*

From facts and assumptions such as those mentioned above, comparisons have been made on all levels – phonological, grammatical, and lexical – of English on both sides of the Atlantic. A few examples follow.

Phonological

One of the most fascinating questions here is that of American /r/. The British usually regard this as a uniformly reverted type of /r/ like the one heard, say, in SW England. This, however, is far from being the case, since, although in most of the USA /r/ is indeed pronounced in all positions in a word, New Englanders, for example, pronounce it only before vowels (*rat, tree, herring, far away*). What linguistic situation in the mother country could have brought this about?

In the English medieval period /r/ was actually pronounced in *every* position in a word (*rat, tree, herring, horse, chair*), but later it began to disappear in St.E. in the *horse, chair* category – though this process was not finally complete for a hundred years or so. In the south and west, and scattered areas of the north, it remains and is still strong today. These are called 'rhotic' areas.

Now, it is usually said that O.E. and M.E. /r/ was everywhere a trill made by the tip of the tongue on the teeth ridge (though I think it more likely to have been a 'reverted' variety in the south and west even at this early period). If this were so, it must have been reduced (except in the rhotic areas) in the post-medieval period to a sound more like that in Pr.E. *rat, herring*, and then, in St.E. and in most of the north and east, ultimately have disappeared altogether. The fact that /r/ is lost in the *horse, chair* class in New England suggests that when the first Puritans left England – most of them from the south and east of the country – English /r/ was in the process of disappearing, so that some (perhaps the earliest or more conservative) of the pilgrims used it, some (perhaps later, or more 'advanced' in speech habits) did not. In the new colony the 'have-nots' won over the 'haves'. This does not, of course, explain the /r/ still present in the more westerly areas of the USA, which were settled by people from different areas of Britain, among whom, in the Middle States, the Scots-Irish were prominent. Quaker adherents from the Midlands and west of England may have also played a role, reinforced by the speech of the Irish, who came to America in large numbers from 1840 onwards.

As a second example, we might instance /(j)u:/ in words of the *Tuesday, tune, blue, suit* class, where the presence or absence of a first element /j/ depends on the other sounds in the word (e.g. it is present in the first two examples, not in *blue*, and in *suit* depends on the speaker). This diphthong seems to have been a 'falling' one /íu/ at first, but there is early evidence (see Dobson, II.185) for its development into a rising diphthong /iú:/ (then /ju:/, except when /j/ is lost). The earlier type /íu/, though confined to the New England settlement area and clearly recessive, is still common in rural northern New England and in upstate New York, with the adjoining counties of Pennyslvania, and has considerable currency in western Massachusetts and Connecticut.

Grammar

This area of American speech has been explored by Professor W. Viereck (as well as by others), basing his work especially on the researches of the late Guy S. Lowman Jr., who carried out his own field-work in the south of England in the 1940s. Viereck's latest analysis of some of Lowman's material provides the following examples:

1. *He does* versus *he do*

The dialectal uninflected 3pr.sg. form *do* – as distinct from St.E. *does* – is typical of the south Midlands of England (especially its eastern parts). Such uninflected forms are, indeed, fairly familiar in these areas, being, according to *LAE* (Maps M34 and M35), especially characteristic of the south (excluding Kent and east Sussex), the west, and East Anglia. The American dialectologist, the late Raven McDavid Jnr., is quoted as saying, 'This feature [i.e. 3pr.sg. *do*] must have been brought to all of the American colonies', but it is unevenly distributed today because of cultural differences: *he do* is predictably retained more widely in the southern colonies, with their predominantly rural economy, much low-grade labour and inferior schooling, while in New England and the Middle Atlantic States *does* is almost universal (Viereck, pp. 252–3).

2. *I am* versus *I are, I be*

The *SED* distribution of these forms, largely confirming Lowman's, is shown on map 15. According to *EDD*, however, *be* was formerly much more widespread, occurring in the entire east up to Lincs and Notts, as well as in the south and south-west. The same is apparently true of 1pr.sg. *are*, which *EDD* gives not only for the Home Counties but also for Lincs and the former county of Rutland.

In the eastern USA, *be* occurs sporadically in New England as a characteristically older form – also in New York, New Jersey and Pennsylvania; *am* occurs everywhere in the eastern USA, where two instances of *are* are also on record. *Is* has considerable currency in southern New England, and is particularly common in eastern Virginia, while a scattering of informants in North and South Carolina also used it. 'Thus almost all the forms recorded in the mother-country (*am*, *are, be* and *is*) crossed the Atlantic; the only exception is *bin*' (Viereck, pp. 253–5).

3. *Going*

Lowman's findings appear on map 16, and are confirmed by both *EDD* and *SED* (though in the latter it occurs only in conventional material). The exotic-looking *gwine* (which is common in parts of SW England), seen on Lowman's map, exists in two separate areas: in New England, and between the Chesapeake Bay and eastern Georgia (with which we might include /w/-less *gine* on the east coast of Virginia, around the Albemarle Sound and the lower Neuse river, which is also recorded by *EDD* for parts of Scotland, and for Yks, where it was still current in the 1970s). In the remaining areas, *going*

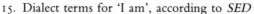

15. Dialect terms for 'I am', according to *SED*

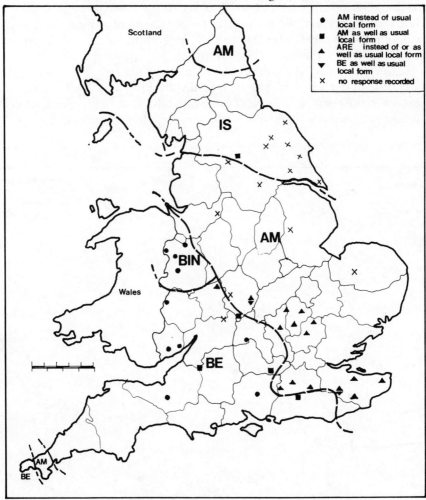

is current. In view of (*a-*)*gwine* as a rather widespread feature of southern British dialectal English, I agree with Viereck and McDavid that this form – so typically found in USA Black English – is unlikely to have originated in Africa as an early mixture of *go* and Akan language forms of *gwa*, *gwo*, *guaá* 'to flee' (Viereck, pp. 255–6).

Vocabulary
The relationship between British and American English on this front is illustrated and explained by maps 17–20 below, and their accompanying captions.

5.9.4 *Conclusion*
One of the most impressive features to emerge from this brief survey is that, although characteristics of the British-English mother tongue survive in the USA on all levels of speech, many of the more prominent dialect characteristics, especially gross dialect traits in pronunciation, have been smoothed out: there is no trace of SW English initial /f, s, θ, ʃ/ voiced to /v, z, ð, ʒ/, the use of /x/ or /f/ in 'gh' words like *bought* and *daughter*, or the northern dialectal /uː/ in *house* and *cow*. Neither is there any trace of the *-en* pl. in *housen*, recorded by *EDD* as general in England except in the north, and by *SED* from Essex and East Anglia and scattered localities in the southerly parts of the west. 'It appears that the weak

16. 'Going'

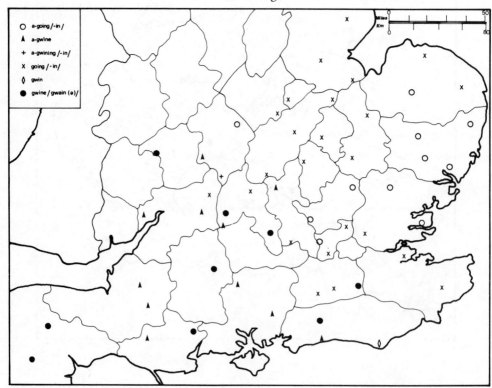

O   a-going /-in /
A   a-gwine
+   a-gwining /-in/
X   going /-in/
◊   gwin
●   gwine / gwain (ə)/

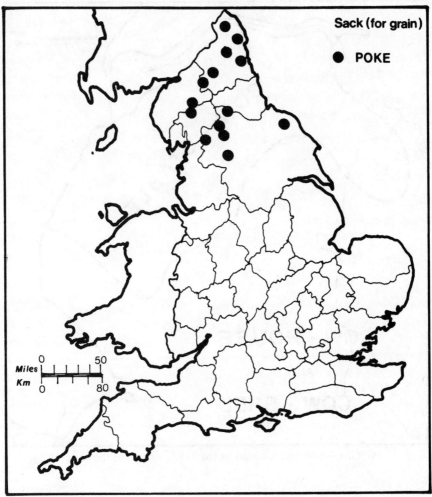

Sack (for grain)

● POKE

17. *Poke* 'Sack for grain': widely used in the USA as the name for a bag of various sorts and sizes.

declension plural form *housen* either did not cross the Atlantic at all or has since died out in the United States' (Viereck, p. 265; for Lowman's recording of *housen*, see Viereck, pp. 265, 293). Many dialect words have left no trace in the USA either, or are at least very rare and sporadic, suggesting perhaps a more extensive currency there in earlier times: *ground* = 'field' now recorded as 'very rare', *tunnel* 'funnel' 'not common' in New England, *shallots* and *young onions* 'spring onions' 'rarely recorded' in New England (see figs. 12, 13 and 24, respectively, in Orton and Wright, Part I, ed. Burghardt).

147

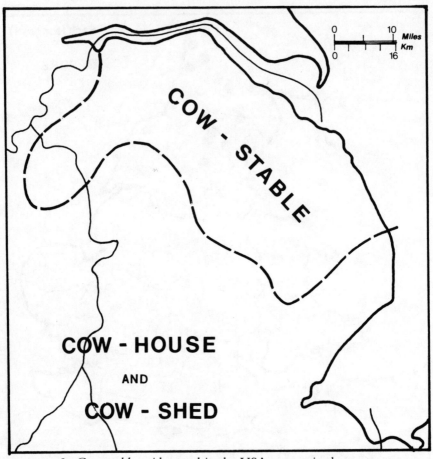

18. *Cow-stable*: widespread in the USA, except in the west

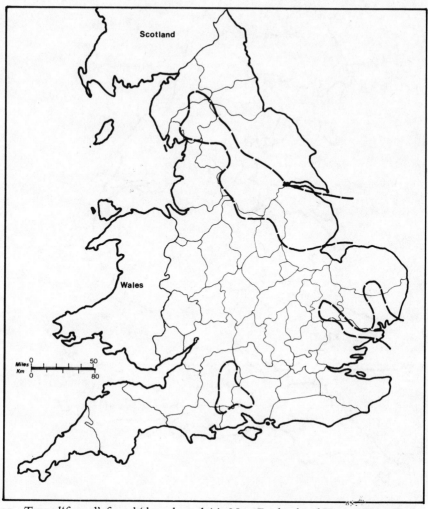

19. *Tunnel* 'funnel': found (though rarely) in New England and Upstate New York

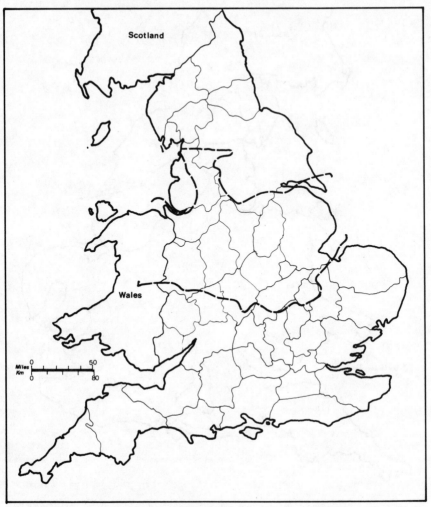

20. *Cade, cade-/cadie-lamb*: found in the USA from Narragansett Bay to Cape Cod

6 *Modern English*

(to the present day)

6.1 Introductory

We have surveyed evidence showing how the English language went through successive periods of change. It is tempting to see the age discussed in this chapter (*c.* 1700–*c.* 1950) as one of comparative stability: pronunciation has changed less quickly than it did in, say, the 300 years between 1200 and 1500, or indeed between 1500 and 1700; spelling and grammar have virtually settled down. There have, however, been copious additions to the vocabulary, especially in the fields of science and medicine, where neologisms have had to be coined (mainly out of Latin and Greek elements) to cope with new concepts and inventions in these fields. And French and other loans from overseas have continued to infiltrate – not least with the opening up of fresh western worlds by travellers and exiles. But the magnitude of such loaning has greatly decreased (especially from French – from, in fact, about 1500) notwithstanding, more recently, the impact of Hollywood and two world wars.

In fact, archaeology is properly the study of 'antiquities', and I do not feel that 1970 or 1980 can come into this category, even though what we call 'history' (of which archaeology is the handmaid) appears to move faster and closer to us than it once did. Having to find an arbitrary point at which to close this account, I have chosen *c.* 1950, on the ground that this gives us a period of about 250 years, which is comparable with the periods covered in earlier chapters; and that the mid-century and the end of the Second World War seem to signal something of a break with the past and to look forward to the sixties and beyond, heralding startlingly new fashions in every sphere, and certainly in methods of analysing language.

We start, as before, by looking at one or two passages. The first should be compared with the text by Sir Thomas Browne on p. 119, written in the same tradition of formal, elegant prose, though some 60 years earlier.

6.1.2 *Texts*

1. Alexander Pope, Preface to the *Iliad* (1721)

1   It is certain no literal Translation can be just to an
     excellent Original in a superior Language: but it is a

great Mistake to imagine (as many have done) that a rash
Paraphrase can make amends for this general Defect; which
5   is no less in danger to lose the Spirit of an Ancient, by
deviating into the modern Manners of Expression. If there
be sometimes a Darkness, there is often a Light in
Antiquity, which nothing better preserves than a Version
almost literal. I know no Liberties one ought to take, but
10   those which are necessary for transfusing the Spirit of
the Original, and supporting the Poetical Style of the
Translation: and I will venture to say, there have not
been more Men misled in former times by a servile dull
Adherence to the Letter, than have been deluded in ours by
15   a chimerical insolent Hope of raising and improving their
Author.

Spellings

We may note only the continued frequent use of capital letters (as in
Browne) and the settled state of final -e. No deductions are possible with
regard to sounds.

Grammar

Be is used as a subjunctive – If there be ... (6–7), now rare in Pr.E. (cf.
B. Foster, pp. 220–22). The one 3pr.sg. preserves (8) has an -s ending
(cf. Browne, serveth).

Vocabulary

Chimerical 'wild, fanciful' (15) is now virtually archaic. No other items.

2. Gilbert White, *The Natural History of Selborne in the County of
Southampton* (1789)
[Humphrey Milford, 1937, p. 132]

Letter IV

Selborne, Feb. 19, 1770

1   Your observation that the cuckoo does not deposit it's
egg indiscriminately in the nest of the first bird that
comes it's way, but probably looks out a nurse in some
degree congenerous, with whom to intrust it's 'young'
5   is perfectly new to me; and struck me so forcibly, that
I naturally fell into a train of thought that led me to
consider whether the fact was so, and what reason there was for it.

3. George Borrow, *The Bible in Spain* (1842)
[Cassell and Company Ltd., 1908, p. 279]

1   We descended from the eminence, and again lost sight of
the sea amidst ravines and dingles, amongst which patches

of pine were occasionally seen. Continuing to descend, we
at last came, not to the sea, but to the extremity of a
5   long narrow firth, where stood a village or hamlet; whilst
at a small distance, on the western side of the firth,
appeared one considerably larger, which was indeed almost
entitled to the appellation of town ... .
    Along a beach of dazzling white sand, we advanced
10 towards the cape, the bourne of our journey.

These extracts show English in its finally crystallised form, the only
exception being certain older spellings in White's book which act as a
contrast to Borrow's work some 50 years later, whose spelling is in total
conformity with that of Pr.E.

In the extract from White, only *it's* (possessive pronoun, 1, 3, 4) is
different from Pr.E. usage in that an apostrophe is still possible; White is
not entirely consistent over this, since *its* also occurs (in Shakespeare's
plays, first printed in the Folio of 1623, there are nine examples of *it's*,
and one of *its*, according to *OED*: there was clearly much fluctuation,
right up to the nineteenth century). Outside the passage there are a
number of spellings different from those of Pr.E.: *scissars, havock, sallad-
oil, phænomena, œconomy*, etc., and occasional grammatical forms also
different, e.g. p.t.sg. *sunk* and adjectival ending *-en* in *beechen woods*
(as in *wooden*, etc.).

In vocabulary, both writers use very occasionally a word which is now
archaic: White has *congenerous* 'of the same genus or family' (4),
apparently a seventeenth-century coinage first recorded in Browne (1646),
and lasting up to the first half of the nineteenth century. Borrow has the
now rather quaint-sounding *dingles* 'wooded hollow, dell, small valley'
(2), and *bourne* 'limit, goal', etc. (10).

6.2 Remarks on English, Standard and non-Standard

For the most persuasive of opinions on the state of English in general
during the eighteenth century, we have to turn first to the leisurely and
considered thoughts of literary men: Dryden, Defoe, Addison, Swift and
Johnson, to mention only the great names. In general, they have two
main interests: 1. to 'correct, improve and ascertain the English Tongue'
(to adapt Swift, writing in 1712); and 2. to found, if possible, an
'Academy' on already-existing Continental models in order to enforce
the proposed regulations. Defoe outlined plans for his proposed Society –
'wholly compos'd of Gentlemen' – just before the opening of the new
century (1697). Rather naively, he thought the existence of an Academy
might help to 'explode the practice' of swearing. He was closely followed
by Swift in his 'Proposal' of 1712, who was not so concerned with
imprecation as with jargon, poetic licence, phonetic spelling, and slang.

He looked back to the supposed 'Golden Age' of Elizabeth I as 'the Period wherein the English Tongue received most Improvement'. In this, of course, he was not the first: William Harrison had claimed as early as 1587 that English 'never came unto the type of perfection, until the time of Queen Elizabeth.' This linguistic utopia was, according to Swift, later corrupted by the racy language used at Court, which has 'ever since continued the worst School in England' for propriety and correctness in speech, and by poetic usage: poets are those responsible for 'manglings and abbreviation' such as *drudg'd, disturb'd, rebuk'd, fledg'd*, presumably owing to the exigencies of their verse. These and other reasons prompted him to argue in favour of some sort of an Academy. (In passing, it is fascinating to note that the 'abbreviations' he so much disliked abound on every page of Defoe.)

Addison (1711) did not like such abbreviations either (he instances *drown'd, walk'd*, and *arriv'd*; also *mayn't, shan't*), or another 'abbreviation', namely the 'substitution' of *s* for *eth* as in *draws, walks, arrives*, or shortened forms like *mob* (from the Latin *mobile vulgus*) and *incog*. A knowledge of the history of the English language was not one of the strong points of the early eighteenth-century literati.

Johnson's (1755) treatment – predictably – is the fullest and sanest. He first ponders how far he has succeeded in 'settling the orthography, displaying the analogy, regulating the structure, and ascertaining the significance of English words'. There is, as usual for the period, much rumination about the past, about eloquence, and about barbarity, but Johnson is at least systematic and lucid in his plans for the great Dictionary. He closes by discussing the causes of change in a language, and with the reluctant admission that 'sounds are too volatile and subtle for legal restraints; to enchain syllables and to lash the mind, are equally the undertakings of pride'. Nevertheless, he concludes that the endeavour to do so is worth something, even if complete success is denied him.

Finally at this point we should mention Noah Webster (1758–1843), known as the progenitor of the modified spelling system much of which has come down to American English. He had already published *A Grammatical Institute of the English Language* in 1783, endeavouring to reform the irrationalities of English spelling, and in the same year *An Elementary Spelling Book*. His *Compendious Dictionary of the English Language* included 5,000 American words not found in Johnson's *Dictionary*. It is the title of the Appendix to his *Dissertation on the English Language* (1789), namely 'An Essay on the Necessity, Advantages and Practicality of Reforming the Mode of Spelling, and of Rendering the Orthography of Words Consistent to the Pronunciation', however, which largely explains his dominant interests: as a spelling reformer, he wanted to make spelling conform to pronunciation by such measures as omitting silent letters (e.g. *k* in *knave, know, gh* in *might, though, g* in *reign*), regularizing the rest (e.g. using *f* instead of *ph* in, e.g., *physic*, *c* instead of *ch* in, e.g., *character*) and adding a few diacritics. Clearly Webster cannot be ignored in any estimate of late eighteenth-century English, especially in its American form.

I have given only a few of the most important samples from writers of this period, but from these it may at least be seen how obsessed with improving English the eighteenth century was. These and lesser works of a like nature are important evidence for our knowledge both of what eighteenth-century English was like and what the most articulate voices thought it *ought* to be like. At the turn of the century, the rise of Comparative Philology, with the consequent abandonment of strictures on what was 'correct' or 'incorrect', and the systematic study of language and languages, caused a much-needed revolution in attitudes towards English. We say good-bye to the old prescriptivism, though even the nineteenth century – and beyond – had to defend English from the fanciful notion that its structure was basically the same as that of Latin, a fiction on which Wallis had poured scorn some 200 years earlier.

6.3 Works on pronunciation and grammar

I have chosen a number of works to illustrate the many analyses of English pronunciation and grammar which appeared during the hundred years between *c.* 1700 and 1800 – what we may, rather crudely, perhaps, call the 'age of prescriptivism' (see, e.g., the views of Lowth, quoted below).

1. John Jones, *Practical Phonography* (1701)
[Ed. E. Ekwall, *Dr. John Jones' Practical Phonography (1701)*, Max Niemeyer (Halle), 1907]

The tedious sub-title of Jones's book is *The New Art of Rightly Spelling and Writing Words by the Sound thereof, and of Rightly Sounding and Reading Words by the Sight thereof, applied to the English Tongue.* Jones was a phonetician, and his aim was to teach beginners 'to sound all words rightly, neatly and fashionably.' The lengthy Chap. III comprises an 'Alphabetical Spelling Dialogue', and notwithstanding numerous defects such as frequent inconsistency, is the most valuable part for students of the history of English sounds. Jones starts from the spoken sounds, going from A to Z as they are represented throughout the alphabet, and sets out rules for their spelling, thus incidentally giving information on contemporary pronunciation. He does not give accurate descriptions of the various sounds, but he does distinguish between different sounds, so that we may often gather what *class* of sound he was thinking of. For example, he tells us that *metre* was pronounced with the same vowel as *see*;

glebe with the same vowel as *the*. Thus, although the exact sounds of the vowels may be uncertain, we do at least know that some sounds are identical. A single page (reproduced opposite from Ekwall's edition) will give an idea of Jones's method.

Jones asks: 'When is the sound associated with the letter *i* spelled *igh, io, is*, and so on?' It is a pity that he could not have devised some form of phonetic alphabet for the first column, since he has to make do with the ordinary alphabet, and thus, here, the letter *i* stands for both /i/ (*biscuit, build, circuit, conduit, guittern*) and /ai/ (the remainder). He is thus imprisoned by a system not intended to represent spoken sounds at all.

More positively, however, as in other places, he gives us valuable information about the various sounds: the item that stands out here is that words spelled *oi* or *oy* may be pronounced /ai/ – 'which some sound as with an *i*.'

Thus Jones takes us through the alphabet. His work was apparently not widely used, perhaps partly on account of its complicated format. But for language 'archaeologists' the book emerges as a meaningful piece of the jigsaw of this period.

2. Samuel Johnson, *Grammar of the English Tongue* (1755)

This essay of eleven and a half folio pages prefaces the *Dictionary*, dividing the treatment into the four conventional divisions of Latin and English grammars, namely Orthography, Etymology (by which, like other contempoary grammarians, he means 'Accidence'), Syntax, and Prosody (i.e. the rules of pronunciation and versification). Under the first heading, it is, again, necessary to attempt a disentanglement of spelling from pronunciation, and to try to cope with Johnson's use of non-phonetic terms to express phonetic concepts – a lack which was not properly remedied until the dawn of phonetic science proper in the twentieth century. Take, for example, the following (p. 31):

OF VOWELS
A has three sounds, the slender, open, and broad.[1]

A slender is found in most words, as, *face, mane*; and in words ending in *ation*, as, *creation, salvation, generation*.[2]

The *a* slender is the proper English *a* ... having a middle sound between the open *a* and the *e*. The French have a similar sound in the word *pais*, and in their *e* masculine.[3]

A open is the *a* of the Italian, or nearly resembles it; as, *father, rather, congratulate, fancy, glass*.[4]

A broad resembles the *a* of the German; as, *all, wall, call*.[5]

Many words pronounced with *a* broad were anciently written

An Alphabetical Spelling Dialogue.

Que*ftions.*		*An*∫*wers.* I.
When is the *Sound* of	*writ-ten*	
		cite, kite, quite, rite (or ceremony) ∫hite, ∫ite (or ∫ituation) ∫mite, ∫nite, trite, white.
i	*igh?*	In ∫even more, viz. — Denbigh, high, nigh, ∫igh, Tenbigh, thigh, tighy.
i	*io?*	See e — io, for they are the ∫ame.
i	*is?*	In four, — I∫land, I∫le, Vi∫count, Vi∫counteß, which are ∫ounded without the ∫.
i	*o?*	See e — o.
i	*oi?*	When it may be ∫ounded oi, or ooi, in the Beginning or middle of Words; as in boil, broil, coil, foil, foi∫t, froi∫e, groin, hoi∫e, join, loin, moil, oilet, poi∫e, poi∫on, ∫oil, ∫poil, tortois, which ∫ome ∫ound as with an i.
i	*oy?*	When it may be ∫ounded oy in the End of Words, or before a Vowel; as Chandois, decoy, &c. — loyal, royal, voyage; ∫ometimes abu∫ively ∫ounded as with an i.
i	*u?*	When it may be ∫ounded u as in Arthur, bu∫y, bu∫ineß, Gladu∫e, Julian, (a Woman's Name) manufacture, manu∫cript. See er — ur; er — ure; ery — ury.
i	*ui?*	In the∫e ten. { beguil | bi∫cuit | build | circuit | conduit | di∫gui∫e | guid | guil | guitttern | Verjuice. See ee — ui; gi — gui?
i	*uy?*	See gi — gui.
i	*y?*	In the End of all Engli∫h Words; as by, cry, dy, &c. none excepted, but tho∫e foreign Words, where i is written i, as above.
i	*y?*	When a Vowel is added to ∫uch as end in y, as crying, dying, &c. Except that generally i is written, when er or e∫t are added to y, as happy, happier, happie∫t; but 'twere more regular to write y always before a Vowel, as i is before a Con∫onant.
i	*y?*	In Bowyer, Lawyer, Sawyer, — loyal, royal, voyage. Always

with *au*, as, *fault*, *mault*; and we still say, *fault*, *vault*. This was probably the Saxon sound, for it is yet retained in the northern dialects, and in the rustick pronunciation; as, *maun* for *man*, *haund* for *hand*[6].

The short *a* approaches to the *a* open, as *grass*.[7]

The long *a*, if prolonged by *e* at the end of the word, is always slender, as *graze*, *fame*.[8]

A forms a diphthong only with *i* or *y*, and *u* or *w*. *Ai* or *ay*, as in *plain*, *wain*, *gay*, *clay*, has only the sound of the long and slender *a*, and differs not in the pronunciation from *plane*, *wane*.[9]

Au or *aw* has the sound of the German *a*, as, *raw*, *naughty*.[10]

1. These categories seem to refer to quality, 'short' and 'long' (further down) to quantity.
2. In all these words the vowel would be /e:/ at this time (on this, and all the following, see Barber, 1976, pp. 292ff.).
3. Presumably = /ɛ/.
4. This would appear to be a lengthened form /æ:/, /a:/ or /a:/ in *father*, *rather*, *glass*, but short /æ/ in *congratulate* and *fancy* (for lengthening before /f, s, θ/, see Dobson II.50, Wyld (1927), para. 219, (1936), pp. 203–4).
5. = /ɔ:/.
6. *au* (/ɔ:/) in these words is of Fr. origin! The dialectal, or 'rustick', pronunciation with *au* is obscure, unless west Midland /ɔ/ before a nasal is meant.
7. *Grass* at this time would have the same vowel as *glass* (note 4, above).
8. As note 2.
9. Ibid. M.E. *ā* and *ai* fell together in /e:/, Pr.E. /ei/.
10. = /ɔ:/ (but ?? 'German *a*').

The above notes show, I think, the considerable ingenuity needed to decipher Johnson's intentions and to translate these into comprehensible modern phonetic terms.

Johnson is on firmer ground with accidence ('etymology'), taking us concisely but thoroughly through the articles, nouns, verbs and the rest, illustrated by examples from those whom he would have doubtless thought of as the 'best writers' (Milton, Pope, *et al.*).
On nouns (p. 35):

The plural is formed by adding -*s*, as *table*, *tables*; *fly*, *flies*; *sister*, *sisters*; *wood*, *woods*; or *es* where *s* could not otherwise be sounded, as after *ch*, *s*, *sh*, *x*, *z*; after *c* sounded like *s*, and *g* like *j*; the mute *e* is vocal before *s*, as *lance*, *lances*; *outrage*, *outrages*.
The formation of the plural and genitive singular is the same.
A few words yet make the plural in *n*, as, *men*, *women*, *oxen*, *swine*, and more anciently *eyen* and *shoon*. This formation is that which generally prevails in the Teutonick dialects.[1]

Words that end in *f* commonly form their plural by *ves*, as, *loaf, loaves; calf, calves.*

Except a few, *muff, muffs; chief, chiefs.* So *hoof, roof, proof, relief, mischief, puff, cuff, dwarf, handkerchief, grief.*[2]

Irregular plurals are *teeth* from *tooth, lice* from *louse, mice* from *mouse, geese* from *goose, feet* from *foot,*[3] *dice* from *die, pence* from *penny,*[4] *brethren* from *brother, children* from *child.*

1. Johnson has confused his categories here: historically, only *oxen, eyen* and *shoon* have the old -(e)n 'weak' ending, and should be joined here by *children* and *brethren. Men* and *women* are 'mutation' plurals, like *goose, geese, mouse, mice,* the -n here being purely incidental.

2. Some of these now have pls. in -*ves.*

3. All these are 'mutation' pls., derived from a change of vowel in Old English (e.g. O.E. *tēþ,* sg. *tōþ; lȳs,* sg. *lūs*).

4. These two are correctly derived, but historically do not belong to this category.

3. Robert Lowth, *A Short Introduction to English Grammar* (1762, new ed. 1769)

A.C. Partridge's final judgement on Lowth (p. 191) – 'As the father of prescriptive grammar, he became the most influential advocate of the doctrine of correctness' – sounds damning to the twentieth century, which has long abandoned prescriptiveness, and is not too enthusiastic about 'correctness' either. According to Lowth, the 'plain way' of teaching us to 'express ourselves with propriety' is by laying down rules illustrated by examples. He writes in terms of 'right' and 'wrong'. Lowth's grammar was probably the most influential and widely-used textbook for the rudimentary instruction of English produced in the eighteenth century. It was the basis for numerous other grammars published between 1763 and 1840, and could claim a distinct authority which no other grammar had before Webster.

Lowth does not deal with pronunciation, but in his 'accidence' he seems to be somewhat indebted to Johnson. Take, e.g., his treatment of the pl. of nouns (pp. 23–4):

In English, the Substantive Singular is made Plural, for the most part, by adding to it *s;* or *es,* where it is necessary for the pronunciation: as, *king, kings; fox, foxes; leaf, leaves;* in which last, and many others, *f* is also changed into *v,* for the sake of an easier pronunciation, and more agreeable sound. Some few Plurals end in *en:* as, *oxen, chicken,*[1] *children, brethren;* and *men, women,* by changing the *a* of the Singular into *e.*★ This form we have retained from the Teutonic;[2] as likewise the introduction of the *e* in the former syllables of two of the last instances; *weomen*, (for so we pronounce it)[3] *brethren*, from *woman*, *brother*: something like which may be noted in some other forms of Plurals; as, *mouse*, *mice*; *louse*, *lice*; *tooth*, *teeth*; *foot*, *feet*; *goose*, *geese*.†

[Lowth's notes:]

★ And antiently, *eyen*, *shoen*, *housen*, *hosen*; so likewise antiently *sowen*, *cowen*, now always pronounced and written *swine*, *kine*.[4]

† These are directly from the Saxon: *mus*, *mys*; *lus*, *lys*; *toth*, *teth*; *fot*, *fet*; *gos*, *ges*.[5]

1. This is the old form of the pl. < O.E. *cicenu*, M.E. *chickene*, etc. See note 1 on p. 128, above.
2. Cf. Johnson, p. 158–9, above.
3. This is, of course, nonsense: *women* was pronounced in 1762, as now, 'wimmen'.
4. *Housen* is a genuine old form, still surviving in dialect. An enormous number of such 'weak' pls. were current earlier in dialect: *EDG*, para. 379, records about thirty different nouns with an -(*e*)*n* ending.
5. Lowth's knowledge of the history of English is superior to Johnson's. He refers here to the pl. 'mutated' forms in Old English; the mutation can be seen in *brethren* (O.E. *brōpor*, original pl. *brēper*), though not in *women* (O.E. *wīfman*, pl. *wīfmen*).

On the 'relation of Possession, or Belonging', Lowth says:

This case answers to the Genitive Case in Latin,[1] and may still be so called; tho' perhaps more properly the Possessive Case. Thus, '*God's* grace:' which may also be expressed by the Preposition; as, 'the grace *of God*.' It was formerly written *Godis* grace: we now very improperly always shorten it with an Apostrophe,[2] even tho' we are obliged to pronounce it fully; as, '*Thomas's* book:' that is, '*Thomasis* book,' not '*Thomas his* book,' as it is commonly supposed.★

[Lowth's note:]

★ '*Christ his* sake,' in our Liturgy, is a mistake, either of the Printers, or of the Compilers.[3]

1. The eighteenth-century grammarians were still addicted to the notion of Latin as The Model for English grammar.
2. This was an innovation of the late seventeenth century.
3. Not a mistake; the use of *his* in possessive constructions arose as early as the O.E. period, but was strengthened by the confusion of *his* with inflexional *-is* in late medieval English, e.g. *Godd-is*, *moder-is*, *chirch-is*, and continued up to the nineteenth century.

In spite of some historical inaccuracies, Lowth works steadily through the structure of English grammar, presenting a clear and uncluttered view. His authority was rightly respected.

6.4 Further excavation of English vocabulary: dictionaries and their adjuncts

One result of the eighteenth-century obsession with cataloguing, describing and 'improving' was the plethora of works on pronunciation and grammar which are now so useful to the language historian; hand in hand with that went the continued production of dictionaries – one might almost call the period the golden age of lexicography – which reached its zenith in the substantial work (1755) of Dr Johnson. His predecessors, however, were many: 'J.K.' (1702) has already been mentioned in the last chapter, but undoubtedly the most popular dictionary before Johnson's was Nathan Bailey's *Universal Etymological English Dictionary* (1721–7), which went into 29 further editions up to 1802. Despite the extremely ambitious and complex nature of Bailey's work, it was followed by others – the craze for dictionaries was evidently insatiable – including most prominently Benjamin Martin's *Lingua Britannica Reformata*, or *A New Universal English Dictionary* (1749), which was largely based on Bailey's two dictionaries and aimed, as had now become the custom, to include 'all the Words in Use'.

Johnson's aim – fully in accord with the dictates of the age – was to produce 'a dictionary by which the pronunciation of the language may be fixed and its attainment facilitated; by which its purity may be preserved, its use ascertained and its duration lengthened'. His illustrative quotations, taken only from 'writers of the first reputation' (mainly from Sir Philip Sidney and those of the Restoration) make it abundantly clear that Johnson's interest is in the *literary* language, though he sometimes condescends to dialect, e.g. in *tole* ('this seems to be some barbarous provincial word') 'to train; to draw by degrees', and *glaver* 'to flatter, to wheedle ... It is still retained in Scotland ... A low word'. Johnson includes, however, obsolete words when they are 'found in authors not obsolete' (e.g., one supposes, Spenser), or 'when they have any force or beauty that may deserve revival'. But of course such obsolete words, although obsolete in St.E., may have been – and often were – still current in regional dialect. A glance at the dialect collection made by Ray-Thoresby (see p. 140, above) shows us that many of Johnson's entries had already appeared there as localized, regionally restricted items.

The later eighteenth century – in spite of Johnson's achievement – saw an unabated flow of dictionaries, for example those of Kenrick (1773), Ash (1775), and Sheridan (1780, 1789). There was now also a marked interest in 'pronouncing dictionaries', aiming to promote good pronunciation and to rid barbarous speakers like those from Wales, Scotland and Ireland of their native dialect (e.g. Sheridan 1780, Walker 1791).

Little of importance in this sphere (Charles Richardson's four-volume work of 1835–7 is perhaps an exception) then appeared before the initiation of what was ultimately to be called the *Oxford English Dictionary* (*OED*) in 1857/8. This great work drew upon all the wisdom and experience of previous dictionary-makers – in comprehensiveness, illustrative quotations, historical principles – and magnificently improved upon them. In our own day it has become the only definitive authority on British English lexical usage, and arguably the world's greatest dictionary, containing between the covers of its 24 volumes (plus supplements in 1933 and 1972–86) the whole history of the English vocabulary from A.S. times to the present day. It is to this work that we have finally to turn in our attempts to 'dig up' the history of the English vocabulary, and even though its outline of a particular word's history will necessarily be skeletal, the entries nevertheless lead us on into deeper exploration of meanings and usage.

Those dictionaries, briefly reviewed here, which had reached the stage of claiming comprehensiveness, allow us in theory to make inferences about the body of work existent in English at any one time. In practice they are only rather rough guides, since even quoting extensively and/or branding words as unsuitable – on whatever grounds – for general use, or designating them 'colloquial', 'low', 'Country Word', etc. does not tell us enough about the social and regional status of an item, so that further exploration is still needed into its social, historical, literary and linguistic background.

We may illustrate this by citing, as something of an excursus, the *OED* treatment of the (now archaic and dialectal) word *kirk* 'church'. I have chosen *kirk* because its history – especially in the Renaissance and later periods – is a peculiarly interesting one, balanced as it was for some hundreds of years between the archaic/poetical and dialectal/'low'.

kirk

O.E. *cyriċe* (ultimately < Gk. *kuriakón* 'Lord's house') is a loan-word in Old Norse, viz. *kirkja*. It was either taken directly back into northern Middle English as *kirke*. etc., or the M.E. *c* /tʃ/ forms were influenced by the Norse forms with /k/ (cf. comparable doublets *chest/kist*, *churn/kern*, *flitch/flick*, *such/sike*). It remained in northern dialect (though over a somewhat reduced area – see map 8, p. 79) up to the 1950s. In Scotland it had long since come to be used of the Presbyterian Church as opposed to the Episcopal Church.

In order to give some idea of the richness of the material at our disposal, I reproduce the full *OED* opposite (though omitting the compounds which follow it (e.g. *kirk-ale*, *kirk-garth*).

Kirk (kɔɪk, *Sc.* kèrk), *sb.* Forms: 3 (*Orm.*) kirrke, 3–7 kirke, 4–6 kyrke, 4–7 kyrk, (4 kirc, 6 kerke, 6–9 kurk), 4– kirk. [Northern form of CHURCH: cf. OE. *circe*, and ON. *kirkja*, Da. *kirke*, Sw. *kyrka*.]

1. The Northern English and Scotch form of the word CHURCH, in all its senses.

a. In Northern English: formerly used as far south as Norfolk; and still extending in dialect use to north-east Lincolnshire: see E. D.D. Frequent in proper names all over its original area.

c **1200** ORMIN 3533 Hallȝhedd inn hiss kirrke. *c* **1330** R. BRUNNE *Chron.* (1810) 92 Clerkes of holy kirke. *a* **1340** HAMPOLE *Psalter* Prol., Þis boke..is mast oysed in halykyrke seruys. *c* **1400** *Melayne* 29 In kirkes and abbayes that there were. *c* **1450** *Mirour Saluacioun* 1422 After the trewe kyrkes vsage. *c* **1550** CHEKE *Matt.* xvi. 18 *note*, Yis word church..coⁱmeth of yᵉ greek κυριακόν..as ye north doth yet moor truli sound it, yᵉ kurk, and we moor corruptli and frenchlike, yᵉ church. **1579** SPENSER *Sheph. Cal.* July 97 To Kerke the narre, from God more farre, Has bene an oldsayd sawe. *a* **1656** USSHER *Power Princes* II. (1683) 234 That place which..all men did call a Kirk. **1674–91** RAY *N. C. Words* 41 *Kyrk*, Church, κυριακόν. **1785** HUTTON *Bran New Wark* (Westmld.) 14 Be serious and devout, net come to kirk with a moon belief. **1802** in Anderson *Cumbld. Ball.* 24 Helter skelter frae the kurk. **1828** *Craven Dial.* s.v., He's as poor as a kirk mouse. **1877** *Holderness Gloss., Kirk,* a church. Not much used. That at Owthorne on the coast is called the 'Sister Kirk'.

b. Used in literary Sc. till 17th c., and still retained in vernacular use in the general sense of 'church'.

1375 BARBOUR *Bruce* II. 71 Quhen he..In-till the kyrk Schyr Ihone haid slayn. *c* **1475** *Rauf Coilȝear* 574 The hie Mes was done, The King with mony cumly out of the Kirk is gane. **1567** *Gude & Godlie B.* (S. T. S.) 11 We trow the kirk Catholik be Ane Faithfull Christin cumpanie. **1643** *Petit. Ass. Kirk Scot.* in Clarendon *Hist. Reb.* VI. § 340 The Kirk of England (which We ought to tender as our own Bowels). **1648** in *Rec. Kirk of Scot.* (1838) I. 507 All the corruptions that have been formerly in the Kirks of God in these Lands [England and Scotland]. *a* **1649** DRUMM. OF HAWTH. *Poems* Wks. (1711) 49 The Scottish kirk the English chúrch do name; The English church the Scots a kirk do call. *a* **1653** BINNING *Serm.* (1743) 607 Unless their prayers do it, or their keeping the kirk. *a* **1704** T. BROWN *Cupid turn'd Tinker* Wks. 1730 I. 112 At play-house and kirk Where he slily did lurk. **1786** BURNS *Twa Dogs* 19 At kirk or market, mill or smiddie. **1894** 'IAN MACLAREN' *Bonnie Brier Bush, Lachlan Campbell* iii. 145 Away on the right the Parish Kirk peeped out from a clump of trees.

c. In official use, the name 'Kirk of Scotland' gave place to 'Church of Scotland' at the date of the Westminster Assembly: see quots. 1645, 1648. But (**d**) in subsequent English (as opposed to Scottish) usage, the term 'kirk' has often been opposed to 'church' to distinguish the Church of Scotland from the Church of England, or from the Episcopal Church in Scotland. So *Free Kirk* for the Free Church of Scotland.

c. **1560** (*title*) The Booke of the Universall Kirk of Scotland. **1637–50** Row *Hist. Kirk* (1842) 3 Instructed..in the exact knowledge of the Estate of this Kirk of Scotland. **1645** in *Rec. Kirk of Scot.* (1838) I. 431/1 Subscribed in name of the General Assembly of the Kirk of Scotland, by the Moderator of the Assembly. [**1648** *Ibid.* I. 506 (*title*) A Declaration and Exhortation of the General Assembly of the Church of Scotland, to their Brethren of England. **1691** (*title*) The principal Acts of the General Assembly of the Church of Scotland conveened at Edinburgh the 16th day of October, 1690.]

d. *a* **1674** CLARENDON *Hist. Reb.* XII. § 121 Nor did she [the queen] prefer the glory of the church of England before the sordidness of the kirk of Scotland. **1708** SWIFT *Sacram. Test* Wks. 1755 II. i. 135 To swear .. as they do now in Scotland, to be true to the kirk. **1791** HAMPSON *Mem. Wesley* II. 19 A member of the kirk. **1831** MACAULAY *Ess., Hampden* (1887) 219 This government..called a general

assembly of the Kirk. **1850** WHIPPLE *Ess. & Rev.* (ed. 3) I. 213 Examples which tell against kirk as well as against church. **1854** KINGSLEY *Let.* 22 Feb. in *Life* xii. (1879) I. 321 Erskine and others think [the lectures] will do much good, but will infuriate the Free Kirk.

2. Sometimes affected to render Du. *kerk*, LG. *kerke*, or Ger. *kirche*.

1673 RAY *Journ. Low C.* 25 Here [Delft] are two large Churches, the one called the old, the other the new Kirk. **1851** LONGF. *Gold Leg.* II. *Village Ch.* 69, I may to yon kirk go, To read upon yon sweet book.

3. Phr. (*Sc. colloq.*) *To make a kirk and a mill of:* to put to any use one pleases, to do what one will with. But Kelly gives what may have been the earlier meaning.

1721 KELLY *Sc. Prov.* 252 Make a Kirk and a Mill of it, that is, make your best of it: It does not answer to the English, 'Make a Hog or a Dog of it': For that means, bring it either to one use, or another. **1822** GALT *Entail* I. xviii. 147 The property is my own conquesting..and surely I may make a kirk and a mill o't an I like. **1837** MRS. ALEXANDER *Mona's Choice* II. vii. 173, I doubt but the man I let the land to is just making a kirk and a mill of it.

4. *attrib.* and *Comb.* (see also, in many cases, corresponding combinations of CHURCH): as *kirk act, bell, door, -goer, government, preacher, rent, steeple, stile, vassal, writer; kirk-greedy, kirklike* adjs.; **kirk-assembly,** Assembly of the Church of Scotland; **kirk-burial,** burial within a church; **kirk-fast,** a fast ordained by the Church; † **kirk-feuar** *Sc.* = *church-feuar* (CHURCH *sb.* 18); **kirk-gate,** the high-way or street leading to a church; **kirk-keeper** *Sc.,* a constant attendant at the kirk; † **kirk-lair** *Sc.,* 'a lair or burial place within a church, the right of burial within a church' (Jam. *Suppl.*); † **kirk-loom,** church machine or utensil; **kirk-shire** (see quot.); **kirk-skail,** **-skailing** *Sc.,* the dispersion of the congregation after divine service; **kirk-work** *Sc.* = CHURCHWORK a.; **kirk-wynd,** the lane leading to a church. Also KIRK-ALE, -GARTH, -YARD, etc.

1605 BIRNIE *Kirk-Buriall* xix, The *Kirk acts against *Kirk-buriall. **1752** CARTE *Hist. Eng.* III. 425 Going..to the *Kirk-assembly at Edenburgh. **1830** GALT *Lawrie T.* VI. ii. (1849) 257 To hear the far-off *kirk-bell ringing. **1814** SCOTT *Wav.* xxx, He would drive a nail for no man on the Sabbath or *kirk-fast. **1820** *Monast.* xvii, The son of a *kirk-feuar is not the stuff that lords and knights are made of. **1643** *Declar. Commons* (Reb. Ireland) 56 Desires for establishing Unity of Religion, and Uniformity of *Kirkgovernment. **1882** J. WALKER *Jaunt to Auld R'eekie*, etc. 42 He neir was godly nor *kirk-greedy. **1815** SCOTT *Guy M.* xi, A constant *kirk-keeper she is. **1606** BIRNIE *Kirk-Buriall* xix, Secluding all from the *Kirk-laire. *c* **1450** HOLLAND *Howlat* 82 The plesant Pacok...Constant and *kirklyk vnder his cler cape, Myterit, as the maner is. **1819** W. TENNANT *Papistry Storm'd* (1827) 201 The mickle pu pit;..was the Cardinal's ain *kirk-loom, He brocht it in a ship frae Rome. **1844** LINGARD *Anglo-Sax. Ch.* (1858) I. iv. 144 *note*, These districts allotted to priests were called priestshires, shrift-shires, or *kirkshires. **1843** BETHUNE *Sc. Fireside Stor.* 283 Hame again At *kirk-skail time she came. **1819** LOCKHART *Peter's Lett.* lxxiii. III. 265 When the service is over..(for which moment the Scotch have, in their language, an appropriate and picturesque term, the *kirk-skailing). **1826** J. WILSON *Noct. Ambr.* Wks. 1855 II. 312 The cock on a 'kirksteeple. **1552** LYNDESAY *Monarche* 4729 Thay bauld the Corps at the *kirk style. **1820** SCOTT *Monast.* iii, To hear ye even the Lady of Avenel to seeking quarters wi' a *kirk-vassal's widow! **1430** in *14th Rep. Hist. MSS. Comm.* App. III. 21 [A penalty of £20 Scots to be paid to the] *kirkwerk [of Glasgow]. **1467** [see CHURCH-WORK]. **1680** G. HICKES *Spirit of Popery* Pref. i, Citing out of the *Kirk-Writers their Papal, ..Schismatical and Rebellious Principles. **1888** BARRIE *When a Man's single* i, A kitchen in the *kirk-wynd of Thrums.

6.5 'Minority' English: the dialectal scene again

In this section, I shall follow more or less the same pattern as in the last chapter, except that it is unnecessary to consider local records since these have far less to tell us in the modern period (though there are exceptions).

6.5.1 *The early observations of writers; and later developments*

These are of various types: they include the random remarks of non-professional itinerant observers, such as Daniel Defoe (in 1724–7), the first to comment on the Northumbrian 'burr' or 'wharle', as he calls it – i.e. the /r/-sound produced at the back of the throat ('which they cannot utter without an hollow jarring in the throat'). On the other hand, they also include various statements of a more 'professional' type, e.g. those of Thomas Sheridan (1780) and John Walker (1791), mentioned above. In 1762, the former compiled a course of *Lectures on Elocution*, which (Chap. 2) tell us something of the 'vices' of 'rustic pronunciation': clearly we have not moved far from Coote's 'barbarous speech of your countrie people' and Daines's 'barbarous custome of the vulgars in their pronunciation'. He tells us:

> Nay, in the very metropolis two different modes of pronunciation prevail, by which the inhabitants of one part of the town are distinguished from those of the other. One is current in the city, and is called the Cockney; the other at the court-end and is called the polite pronunciation.

The fashion at Court, he is convinced, is bound to triumph:

> All other dialects are sure marks, either of a provincial, rustic, pedantic, or mechanic education; and therefore have some degree of disgrace annexed to them.

He goes on to instance various Anglo-Irish and Cockney 'defects'. But (more significantly) some rustic pronunciations, he tells us, apparently still prevailed among the country gentry and the educated in different counties, and it is interesting to compare Puttenham's remarks (p. oo, above) on this very subject, made about 170 years earlier.

Some twenty years later (1780) – anxious to promote 'good' pronunciation – Sheridan in his *Dictionary* pompously provided some 'Rules to be observed by the Natives of Ireland in order to attain a just pronunciation of English', and also included useful hints for the Scots and Welsh to enable them to 'get rid of their provincial dialect', and a concluding paragraph on the voicing of initial /f/ and /s/ in Soms. To similar points of guidance, Walker adds four 'faults of the Londoners' (i.e. Cockneys).

It is unnecessary to trace in detail the systematic study of English dialect from its beginnings, through the founding of the English Dialect Society (1873), the compilation of the *English Dialect Dictionary* and the

English Dialect Grammar (1898–1905) by Joseph Wright, and A.J. Ellis's monumental *On Early English Pronunciation* (*EEP*, 1889), to its culmination, this century, in the Survey of English Dialects; such basic works, and the various writings on individual dialects produced during more or less the same period, are the essential guides to the non-Standard English of the last hundred years. Basing their method firmly on historical principles, as well as describing the nineteenth- and twentieth-century dialect sounds as they then were, they painstakingly traced the M.E. sounds down to their end results, being concerned only with 'genuine' (i.e. traditional, historical) pronunciations, and regarding 'non-genuine' forms as intrusions from other dialects, especially from St.E. However 'old-fashioned' such treatments may appear to a modern generation of dialectologists, concerned mainly with urban sociological distinctions in speech, they constitute an essential background from which all modern dialect studies inevitably descend.

6.5.2 *Literary dialect and dialect on the stage*
We traced the earliest beginnings of this phenomenon and that of dialect literature in the last chapter. In the age being considered here, both blossom in profusion. There is not space to list all the writers who used dialect in their works, but a selection of the most distinguished would include (as well as those treated in more detail below): John Clare (1793–1864; Northants), Elizabeth Gaskell (1810–65; Lancs), Charles Dickens (1812–70; Yks, Lancs, East Anglia), Emily Brontë (1818–48; North Yks), George Eliot (1819–80; Warwickshire), Thomas Hardy (1840–1928; 'Wessex'), Rudyard Kipling (1865–1936; Cockney in *Barrack-Room Ballads*), Arnold Bennett (1867–1931; the Potteries), and more recently the northern/north Midland writers Phyllis Bentley and J.B. Priestley.

Here, as before, I will consider 'literary dialect' and 'dialect literature' separately, and commence, again, with the stage.

In the field of popular theatre the 'masque' tradition, as seen in *The King and Queenes Entertainement at Richmond* (1636), is continued in pieces such as *The Obliging Husband and Imperious Wife or, The West Country Clothier* (1717), in which the dialect element is provided by 'Honest Humphrey', the clothier's 'man', whose speeches are couched in a Devonian dialect. Here, Honest Humphrey expresses his opinion of women and marriage (pp. 12–13):

1 Why then, Meister, you mun[1] know that my Meister Hawkins
   was zike[2] another young Man then, as you be now; he had
   good Means to live on, and wanted vor nought; but as it
   shou'd zeem, he was troubled with a rumbling in his Codpice,
5 as me hap[3] you may be, Meister, and he'd'n have a Wife; not
   only to lay the Surrection,[4] che think they call it, o' the

bottom of his Belly, but to make'n a good Husband, that he
might'n prevent idle Expences, and get a good Vortune beside.

[1]must [2]such [3]mayhap (i.e. perhaps) [4]i.e. erection

The main features are conventional: voicing of initial /f, s, ʃ/, e.g. *vor*
(3), *vortune* (8), *zike* (2), *zeem* (4); *che* 'I' (6), plus some other well-
known SW dialect words and forms: *meister* 'master' (1; still widespread
/meːstər/ in Pr.E. dialects); *you be* (2); *nought* (3); 'n attached to *he'd*
(5), *make* (7), *might* (8), etc., is obscure, but was presumably a feature
of eighteenth-century Devon speech. *Surrection* 'erection' is a deliberate
malapropism. A few words seem to be of northern origin: *zike* (2), the
northern form of 'such' also occurs in line 2 of Meriton's *Dialogue* (p.
137, above; *himsen*, which occurs later, is also a northern and Midland
form). But such an admixture of northern forms in SW dialect is not by
any means unknown.

The second specimen is a much later one – but the period between the
early eighteenth century and the mid-nineteenth displays little enthusiasm
for stage dialect. Since it is by an author with a deep interest in language,
especially in its social context, it can reliably tell us something about early
Cockney – at least as presented for the stage. It is from one of Mr
Drinkwater's speeches in Bernard Shaw's *Captain Brassbound's Conversion* (1899):

1   Bless your awt,[1] y' cawnt be a pawrit[2] naradys.[3] Waw,[4]
the aw[5] seas is wuss pleest[6] nor Piccadilly Suckuss.[7]
If aw was to do orn[8] thet there Hetlentic Howcean the
things aw did as a bwoy in the Worterleoo Road, awd ev
5   maw[9] air cat[10] afore aw could turn maw ed. Pawrit be
blaowed! Awskink yr pawdin, gavner.

[1]heart [2]pirate [3]nowadays [4]Why! [5]high [6]policed [7]Circus [8]on [9]my [10]cut

Shaw, as compared with earlier playwrights, gives his sound-system
in some detail: *aw* = /ɔː/ (R.P. /aː/) in *awt* (1), *cawnt* (1), *awskink* (6),
pawdin (6), (R.P. /ai/ in *pawrit* (1, 5), *waw* (1), *aw* ('high', 'I', 2, 3), etc.
(i.e. the sounds equivalent to R.P. /aː/ and /ai/ have apparently coalesced
in this dialect), R.P. /əu/ in *Howcean* (3); but *y* or *i* = /ai/ (R.P. /ei/)
in *naradys* (1), etc.; *a* = /a/ (R.P. /ʌ/) in *cat* (5), *gavner* (6): *e* = /ɛ/
(R.P. /a/) in *ev* (4), *thet* (3), etc.; *aow* = /æu/ (R.P. /əu/) in *blaowed* (6).
Shaw thus gives Cockney equivalents for over six vowels and diphthongs
even in this short extract, to which we may add items like *bwoy* (4; with
/w/ after /b/), *awskink* (6; with 'excrescent' /k/), and *naradys* (1; with /r/
instead of /w/); and also dialectal *nor* 'than' (2).

Turning to other forms of literary dialect, here are examples from four
authors – out of a very great many. First:

1. Robert Burns (1759–96), 'Tam o' Shanter' (1790)

1   But to our tale, Ae[1] market night,
     Tam had got planted[2] unco[3] right,
     Fast by an ingle,[4] bleezing[5] finely,
     Wi' reaming[6] swats,[7] that drank divinely;
5   And at his elbow, Souter Johnny,
     His ancient, trusty, drouthie[8] crony;
     Tam lo'ed him like a very brither;[9]
     They had been fou[10] for weeks thegither.
     The night drave on wi' sangs and clatter,
10   And aye the ale was growing better.

[1]one [2](i.e. firmly in their seats) [3]just ('right'; *unco* short for *uncommonly*) [4](a fireside nook) [5]blazing [6]creamy [7]new ale [8]thirsty [9]brother [10]drunk

The chief interest here is the vocabulary – *unco* (2), *reaming* (4), *drouthie* (6), and so on, but Burns tries to give some idea of the sounds of the dialect, e.g. /i/ in *brither* (7), *sangs* (9; with typical northern /a/ before /ŋ/), and, more importantly, *a* in *drave* (9), showing the continuation of the retention of O.E. $\bar{a}$ (O.E. *drāf*) to M.E. *a*, ultimately to > /e:/, as doubtless here (elsewhere in the poem there are *stane* 'stone', *hale* 'whole', etc.); *bleeze* is a Scots and northern form of 'blaze'.

2. Alfred, Lord Tennyson (1809–92), 'The Northern Cobbler' (1879–80)

Tennyson wrote a number of Lincs dialect poems apart from this one, beginning with 'Northern Farmer, Old Style' in 1864, and adding a further five up to his death in 1892. He spent all of the first 28 years of his life in the neighbourhood of Somersby, a small village in the south Lincs Wolds, and the dialect of the poems is presumably intended to be of that area in the early nineteenth century. The cobbler tells of his early drinking habits:

1   Meä an' thy sister was married, when wer it ? back–end o' June,
     Ten years sin', and wa 'greed as well as a fiddle i' tune:
     I could fettle and clump[1] owd booöts and shoes wi' the best
                             on 'em all,
     As fer as fro' Thursby thurn[2] hup to Harmsby and Hutterby Hall.
5   We was busy as beeäs i' the bloom an' as 'appy as 'art could think,
     An' then the babby wur burn, and then I taäkes to the drink.
     . . . .
     An' Sally she weshed foälks' cloäths to keep the wolf fro' the dour,
     Eh, but the moor she riled[3] me, she druv me to drink the moor,

Fur I fun',[4] when 'er back wur turned, wheer Sally's owd stockin'
wur 'id,
10 An' I grabbed the munny she maäde, and I weäred[5] it o' liquor, I did

[1]mend and sole [2]thorn [3]angered [4]found [5]spent

Tennyson ingeniously used the diaresis to express Lincs diphthongs
which had developed out of the M.E. sounds (cf. Barnes, below):
eä (= /iə/) in 'me' (1), 'bees' (5; both containing M.E. $\bar{e}$); *aä*
(= /ɛə/) in 'takes' (6), 'made' (10; M.E. $\bar{a}$; also in 'weared' (10),
with M.E. $\bar{e}$); *ooö* (apparently a very long form of /u:/ in 'boots'
(3; M.E. $\bar{o}$); *oä* (perhaps = /oə/) in 'folks' (7), 'clothes' (7; M.E. $\bar{o}$).
This is the most important of his usages as seen here, but he also
suggests one or two 'special' Lincs pronunciations: *sin*' (2), *thurn (4)*
and *burn* (6; /ur/ for R.P. /ɔ:/), *weshed* (7), *moor* (8), *fun*' (9).
These, plus a number of shortened forms, incorrect use of *h*, and so
on, are intended, collectively, to give the impression of rural northern
speech. *Thy* (1) has continued in dialect use to the present day.

3. William Barnes (1801–86), 'The Pillar'd Geate'
[from *Poems of Rural Life in the Dorset Dialect*, 1879]

Our next example is from another poet who, as befits a philologist,
went to some pains to convey the sounds of his local dialect though,
like Tennyson and Hardy, he experienced some doubts as to how
far he could go in presenting it in detail. He tried varied spellings
in his dialect poetry at first, but a second, simplified, system came
into full use in *Hwomely Rhymes* (1859). He was a prolific author
from the age of 19, and wrote two grammars of the Dorset dialect
(1863, 1886), besides contributing information to Ellis's *EEP* (1889).

1   As I come by, zome years agoo,
     A-burnt below a sky o' blue,
     'Ithin the pillar'd geäte there zung
     A vaïce a-sounden sweet an' young,
5   That meäde me veel awile to zwim
     In weäves of jaÿ to hear its hymn;
     Vor all the Zinger, angel-bright,
     Wer then a-hidden vrom my zight,
     An' I wer then too low
10   To seek a meäte to match my steäte
     'Ithin the lofty-pillar'd geäte,
     Wi' stwonen balls upon the walls:
        On, no ! my heart, no, no.

Most of the features relate to sounds: voicing of /f/ and /s/ (*veel* (5),
vrom (8), *zome* (1), *zinger* (7), etc.); *eä* (? = /iɛ/: *geäte* (3), *meäde* (5),

steäte (10), etc.): *aï* and *aÿ* (? = /ai/: *vaïce* (4), *jaÿ* (6) – these also showing unrounding of the first element in /ɔi/); *oo* (= /u:/: *agoo* (1)); loss of /w/ in '*ithin* 'within' (3), but /w/-glide in *stwonen* 'stone' (adj., 12). Some grammatical features also appear: *a-* + p.p. and pr.p. – *a-burnt* (2), *a-hidden* (8);
a-sounden (4). No specifically dialect vocabulary appears here out of Barnes's stock of some 500 words.

3. D.H. Lawrence (1885–1930), *Lady Chatterley's Lover* (1928)

I close with a more recent passage of dialect writing. D.H. Lawrence's novel centres around a love-affair between Lady Constance Chatterley and her husband's gamekeeper Mellors who, although having been a lieutenant in the Indian Army, still speaks, as Constance says, 'broad Derbyshire' when it suits him. The passages in dialect and about dialect are especially interesting in that they reflect the 'bi-dialectalism' still often characteristic of dialect speakers in this century. This episode occurs early on in the relationship between Constance and Mellors.

Mellors takes the key of his hut from his pocket:

1   'Appen[1] yer'd better 'ave this key, an' Ah[2] mun[3]
       fend[4] for t'bods[5] some other road.'[6]
       She looked at him.
       'What do you mean ?' she asked.
5   'I mean as 'appen Ah can find anuther pleece[7] as'll
       du for rearin' th' pheasants. If yer want to be 'ere,
       you'll no[8] want me messin' abaht a' th' time.'[9]
       She looked at him, getting his meaning through
       the fog of the dialect.
10   'Why don't you speak ordinary English ?' she said coldly.
       'Me ! Ah thowt[10] it *wor*[11] ordinary.'

[1]happen (= 'perhaps') [2]I [3]must [4]make provision [5]the birds [6]may [7]place [8]not [9]all the time [10]thought [11]were (i.e. was)

Lawrence makes a clear attempt to convey the effect of the Derbyshire dialect in its sounds, grammar and vocabulary. Examples are: phonological – reduced form of *the* (to *t'* before *bods* (2) and to *th'* before *pheasants* (6), *time* (7)); /ɔ/ for R.P. /ə:/ in *bods* (2); *u* in *anuther* (5) = /u/; *ee* in *pleece* (5) probably = /ɛ:/ or /e:/; in *du* 'do' (6) *u* probably means something like /ʏ:/ (i.e. a fronted form of /u:/); *ah* in *abaht* (7) = /a:/ (also in *Ah* 'I' (1), perhaps short /a/ or /a/; loss of /l/ in *a'* 'all' (7)); in *thowt* 'thought' (11) *ow* probably = /au/. Grammatical – *wor* 'was' (11; perhaps < O.N. *váru* 'were' pl.).

Lawrence, who was interested in language as an indicator of character and class, is using dialect here not only to place his gamekeeper in the regional context of Derbyshire, but also to draw attention to his social background and thus to differentiate him from Constance Chatterley, with her high-class brand of Standard English characteristic of the 'well-to-do intelligentsia' to which she belonged. So, in addition to his specifically regional dialect, the gamekeeper has several class-indicators, features which are just generally non-Standard without being restricted to any particular area, e.g. *yer*, unstressed form of 'you'; loss of /h/ in *'appen, 'ave, 'ere*; *will* shortened to *'il*; loss of final /d/ in *an'*; and /ŋ/ reduced to /n/ in *messin'*.

6.5.3 *Dialect literature*

Dialect literature is, as we have seen, written to show the features of a dialect, often for antiquarian or linguistic purposes or to promote the preservation of a dialect. Although the linguistic accuracy of such pieces is often dubious (many dialect writers, for example, write in an old-fashioned mode removed from that of their own generation), these popular works can often extend our knowledge of dialect vocabulary as it existed in, say, 1750 or 1870, so we shall look at a few samples.

1. Anon [? Revd. Joshua Hole], 'Exmoor Courtship. Or, a Suitoring Discourse, in the Devonshire Dialect and Mode, near the Forest of Exmoor', *The Gentleman's Magazine*, 16 (1746), pp. 297–300

This humorous short dialogue was first printed as cited above, together with a second, the 'Exmoor Scolding'. Both clearly proved popular, since numerous editions were printed up to 1839. The dialogue, couched in somewhat argumentative tones, is spoken between a young farmer, Andrew Moorman, and his sweetheart, Margery Vagwell, and is intended to be that of rural north Devon.

> [He takes hold of her, and paddles in her neck and bosom.]
> 1   *M.* Come, be quiet – be quiet – ees[1] zay. A-grabbing o' wone's
> tetties ! Eees won't ha' ma tetties a-grabbed zo; ner[2] ees
> won't be zo mullad[3] and soulad.[4] Stand azide; come, gi' o'er.
> *A.* Lock, lock[5] ! How skittish we be now ! Yow weren't zo
> 5   skittish wey[6] Kester Hosegood up to[7] Daraty Vuzz's up-zetting[8]
> – no, no, yow weren't zo skittish than, ner zo squeamesh
> nether. *He* murt[9] mully and soully tell ha wos weary.
> *M.* Ees believe the vary dowl's[10] in voke vor leeing.[11]
> *A.* How ! zure and zure, you won't deny et, wull ye, whan oll
> 10   the voaken[12] took noteze o' et ?
> *M.* Why, cozen Andra, thes wos the whole sump[13] o' tha bezneze.[14]
> Chaw'r[15] in wey en to donce; and whan tha donce was out,
> tha crowd[16] cry'd 'Squeak, squeak, squeak, squeak' (as ha
> uzeth[17] to do, you know), and ha cort ma about tha neck, and
> 15   wouden't be, a zed,[18] bet[19] ha would kiss ma, in spite o' ma,

do what ees coud to hender en. Ees coud a borst tha crowd
in shivers,[20] and tha crowder[21] too, a foul slave[22] as ha
wos, and hes veddlestick to tha bargen.

A. Well, well, es ben't[23] angry, mun,[24] and zo let's kiss and
20   vriends.

[1]I [2]neither [3]moiled [4]soiled [5]look [6]with [7]at [8][obscure] [9]might [10]devil's
[11]lying [12]folks [13]core [14]business [15]I were [16]fiddle [17]as he is accustomed
[18]wouldn't rest, he said [19]unless, except [20]fragments [21]fiddler [22]wretch
[23]am not [24][familiar term of address]

Many of the spellings here, as in other dialect writings, actually
mean nothing in real phonetic terms (e.g. *wone's, yow, wos, woud*
and *coud, bargen*), but are meant to give an impression of broad
dialectal speech; but some others clearly do indicate north Devonshire
pronunciations. The most important examples are: conventional voicing of /f, s/ to /v, z/ is shown initially and sometimes medially (*passim*) –
also /ʃ/ appears as /z/ in *zure* (9), suggesting /ʒ/; 'I' appears in the
form *ees* (1, etc.; unless this is really a form of 'us', as has been
suggested), but as *ch* in the odd-looking form *chaw'r* 'ich were' (12);
/i/ is spelled *e* (*tetties* (2, 2), *tell* (7), *thes* (11), *hender* (16), etc.), another
familiar SW feature, and similarly /ɔ/ as *a* (*Daraty* (5) = 'Dorothy').
Individual forms of interest are: *murt* 'might' (7; *r* is customarily used
in this work to express the fricative consonant /x/ or /ç/); in *vary* (8),
/ɛ/ is lowered to /a/ – a not unusual SW feature, but *than* (6) and
whan (9) may derive directly from O.E. *þænne* and *whænne* (in both of
which O.E. æ > /ɛ/ in R.P. instead of /a/); *leeing* 'lying' (8) shows a
vowel sound /iː/, which occurs in other words of this class in SW
dialect (*sheen* 'shine', *leeke* 'like', etc., see p. 138–9, above); *dowl*
'devil' (8) is another common SW form (ultimately < Lat. *diabolus*);
wull (9) suggests /u/ or /ʌ/ from /i/ under the influence of both /w/
and /l/; *donce* (12), like *leeing*, is another controversial form typical
of early SW documents of this nature. Finally, *cort* 'caught' (14), unless
a meaningless spelling, may actually represent a pronunciation of the
word with /r/ inserted, as often in SW dialect. Also note the numerous
reduced and unstressed forms – *o', ha', ma, gi', (h)a* 'he', etc.

Grammatical features: *a-* + pr.p. (*a-grabbing* 1) and p.p. (*a-grabbed*
2); *be* pr.pl. (4) and *ben't* 1pr.sg. (19); 3pr.sg. of the verb in *-eth* (*uzeth*
14); pronouns *ye* (9), and *en* 'him' (12); *-n* pl. of the noun in *voaken*
(10).

2. 'A Norfolk Dialogue' (from *Erratics by a Sailor*, by the Revd.
Joshua Larwood (London, 1880, pp. 69–74)
[Reprinted in *Nine Specimens of English Dialects*, ed. W.W. Skeat
(EDS, 1896).]

Another comic dialogue, in the familiar style, this one takes place between two neighbours who discuss the iniquity and misfortunes of one Ursula, 'the knacker's mawther' (the collar-maker's daughter). Phonetic representation is almost entirely subjugated to the desire to include as many dialect words as possible. The following is typical:

1   *Rabbin.* She's a fate mawther,[1] but ollas in dibles[2]
    wi' the knacker[3] and thakster;[4] she is ollas a-ating
    o' thapes[5] and dodmans.[6] The fogger[7] sa she ha the
    black sap:[8] but the grosher[9] sa she have an ill dent.[10]

5   *Tibby.* Why ah ! tother da[11] she fared stounded;[12] she
    pluck'd the pur[13] from the back-stock,[14] and copped[15]
    it agin the balk[16] of the douw-pollar,[17] and barnt it;
    and then she hulled[18] at the thackster, and hart[19] his
    weeson[20] and huckle-bone.[21] There was nothing but

10 kadders[22] in the douw-pollar, and no douws; and so,
    arter she had barnt the balk, and the door-stall,[23] and
    the plancher,[24] she run into the paryard,[25] thru the
    pytle,[26] and then swounded[27] behinn'd a sight[28] o'
    gotches[29] o' beergood.[30]

[1]clever girl [2]troubles [3]collar-maker [4]thatcher [5]gooseberries [6]snails [7]man at the chandler's shop [8]consumption [9]grocer [10]is out of her senses [11]day [12]appeared struck mad [13]poker [14]stove-back [15]flung [16]beam [17]pigeon-house [18]threw [19]hurt [20]throat [21]hip-bone [22]jackdaws [23]door-frame [24]floor [25]cow-yard [26]small field [27]fainted [28]great quantity [29]pitchers [30]yeast

Almost all the dialect flavour here is due to the vocabulary, but there are also one or two phonological and grammatical items: of the first, note *ollas* 'always' (1, 2), *a-ating* (2; with something like /ei/ or /e:/ in the stressed syllable), *sa* 'say' (3, 4) and *da* 'day' (5), *agin* (7), *ar* (= /ar/) in *barnt* 'burnt' (7), *hart* 'hurt' (8); *arter* 'after' (11), *behinn'd* (13), together with shortened forms like *o'* and *wi'*. Most of these are common in dialect (though the pronunciation of *sa* and *da* is doubtful). Grammatical: *a-* + pr.p. (*a-ating* 2, plus otiose *o'*), *she have* (4; and shortened form *ha* 3), *she run* p.t. (12).

3. Elizabeth Webber, 'Owd Scrawmer' (1934)

Elizabeth Webber was born near Bury, Lancs, and wrote verse from the age of 11. The poem printed here (the first two verses only) was awarded second prize by the Manchester Lyric Club for dialect verse in 1934, and is a good example of the body of dialect writings which became, from the nineteenth century onwards, such a dominant aspect of what has been called 'provincial self-consciousness in Lancashire'.

1   Yo' o'[1] know a mon co'ed[2] Owd Scrawmer,
     He wer' a practical joker, yo' know;
     Aw've yerd o' mony a prank ov his,
     But last ut[3] he's done caps[4] o'.
5   He yerd as they had at a farmheawse nearby
     Sum whoam's cured[5] bacon an' good,
     So he thowt ut he'd like sum to thry[6] for hissel,
     Aye, an' gerr[7] it for nowt if he cud.
     He geet[8] to th' farmheause an' knocked uppo th' door,
10   An' when th' missis coom[9] sed, 'Hello !
     Aw've yerd yo'n[10] sum very nice bacon just neaw,[11]
     An' nobry[12] con cure it like yo' con, aw know.'
     That pleased t'farmer's wife reet away an' hoo[13] said:
     'Come in, an' ceawer[14] deawn for a bit,
15   Aw'll fotch[15] t'bacon eaut an' cut what yo' like,
     Aw'm sure yo'll be suited[16] wi' it.'

[1]all [2]called [3]at (i.e. 'that') [4]beats [5]home-cured [6]try [7]get [8]got [9]come (i.e. 'came') [10]you have [11]now [12]nobody [13]she [14]sit [15]fetch (i.e. bring) [16]pleased

Phonological features (only the most important): west Midland *o* (= /ɔ/) before /n/ in *mon* (1), *mony* (3), *con* (12); northern and Midland *oo* (= /u/) in *coom* (10: not consistent; note also *sum* (11) and *come* (14); *eaw* and *eau* both express a Lancs diphthong equivalent to R.P. /au/ in *-heawse* (5) and *-heause* (9), *neaw* (11), *ceawer* (14), *deawn* (14), *eaut* (15); *aw* (= /ɔ:/) in *aw've* 'I've' (3), *aw'll* 'I'll' (15), *aw'm* 'I'm' (16). Individual items include: *yo'* (1, 2, etc., Lancs pronunciation of 'you'); *o'* 'all' (4) and *co'ed* 'called' (1) show typical loss of /l/, as does *owd* 'old' (1); *yerd* 'heard' (3) shows /j/ at the beginning, typical of western dialects, and likewise *whoam* (6) shows initial /w/; *thowt* 'thought' (7) is local pronunciation /θaut/; *th* in 'try' (7) represents the NW variety of /t/ before /r/; /r/ indicated in *gerr* (8), *nobry* (12) is a very common dialect substitution for /t/ and /d/; *geet* (9) is a Lancs form of 'got'; *reet* (13) has northern /i:/ instead of R.P. /ai/. There are also some common 'reductions' like *an'*, *th'* (and more typically northern *t'*), *wi'*.

Grammatical features: northern *hissel* (7): west Midland *yo'an* (11),

---

(*Overleaf*) A page from *Back o't Mooin Olmenac*, 1868. The comic dialect almanac is a unique Yorkshire (especially former West Riding) phenomenon, starting with Charles Rogers' *Bairnsla* [Barnsley] *Foak's Annual* in 1840. Although an 'amateur job', the spellings often represent old dialect sounds with some accuracy. Note, for example: *fooil, stoane, dahn, reight, onny, macks* in the first two paragraphs alone.

APRIL hez 30 Days.

7t.—Full mooin, 7h. 16m. morn.	22d.—New mooin, 8h. 19m. neet.
14t.—Last quarter, 10h. 34m. neet.	29t.—Furst quarter, 6h. 18m. after.

1	W	April fooil day, for them at's no more sense.
2	Th	Furst stoane laid ov Bradforth Mechanics' Institute, 1839.
3	F	Lenkashire an Yorkshire Railway Co.'s warehus at Huthers-
4	Sa	field Station burned dahn, 1867, an abaht £15,000 damage.
5	S	Paum Sunday.] W. E. Foster nominated M.P. for Bradforth '61.
6	M	There is a chap at Huthersfield at says he's reight dahn stall'd
7	Tu	ov tailyers, for when onny on em macks him onny trowsers
8	W	they all mak em nock-a-need.
9	Th	T''new covered market at Leeds wor oppened, 1857.
10	F	Gooid Friday.] Hay, it's gooid for t'shop lads, kos the'v halliday.
11	Sa	Iv Jack happens to be e love he's net a judge ov Jill's bewty.
12	S	Easter Sunday.] A poor Lenkashire man at hed gooan to
13	M	Thornton, near Bradforth, deed and wor burried as follas :
14	Tu	A coil cart for a hearse, t'chief mourner wor a chap set on't
15	W	coffin smokin, an e gooin he called at two public-hahces to
16	Th	get his guzzil ; one on em wor kept bit coffin macker, 1866.
17	F	A ox went intul a lawyer's office e Heckanwauk an started ov
18	Sa	walkin upstairs as clever as if it wor gooin to ax advice, bud
19	S	afore it gate tut top some chaps pooled it dahn bit tail, with-
20	M	aht givin him a chonce to state his case, 1867.
21	Tu	Theare's a woman at lives at Dawgreen at they say hez sich a
22	W	' wide mahth at they can cram a bairn intul it.
23	Th	Furst stoane ot new Catholic Church, Dewsbre, wor laid, 1867.
24	F	Theare wor a owd man at lived at Bradforth, at when he wor
25	Sa	asleep he used to snoar like a pig at wor brussen up wi fat.
26	S	One time he went off for a toathree days an left t'wife at
27	M	hooam, bud when sho gate to bed at neet sho cuddant sleep
28	Tu	for t'life on hur, kos t'owd chap worrant theare to lull hur
29	W	asleep wi his snoarin. Hur two dowters consulted together
30	Th	what wor to be done abaht it ; at last they bethowt em on a

plan at ad do ; they gate t'coffee miln an filled it wi coffee, an went tul hur bed side on started ov grindin away as hard as they could, and wi that they sooin gate t'owd lass asleep.

Year.	REMARKABLE EVENTS.

1691.—T'gurt bell e Halifax steeple wor cast, on which is t'follahin words :—
    All you that hear my mournful sound
    Repent before you lye in ground.

1739.—April. Dick Turpin, t'heeway robber, wor henged at York, an t'next mornin his body wor berried, bud at Tuesday mornin after abaht three o'clock, it wor tayed up bi "resurrection men" an hid in a garden, wheare it wor fun bi a mob an some ov his mourners, an they carried it thro't city e triumph, and put it in a coffin an covered it up wi wick lime so at it woddant be fit for't dissectin fowks, an then filled up t'grave.

with /n/ ending of the verb; *hoo* (13) is west Midland 'she', originating in O.E. *hēo*.

6.6 Nineteenth-century and subsequent developments

The nineteenth century takes us almost as far as we wish to go with 'archaeology', since the twentieth has developed a different sort of interest in language studies, namely the approach labelled by F. de Saussure (1857–1913) as 'synchronic': that is, the study of languages as communication systems at one particular point in time, as distinct from that of their historical progression ('diachronic' or historical linguistics, or, more broadly, 'philology') which was the prime interest of the nineteenth century.

The latter dominated nineteenth-century language research, gaining its first impetus in Germany, and paralleling 'the general intellectual and artistic movement of late-eighteenth to mid-nineteenth-century Germany known as Romanticism.' But the historical outlook was also related to contemporary thought, taking its inspiration especially from physics (whence the idea of describing the history of sound-change in a language in terms of universal 'laws', rather like, in physics, the practice of describing all phenomena in terms of laws of force and motion) and biology (whence the idea of languages as organic bodies formed in accordance with definite laws and bearing within themselves a principle of life which grows and develops). In the latter domain, Darwinism was an important influence: the 'family tree' theory of linguistic evolution was first formally expressed by August Schleicher in 1861, at almost the same time as the appearance of Darwin's *Origin of Species* (English edn. 1859, German translation 1860), while the suggestion that the discipline closest to the new science of 'comparative grammar' was comparative anatomy had been made as early as 1808 (by Friedrich von Schlegel) and 1819 (by Jacob Grimm, one of the founders of Germanic linguistics).

Towards the end of the nineteenth century, the historical approach to language studies looked as if it might be the frontier from which further advances would be made. However, this proved not to be the case, partly because the notion of linguistic change as having a *scientific* direction became less popular, and thus the Darwinian concept of 'natural selection' could not be applied to language: the idea of the 'simplest', most functional, etc. language surviving at the expense of complicated dinosaurs was seen not to work. Then there was the further doubt about the *causes* of change in language, which came increasingly to be seen as local (and therefore needing 'local' explanations, e.g. by non-linguistic factors such as geographical or climatological conditions) rather than universal.

Saussure's scholarship was mainly on traditional, historical lines, but he was the first to define the notion of 'synchronic linguistics' – in the posthumous volume of his lecture notes, the *Cours de Linguistique*

Générale (1916). This one work had a decided and lasting effect on the development of linguistics in the twentieth century, the fruits of which need to be pursued in the work of scholars like the American Edward Sapir (1884–1939) and Benjamin Lee Whorf (1897–1941), of the 'Prague School' in the first half of this century, of Noam Chomsky (1928–), and so on. However, their work need hardly concern those of us trying to uncover the historical foundations of the English language, preoccupied as these scholars are with the structure of language as an abstract entity rather than with the 'physical' nature of items like inscriptions, manuscripts, and books on grammar.

Henry Sweet (1845–1912) was the greatest of the few British historical linguists of the nineteenth century but, unlike his German contemporaries, he based his historical studies on a detailed understanding of the workings of the vocal organs: he was a phonetician as well as a philologist. His *Handbook of Phonetics* (1877) marked virtually the beginning of that discipline as a modern science, but he also wrote *A New English Grammar: Logical and Historical* (1891–8). A sentence in his Preface (p. x) – 'In this grammer I have taken pains to make the Old English formulation as sound as possible' – indicates the orientation of the work, but this by no means overshadows the element of pure description of nineteenth-century English in it, an account for which we may be grateful.

In historical grammars, Otto Jespersen's *Modern English Grammar on Historical Principles*, in seven volumes (1909–49), may be seen as the logical successor to Sweet's work. But most of the grammars produced this century (e.g. those listed in the bibliography to Quirk *et al.*, *Grammar of Contemporary English*, 1972) are unashamedly 'descriptive', and find their apotheosis in the last-mentioned magisterial work, whose field 'is no less than the grammar of educated English current in the second half of the twentieth century in the world's major English-speaking communities' (p. v). Meanwhile, American English has been most competently covered by scholars such as W.N. Francis (*The Structure of American English*, 1958), C.C. Fries (*American English Grammar*, 1940), and H.L. Mencken (*The American Language*, rev. ed., 1963).

The foregoing bibliographical summary is intended merely to tie up loose ends left over from my treatment of the sources for our knowledge of the history of English, in this and previous chapters. It is self-evidently selective rather than comprehensive.

References and Select Bibliography

Chapter 1 pp. 13–32
[Note: works dealing with specific topics covered at greater length later in the book are listed in the bibliography to the appropriate chapter, rather than here.]

1.1 *Linguistic change*
BARBER, C., *Linguistic Change in Present-day English*, Oliver and Boyd, 1964.
FOSTER, B., *The Changing English Language*, Penguin, 1970, p. 9.
STRANG, B.M.H., *A History of English*, 2nd rev. edn., Methuen, 1972. (See Part I.)
STURTEVANT, E.H., *Linguistic Change: an Introduction to the Historical Study of Language*, new edn., with an Introduction by E.P. Hamp, Chicago University Press, 1961.

1.2 *The Anglo-Saxon invasion and settlement*
Standard works:
BLAIR, P.H., *An Introduction to Anglo-Saxon England*, Cambridge University Press, 1956.
CAMPBELL, J. (ed.), *The Anglo-Saxons*, Phaidon, 1982.
HODGKIN, R.H., *A History of the Anglo-Saxons*, 2 vols., Clarendon Press, 1935.
JACKSON, K.H., *Language and History in Early Britain*, Edinburgh University Press, 1953. (See Chap. 6.)
MYRES, J.N.L., *The English Settlements*, Clarendon Press, 1986.
STENTON, F.M., *Anglo-Saxon England*, 3rd rev. edn., OUP, 1971.
Celtic survival:
JACKSON, K.H. (above), Chap. 6, and especially pp. 234ff.
WAKELIN, M.F., *English Dialects: an Introduction*, 2nd rev. edn., Athlone Press, 1977, pp. 15–16, and further references, p. 171.
On the history of the 'Celtic fringe' (Wales, north Scotland, etc.):
PRICE, G., *The Languages of Britain*, Edward Arnold, 1984.

1.3 *Primitive Germanic and Indo-European*
See the standard histories of English, of which this is a selection:
BARBER, C.L., *The Story of Language*, Pan Books, 1964.
BAUGH, A.C., and CABLE, T., *A History of the English Language*, 3rd rev. edn., Routledge, 1978.
JESPERSEN, O. (below).
WRENN, C.L., *The English Language*, Methuen, 1949, 1952.
WYLD, H.C., *A Short History of English*, 3rd rev. edn., John Murray, 1927. (Especially useful for the history of sound-change.)

WYLD, H.C., *A History of Modern Colloquial English*, 3rd rev. edn., Basil
  Blackwell, 1936.
STRANG, B.M.H. (above).
[Note: the standard histories of English may be consulted for almost all sections of this
and the following chapters, and will not be referred to further.]

1.7 *Borrowings from other languages*
The following are standard treatments:
BLISS, A.J., *A Dictionary of Foreign Words and Phrases*, Routledge and
  Kegan Paul, 1966.
JESPERSEN, O., *Growth and Structure of the English Language*, 9th edn., Basil
  Blackwell, 1972, Chaps. IV–VII.
SERJEANTSON, M.S., *A History of Foreign Words in English*, Kegan Paul,
  Trench, Trubner and Co. Ltd, 1935.
SHEARD, J.A., *The Words we Use*, Deutsch, 1954.
On Celtic and Latin loan-words, see more specifically:
JACKSON, K.H. (above).
WAKELIN, M.F. (above), pp. 126–30 (on Celtic element in dialect).
On Scandinavian settlements and loan-words, see 3.9ff., below.

1.9 *Who spoke and wrote what?*
WILSON, R.M., 'English and French in England 1100–1300', *History*, N.S., 28,
  1943, pp. 37–60.

Chapter 2 pp. 33–43
2.1 *The reconstruction of languages*
WYLD, H.C., *The Universal Dictionary of the English Language*, George
  Routledge and Sons Ltd, 1934 (Introduction). See also below.

2.2 *Who were the Indo-Europeans?*
CROSSLAND, R.A., 'Indo-European Origins: the Linguistic Evidence', *Past and
  Present*, 9, 1957, pp. 16–46. (Has detailed bibliographical notes.)
LOCKWOOD, W.B.L., *A Panorama of European Languages*, Hutchinson, 1972.
RENFREW, C., *Archaeology and Language: the Puzzle of Indo-European
  Origins*, Cape, 1987.
THIÈME, P., 'The Indo-European Language', *Scientific American*, 199, 1958,
  pp. 63–74.

2.3 *The Germanic languages*
PROKOSCH, E., *A Comparative Germanic Grammar*, Linguistic Society of
  America, University of Pennsylvania, 1939.
STREADBECK, A.L., A Short Introduction to Germanic Linguistics, Pruett
  Press, Boulder, Colorado, 1966.

2.3.1 *North Germanic*
For introduction and some early Norse inscriptions:
GORDON, E.V., *An Introduction to Old Norse*, 2nd edn., rev. A.R. TAYLOR,
  Clarendon Press, 1957, pp. 179–93.
HAUGEN, E., *The Scandinavian Languages: an Introduction to their History*,
  Faber and Faber, 1976.

2.3.2 *East Germanic*
See 2.5, below.

2.3.3 *West Germanic*
See bibliography for Chap. 3.

2.4 *Primitive Germanic inscriptions*
ELLIOTT, R.W.V., *Runes: an Introduction*, Manchester University Press, 1959.

2.5 *Gothic*
WRIGHT, J., *Grammar of the Gothic Language*, 2nd edn., with supplement, by O.L. SAYCE, Clarendon Press, 1954. (Contains the Gothic version of St Mark's Gospel, with full glossary.)

Chapter 3 pp. 45–84

3.1 *Introductory*
Standard works and books of selections:
CAMPBELL, A., *Old English Grammar*, Clarendon Press, 1959.
BROOK, G.L., *An Introduction to Old English*, Manchester University Press, 1955.
MITCHELL, B., and ROBINSON., F.C., *A Guide to Old English*, 4th rev. edn., Basil Blackwell, 1986.
SWEET, H., *An Anglo-Saxon Primer*, 9th edn., rev. N. DAVIS, Clarendon Press, 1953.
SWEET, H., *A Second Anglo-Saxon Reader*, rev. T. HOAD, Clarendon Press, 1978.
QUIRK, R., and WRENN, C.L., *An Old English Grammar*, 2nd edn., Methuen, 1957.

3.2 *The formative influences behind late West Saxon*
See the relevant sections in BLAIR, HODGKIN and STENTON (1.2, above), STRANG (above, Chap. VI).

For *Beowulf*, see the following standard edns., both with excellent introductions, notes, glossaries, and bibliographies:
KLAEBER, F., *Beowulf and the Fight at Finnsburg*, 3rd edn., Boston, D.C. Heath and Co., 1936 (with Supplements 1941, 1950).
WRENN, C.L., *Beowulf, with the Finnesburg Fragment*, 3rd edn., rev. W.F. BOLTON, Harrap, 1973.

Translations are to be found in:
GORDON, R.K., *Anglo-Saxon Poetry*, 2nd rev. edn., Dent: Everyman's Library, 794, 1954, pp. 1–62.
BRADLEY, S.A.J., *Anglo-Saxon Poetry*, Dent, 1982, pp. 405–94.

Selections from *Beowulf* are given in many of the Readers, and there is a facsimile by:
ZUPITZA, J., *Beowulf, Reproduced in Facsimile ... With a Transliteration and Notes*, 2nd edn., EETS, O.S. 245, 1959.

3.3 *The rest of the O.E. manuscript tradition*
On the O.E. dialects:
BROOK, G.L., *English Dialects*, 2nd edn., Deutsch, 1965.
CAMPBELL, A. (above).
WYLD, H.C., *Short History* (above).

The chief O.E. dialectal texts are found in:
SWEET, H. (rev. HOAD), *Second Anglo-Saxon Reader* (above).

On the alphabet, see:
DENHOLM-YOUNG, N., *Handwriting in England and Wales*, Cardiff, 1954 (with 31 plates).
SCRAGG, D.G., *A History of English Spelling*, Manchester University Press, 1974, Chap 1.

3.4ff. *Runes*
See ELLIOTT, R.W.V. (above), and also:
PAGE, R.I., *An Introduction to English Runes*, Methuen, 1973. (See
  bibliographies in both Elliott and Page for the individual inscriptions.)
On the O.E. runes in manuscripts, see the above, and:
DEROLEZ, R., *Runica Manuscripta: the English Tradition*, Bruges:
  Rijksuniwersiteit te Gent, 1954.
DICKINS, B., *Runic and Heroic Poems*, Cambridge University Press, 1915.
SISAM, K., 'Cynewulf and his Poetry', *Proceedings of the British Academy*,
  18, 1932, pp. 303–31.

3.4.5 *The Ruthwell Cross*
The most modern edns. of *The Dream of the Rood*, which also deal with the
  Ruthwell inscription, are those of:
DICKINS, B., and ROSS, A.S.C., Methuen's Old English Library, 4th edn., 1954,
  and SWANTON, M.J., Manchester University Press, 1970.
See also:
FORBES, M.D., and DICKINS, R., 'The inscriptions of the Ruthwell and
  Bewcastle Crosses and the Bridekirk Font', *Burlington Magazine*, 25, 1914,
  pp. 24–9.

3.5 *Non-runic inscriptions*
The definitive edn., with many photographs, is:
OKASHA, E., *Hand-List of Anglo-Saxon Non-Runic Inscriptions*, Cambridge
  University Press, 1971.

3.6 *Coins*
BLACKBURN, M., ed., *Anglo-Saxon Monetary History*, Leicester University
  Press, 1986.
COLMAN, F., 'Anglo-Saxon Pennies and Old English Phonology', *Folia
  Linguistica Historica*, 5.1, 1984, pp. 91–143 (with important references).
DOLLEY, M., *Anglo-Saxon Pennies*, Trustees of the British Museum, 1970.
VON FEILITZEN, O., and BLUNT, C., 'Personal Names on the Coinage of
  Edgar', in CLEMOES, P., and HUGHES, K., eds., *England before the
  Conquest*, Cambridge University Press, 1971.
THOMPSON, J.D.A., *Inventory of British Coin Hoards A.D. 600–1500*, no. 1,
  1956.
Note, finally, the important ongoing series of catalogues and photographs of
A.S. and other coins:
Sylloge of Coins of the British Isles, published for the British Academy by
  OUP and Spink and Son Ltd. About 30 vols. so far produced. See, for
  names, especially, Vol. 28, 1981.
On runic names on coins, see PAGE (above), Chap. 9.

3.7 *Summary*
On the late O.E. spelling- and sound-system, see STRANG (above), para. 159.

3.8 *Addendum: place- and personal names in manuscripts*
Anglo-Saxon Chronicle:
A new collaborative edn. of all the versions is in progress (together with
  associated texts in English and Latin), general editors DUMVILLE, D., and
  KEYNES, S., published D.S. Brewer, 1982–. There is also a new translation,
  with commentary and illustrations, by Anne Savage, Macmillan, 1982.
Of the many earlier versions, note:

PLUMMER, C., *Two of the Saxon Chronicles Parallel*, 2 vols., Clarendon Press, 1892–9 (reprinted, 1952; still standard and indispensable).

SMITH, A.H., *The Parker Chronicle (832–900)*, Methuen's Old English Library, 1935 (with valuable introduction and bibliography).

Domesday Book:

The Phillimore edition (general editor, MORRIS, J.), with translation, in 40 county vols. is very convenient; but note also the new complete facsimile, with translation, published for the Public Record Office, 1986, by Alecto Historical Editions (London).

HOLT, J.C., ed., *Domesday Studies*, Boydell and Brewer Ltd., 1986.

Place-name treatments:

CAMERON, K., *English Place-names*, rev. edn., Batsford, 1988.

DODGSON, J. McN., 'Domesday Book: Place-names and Personal Names', in HOLT, J.C., ed., above.

EKWALL, E., *The Concise Oxford Dictionary of English Place-Names*, 4th rev. edn., Clarendon Press, 1960. (Indispensable, together with the vols. of the English Place-name Society.)

REANEY, P.H., *The Origin of English Place-Names*, Routledge and Kegan Paul, 1960.

3.9 *The Scandinavian impact*

For *ASC*, see under 3.10, above.

For the *Treaty of Alfred and Guthrum* and the other documents mentioned, see:

WHITELOCK, D., ed., *English Historical Documents*, Vol. I: *c. 500–1042*, Eyre and Spottiswoode, 1955. (Has excellent bibliographies and introductory summary of the period.)

The York excavations have been covered in a very readable manner in:

HALL, R., *The Excavations at York: the Viking Dig*, The Bodley Head, 1984.

3.9.3 *Scandinavian runes*

ELLIOTT, R.W.V. (Chap. 3) and PAGE, R.I. (Chap. 12), under 3.4 (above).

On the Bridekirk font:

FORBES, M.D., and DICKINS, B., under 3.4.5 (above).

See also:

PAGE, R.I., 'How long did the Scandinavian language survive in England? the epigraphical evidence', in CLEMOES, P., and HUGHES, K., *England Before the Conquest*, Cambridge University Press, 1971. (Makes reference to E. Ekwall's article of the same title (1930), which considered place-names and loan-words, as well as inscriptions.)

3.9.4 *Scandinavian loan-words:*

ORTON, H., and WRIGHT, N., *A Word Geography of England*, Seminar Press, 1974, pp. 14–17.

WAKELIN, M.F., *English Dialects*, 2nd rev. edn., Athlone Press, 1977, pp. 130–38 (and bibliographical references, p. 178).

Scandinavian place-names:

See REANEY, P.H., under 3.8, above (Chap. 7), and CAMERON, K., ibid. (Chap. 6).

3.10 *The Norman Conquest*

DOUGLAS, D.C., and GREENAWAY, G.W., *English Historical Documents*, Vol. II: *1042–1189*, Eyre and Spottiswoode, 1953.

The Peterborough Chronicle, 1070–1154, CLARK, C., ed., OUP, 1958. For the latest collaborative edn. of *ASC*, see under 3.8, above.

Chapter 4 pp. 85–107
4.2 *Manuscripts*
IRWIN, R., *The Origins of the English Library*, George Allen and Unwin, 1958.
McINTOSH, A., SAMUELS, M.L., and BENSKIN, M., *A Linguistic Atlas of Late Mediaeval English*, 4 vols., Aberdeen University Press, 1986.
SISAM, K., *Fourteenth-century Verse and Prose*, Clarendon Press, 1921 (Introduction).
WORMALD, F., and WRIGHT, C.E., eds., *The English Library before 1700: Studies in its History*, Athlone Press, 1958.

4.4 *Summary*
See the excellent summaries of M.E. grammar in Dickins and Wilson, Bennett and Smithers, and Sisam (p. 00, above).

On Irish Middle English, see:
SAMUELS, M.L., 'Prolegomena to a Study of Mediæval Anglo-Irish', *Medium Ævum*, 37, 1968, pp. 1–11. (Valuable lists of texts and linguistic features.)

4.5 *Late M.E. dialects and the rise of a written standard*
On 'standards' previous to Chancery, and on Chancery itself, see:
SAMUELS, M.L., Some Applications of Middle English Dialectology', *English Studies*, 44, 1963, pp. 1–11; and then:
FISHER, J.H., RICHARDSON, M., and FISHER, J.L., *An Anthology of Chancery English*, University of Tennessee Press, 1984.

4.6 *Latin manuscripts:*
On place-names, see under 3.8.

Chapter 5 pp. 109–150
5.2 For grammarians mentioned here, see:
DOBSON, E.J., *English Pronunciation 1500–1700*, 2 vols., 2nd edn., Clarendon Press, 1968, Vol. I. (Their 'evidence' is presented in Vol. II.)
Individual writers in order of appearance (N.B. the abbreviation 'S.P.' below refers to a facsimile reproduction in the Scolar Press series, *English Linguistics 1500–1800*):

NOWELL: see MARCKWARDT, A.H., *Laurence Nowell's Vocabularium Saxonicum*, Ann Arbor, 1952; WAKELIN, M.F., *English Dialects* (1.2, above), pp. 43–4.
SOMNER: *Dictionarium Saxonico-Latino-Anglicum*, 1659 (though compiled from earlier sources; S.P. 247, 1970.)
HICKES: *Linguarum Vett. Septentrionalium Thesaurus Grammatico-Criticus et Archaeologicus* is reprinted in *Anglistica and Americana*, 64, George Olms, Hildesheim and New York, 1970; S.P. 248, 1970.
COOTE: *The English Schoole-Master*, 1596; S.P. 98, 1968.
JONSON: see NEUMANN, J.H., 'Notes on Ben Jonson's English', *Publications of the Modern Language Association of America*, 54, 1939, pp. 736–63.
GIL: *Logonomia Anglica*, 1619, 2nd edn. 1621; ed. JIRICZEK, O.L., K.J. Trübner (Strassburg), 1903.
DAINES: RÖSLER, M., and BROTANEK, R., eds., Max Niemeyer (Halle), 1908; S.P. 31, 1967.

COOPER: see SUNDBY, B., *Christopher Cooper's English Teacher (1687)*, C.W.K. Gleerup (Lund) and Ejnar Munksgaard (Copenhagen), 1953; S.P. 86 (1685 edn.), 1968; S.P. 175 (1687 edn.), 1969.

On dictionaries and their compilers, see:
BURCHFIELD, R., ed., *Studies in Lexicography*, Clarendon Press, 1987.
MATTHEWS, M.M., *A Survey of English Dictionaries*, OUP, 1933.
STARNES, DE W.T., and NOYES, G.E., *The English Dictionary from Cawdrey to Johnson 1604–1755*, Chapel Hill, 1946.

Individual lexicographers (in chronological order):
LEVINS: *Manipulus Vocabulorum*, 1570, ed. WHEATLEY, H.B., EETS, O.S. 27, 1867, 1937. S.P. 195, 1969.
CAWDREY: *A Table Alphabeticall*, 1604 (see p. oo, above).
SKINNER: *Etymologicon Linguæ Anglicanæ*, 1671.
COLES: *An English Dictionary*, 1676. S.P. 268, 1971.
KERSEY: 6th rev. edn. of EDWARD PHILLIPS' (1658) *The New World of Words*, 1706; *Dictionarium Anglo-Britannicum*, 1708 (S.P. 156, 1969); and (probably) as 'J.K.' *A New English Dictionary*, 1702.
BAILEY: *An Universal Etymological English Dictionary*, 1721; Vol. II, 1727. Vol. I is reprinted in *Anglistica and Americana* 52, Georg Olms (Hildesheim and New York), 1969.
JOHNSON: *A Dictionary of the English Language*, 1755.

5.3 *Different types of English*
DOBSON, E.J., 'Early Modern Standard English', *Transactions of the Philological Society*, 1955, pp. 25–54. (All the writers cited in this chapter are documented in this article.)

5.4 *Vocabulary and the 'Inkhorn Controversy'*
BOLTON, W.F., ed., *The English Language: Essays by English and American Men of Letters, 1490–1839*, Cambridge University Press, 1966.
JONES, R.F., *The Triumph of the English Language*, OUP, 1953.
MOORE, J.L., *Tudor-Stuart Views on the Growth, Status and Destiny of the English Language*, Max Niemeyer (Halle), 1910.

5.5 *Analyses of English: 1. Sounds*
On Gil, Daines and Cooper, see above. On all writers cited in this chapter:
PARTRIDGE, A.C., *Tudor to Augustan English*, Deutsch, 1969.

For Hart, see:
DANIELSSON, B., ed., *John Hart's Works on English Orthography and Pronunciation [1551 · 1569 · 1570]*, Almqvist and Wiksell (Stockholm), 1955–63.
WALLIS: reprinted S.P. 142, 1969.

Summary of early Mod.E. sound system:
BARBER, C.L., *Early Modern English*, Deutsch, 1976, Chap. 6.

5.6 *Analyses of English: 2. Grammar*
See BARBER (above), Chap. 5.

5.7 *Occasional spellings:*
WYLD, *H.C., 1927, 1936, 1.3 (above).*

5.8.1 *Dialectal spellings* (in order of appearance)
ORTON, H., *The Phonology of a South Durham Dialect*, Kegan Paul, Trench, Trubner and Co. Ltd, 1933.

HEDEVIND, B., *The Dialect of Dentdale in the West Riding of Yorkshire*, University of Uppsala: *Studia Anglistica Upsaliensia*, 5, 1967.

KÖKERITZ, H., *The Phonology of the Suffolk Dialect*, University of Uppsala, 1932.

MATTHEWS, W., 'South Western Dialect in the Early Modern Period', *Neophilologus*, 24, 1939, 193–209.

VIKAR, A., *Contributions to the History of the Durham Dialects*, Röhr (Malmö, Sweden), 1922.

5.8.2 *Observations of writers*
For Carew, see:
HALLIDAY, F.E., *Richard Carew of Antony: The Survey of Cornwall*, Melrose, 1953. (This also includes the *Excellency*.)

For Puttenham, see:
DOBSON, under 5.3, above; ed. WILLCOCK, G.D., and WALKER, A., Cambridge, 1936, reprinted 1970; S.P. 110, 1968.

For Coote and Gil, see 5.2 (above).

5.8.3 *Dialect in literature and on the stage*
On Chaucer, see:
TOLKIEN, J.R.R., 'Chaucer as a Philologist: *The Reeve's Tale*', *Transactions of the Philological Society*, 1934, pp. 1–70.

On Shakespeare, see:
KÖKERITZ, H., 'Shakespeare's Use of Dialect', *TYDS*, 9, Part 51, 1951, pp. 10–25.

On Jonson, see NEUMANN (above).

On SW literary dialect, see:
WAKELIN, M.F., *Varieties of English around the World: T5, The Southwest of England*, John Benjamins Publishing Company, 1986, para. 1.7, and Texts 11 and 43 (also gives the Shakespeare scene, p. 15).

On Stage Cockney, see KÖKERITZ, above.

5.8.4 *Dialect literature*
On Meriton's *Dialogue*, in addition to Cawley's edn., see:
DEAN, C., *The Dialect of George Meriton's 'A Yorkshire Dialogue (1683)': Studies in the Stressed Vowels'*, Yorkshire Dialect Society Reprint III, 1962.

5.8.5 *Dictionaries and glossaries*
WAKELIN, M.F., 'The Treatment of Dialect in English Dictionaries', Chap. 9 in BURCHFIELD, R., ed., 5.2 (above).

5.9 *English abroad*
KURATH, H., 'The Origin of the Dialectal Differences in Spoken American English', *Modern Philology*, 25.4, 1928, 385–95; and also 'Some Aspects of Atlantic Seaboard English considered in their Connection with British English', c. 1965; both reprinted in *A Various Language: Perspectives on American Dialects*, ed. WILLIAMSON, J.V., and BURKE, V.M., Holt, Rinehart and Winston Inc., 1971.

VIERECK, W., 'On the Interrelationship of British and American English: Morphological Evidence', in VIERECK, W., ed., *Focus on England and Wales*, John Benjamins, 1985.

WAKELIN, M.F., 'English on the Mayflower', *English Today*, 8, October, 1986, pp. 30–33.

Chapter 6 pp. 151–76
6.1ff.
BARBER, C.L. (above).
BOLTON, W.F., and CRYSTAL, D., eds., *The English Language*, Vol. 2,
  Cambridge University Press, 1969.

6.3
Jones is S.P. 167, 1969.
On Lowth, see PARTRIDGE, A.C (above); S.P. 18, 1967.

6.4 *Dictionaries*
See under 5.2.

6.5ff. *Dialect*
DEFOE *et al.*: WAKELIN, M.F., English Dialects (above), pp. 40–42.
SHERIDAN: *A General Dictionary of the English Language*, 1780. S.P. 50,
  1967.
WALKER: *A Critical Pronouncing Dictionary*, 1791. S.P. 117, 1968.
Eighteenth and nineteenth-century monographs, glossaries and dictionaries:
WAKELIN, M.F. (above), pp. 43–6, and, for bibliographical details of all works
  cited in this section, ibid., p. 173.

6.5.2 *Literary and stage dialect*
The Obliging Husband: WAKELIN, M.F., *The Southwest of England*, above,
  Text 12.
TENNYSON: TILLING, P.M., 'Local Dialect and the Poet', in WAKELIN, M.F.,
  Patterns in the Folk Speech of the British Isles, Athlone Press, 1972.
BARNES: WAKELIN, M.F., *Southwest England*, (above), Text 36 (and refs.).

6.5.3 *Dialect literature*
Exmoor Courtship: WAKELIN, M.F (above), Text 13.

6.6 *Nineteenth-century and subsequent developments*
On all authors and subjects treated here, see:
SAMPSON, G., *Schools of Linguistics: Competition and Evolution*, Hutchinson
  University Library, 1980.

Index